Kemar Duhaney was killed on 11 July 2012, aged 21.

He came to the UK from Jamaica at the age of eleven and had severe difficulties with literacy and numeracy. He got into trouble at school and eventually joined the London Boxing Academy Committee Project (LBACP).

At the LBACP, we taught many challenging students. Kemar, however, was different. He was charming, warm and positive. Those who came to know him always went out of their way to help him, because he was so rewarding to help. He was secretly all the staff's favourite – a friendly, funny and genuinely decent young guy trying to improve himself and his lot in life.

Those are some of the reasons why it was such a tragedy that Kemar died in the way that he did. He was stabbed in the chest, after being confronted by the former partner of a girl he was seeing at the time. He later died at the Royal Free Hospital after five hours of open-heart surgery. Kemar had nothing to do with gangs, drugs or anything illegal. He had done no wrong. That is why Kemar's friends and family are in such utter shock that he was taken in that way.

As you may know, funerals are very expensive. Kemar's mum, Diana, needs help to fund a fitting memorial. It will cost at least five thousand pounds to make that happen. Any contribution towards that target would be an enormous help to Kemar's family.

Visit www.gofundme.com/helpkemar

Or donate directly: sort 20-71-45, account 73238385

Boxing Clever

To Katie

Here's to the future!

Tom x

Boxing Clever

How one alternative-provision school for excluded
teenagers used traditional teaching,
personal relationships and sport to fight gangs,
unhappiness and educational failure in a battle for
the future of its pupils.

Tom Ogg

Foreword by

Lord Glasman

Civitas: Institute for the Study of Civil Society
London

First Published September 2012

email: books@civitas.org.uk

ISBN 978-1-906837-43-3

Independence: Civitas: Institute for the Study of Civil Society is a registered educational charity (No. 1085494) and a company limited by guarantee (No. 04023541). Civitas is financed from a variety of private sources to avoid over-reliance on any single or small group of donors.

All publications are independently refereed. All the Institute's publications seek to further its objective of promoting the advancement of learning. The views expressed are those of the authors, not of the Institute.

Typeset by
Civitas

Printed in Great Britain by
Berforts Group Ltd, Stevenage SG1 2BH

Contents

Author

Tom Ogg grew up in South London, where he attended a local comprehensive school before joining the sixth form of Graveney School in Tooting. He read philosophy, politics and economics (PPE) at Corpus Christi College, University of Oxford, before completing a MSc in sociology at Nuffield College, University of Oxford.

Tom joined the staff of the social-policy think-tank Civitas in 2007, for whom he worked on the London Boxing Academy Community Project until 2010. He has since taught for Civitas on their Civitas Schools programme and at Footsteps Football Academy. He is also a governor of the East London Science School, a Free School due to open in September 2013.

Tom is now a pupil barrister at a leading commercial set of chambers in the Temple, London. Whilst training to be a barrister, Tom set up the City/4-5 School Exclusions Project (www.city.ac.uk/schoolexclusions), which provides representation to pupils who are appealing against their permanent exclusion from mainstream schools. He was also part of the miscarriage of justice campaign for Sam Hallam (www.samhallam.com), who was released from prison in 2012 following the quashing of his conviction for murder by the Court of Appeal.

In memory of

Kemar Duhaney

1991 – 2012

Acknowledgements

There are a number of people to whom I owe my thanks. I would first like to thank all of the students whom I taught at the LBACP: thank you for being so stimulating, challenging and entertaining. Thank you to everyone I worked with at the LBACP. The most important figure in my narrative is Chris Hall, for reasons that will become apparent to the reader, but I would like to acknowledge the important contribution made to the project by Simon Marcus, without whose involvement it wouldn't have happened in the way and at the time it did. It was Simon who first made contact with Civitas, which led to my involvement, and who was able to raise the profile of the work in public policy circles. This was an important element in the development of LBACP. Thanks to my other LBACP colleagues Peter Haymer, Richard Ross, Caroline Jarrett, Ervis Jegeni, Terri Kelly, Carmel Cadden, Angie Despong, Frank Brinkley, Rachel DeJong, Daniel Sandle-Brownlie, Danny Coklie, Anna Cain, Paulo Muphungo, James Woodward, Eric Ochieng, Michael Grant and John Beckles; and to my Civitas colleagues Will Hodson and Pete Quentin. Thank you also to all the volunteers who helped at the LBACP, who include Richard Abraham, David Sooby, Ganan Sritharan, Jonathan Broad, Lorna Price, Emily Kaill, Beth Haines, Tsz San So, Claire Mullarkey, Aylete Fpiro and John Graham. Special thanks to Jan and Laurie Whelan who gave their time to work with a special student.

The assistance that Civitas provided for the work of the LBACP was made possible by the generous response to appeals which were made to Civitas supporters. Thanks are also due to the Tom ap Rhys Pryce Trust; Sir Stephen Waley-Cohen for his generosity in helping our students to go to the theatre courtesy of Mousetrap Theatre Projects; and Lord Feldman for funding our trips to Parliament, amongst many other trips. I would also like to thank the following people: Harriet Pickering of the London Russian Ballet School for being so keen to spread the joy of ballet; both the Oxford University Amateur Boxing Club (Richard Pickering in particular) and Corpus Christi College Boat Club (Gregor Jotzu in particular) for giving us great work-outs; the Oxford Union for hosting the former mentioned work-out; Corpus Christi and St John's Colleges at Oxford University for receiving us on trips; Maria Allen for organising our trip to Parliament; Dwayne Chambers, Jim Pope and Jesse Armstrong for taking the time out to visit us; PGL camps and Atholl Adventures for hosting us in Devon and Scotland respectively; the Bank of England and its Governor Mervyn King; OnlyConnect; and the Tottenham Community Sports Centre, and particularly Malcolm Springthorpe, for hosting us.

I would like to thank all those who have kindly read chapters of the book, or served as a sounding board for my ideas. Thank you to Harry Ogg, Richard Abraham, Charlynne Pullen, Eleanor Rogerson, Anastasia de Waal, James Easy, Brandon Terry, Richard Kidd, Polly Hunt, Rowenna Davis, Kiri Crequer, Alex Sutherland, Lee Jones, George Hoare, Andrew Flint, Helen Cowen, Zenobe Reade, Rob Howsam, Juliet Grames, David Sooby, Nick Cowen, Carl Parsons, Sue Tallon, Samuel Gartland, and Vidya Kumar. Thank you also to the Institute of Ideas Education Forum for hosting a discussion about the LBACP in mid-2010. Particular thanks are due to Gemma Glyn, James Woodward, and Mike Rivers-Bowerman for their detailed comments. I am also grateful to those who participated in the anonymous refereeing process for their helpful comments. Special thanks are due to Rob Howsam and Purpose for designing the cover.

My greatest thanks must go to the following people. To my parents, without whom none of this would have been possible. To David Green, the director of Civitas, whose vision and wise steering of the project were crucial, and who I think should receive credit for plunging his think-tank into the messy business that is the sharp end of education in the UK. As will become clear, this book is in large part a tribute to the work and achievements of Chris Hall, without whom this book would not have been written. It was Chris's idea to turn his boxing gym into a school, and I am just one among of thousands who are grateful to him for doing so. I owe my thanks to him also.

Finally, the person to whom this book and my work in Tottenham owes most is Robert Whelan. Robert guided me through my time at the LBACP and has done since. It was at his suggestion that I first began keeping the diaries that form the basis for the book, and not only did he edit it, he shepherded me through the entire process. It was Robert's belief in and commitment to the project that kept the show on the road at the most rocky of moments. I owe Robert a great deal. Thank you, Robert.

Tom Ogg
London, August 2012

Foreword

There are several reasons why I feel honoured to write this foreword.

The first is the great respect I have for David Green, the director of Civitas. He has been concerned for a lifetime with the everyday virtues of how ordinary people support and protect each other and preserve their sense of humanity. He is a rare thing in the contemporary political scene, an intelligent man fearlessly committed to the good. This permeates the work that Civitas does, a prime example of which is Tom Ogg's *Boxing Clever*.

The second is that it is set in 'my' London, on a straight line north of the City up the A10. Dalston, Tottenham and Edmonton are the areas the students come from and I have seen these places transformed by immigration, manufacturing decline and technological change in my lifetime. I live in Hackney and have a strong commitment to the good of these places. This is intensified by the fact that the London Boxing Academy is in Tottenham, the home of the football team I have supported for as long as I can remember. Every visit to White Hart Lane, mysteriously located on Tottenham High Street, has a childhood sense of wonder with something of the pilgrimage about it. At least when I arrive. After watching the match, a related emotion of heartbroken disenchantment can gain the upper hand. The intensity of my reaction when Spurs announced that they wished to move to Stratford is still something that surprises me and gives an insight into the raw grief that a sense of powerless dispossession can generate. In my mind, the destinies of the club and of the place are inextricably linked, and this book gives a unique insight into its reality.

The third is a long-standing interest in boxing. Boxing is a demanding vocation. It requires dedication and speed, skill and strength. It is extreme in its virtues and vices, combining violence and intelligence, greed and self-sacrifice, glory and humiliation, risk and reward. There was a time when British politics, adversarial, personal and heroic, was compared favourably with boxing, the truth of the contenders being decided in the 'bear-pit' of Parliament, but these are not such times. As politics has become more procedural, boxing ceases to look like an arena for virtue and more like an untidy remnant from a disagreeable past, based upon violence, antagonism and blood lust. I think that there is still a great deal that we can all learn from boxing and this book interested me for that reason.

Those are the reasons I had for agreeing to write the foreword but they did not prepare me for the quality of what I read. The prose is strong, the story compelling and the political implications profound. In Community Organising, I was taught that the better you understand the world as it is, the better your chances of acting in such a way as to change it into the world as it should be. This is a story about a new institution with a strong sense of moral purpose, in the words of contemporary political theory, upholding good practice and a sense of virtue in an ecology of broken relationships, instant gratification and a widespread sense of estrangement. Tom Ogg tells his story, particularly relating to his father's mental illness, with skill and force, and the connection and disconnection between his own life and those of the students he teaches adds to the book being both educational and moving.

The London Boxing Academy begins its work where the mainstream educational system stops. The 'alternative-provision projects' are those programmes that deal with the permanently excluded. They are not inspected by Ofsted, do not follow the national curriculum and up until now remain fundamentally unregulated. For those reasons they are also places of truth and innovation where things that are not allowed to happen in mainstream education can occur. They are deeply local and relational. The London Boxing Academy was located in the Tottenham Community Sports Centre which was held in trust to provide sporting facilities for the young people of Tottenham and was previously used by the Territorial Army. It could not be privatised and the importance of endowment and trust in the preservation of a non-commercial and non-state institution in such an environment is significant. A space was preserved in Tottenham where a mutual good could grow. A sense of place is important in Tom Ogg's own story, in which his own postcode lottery left him in what Alasdair Campbell might call a 'bog standard' comprehensive in Mitcham, where the only connection with institutional excellence was that the school provided six ball boys a year to the Wimbledon Championships. It was that connection and experience which galvanised the young Tom to want something different, and he changed school for the sixth form and went on to Corpus Christi College in Oxford to study PPE.

It is greatly to the credit of Tom Ogg that he does not portray himself as the hero of the book and is honest about his dilemmas and weaknesses when confronted with the relentless grief and disappointment, interspersed with hope and possible redemption that gave meaning to his experience as a teacher in Tottenham. The central character is Chris Hall. Mr Hall co-founded the Academy and developed its particular ethos. An ex-amateur boxing champion and coach and a deeply committed Christian, Chris is driven by a calling to love the unloved and utters the defining words of this book, which exposes all the limits of New Labour and Conservative welfare reform. He said: 'Rules without relationships ain't worth toffee'.

I would like to see those words printed out on bold banners in every school, social security office and hospital in the country. The overwhelming lesson of Tom Ogg's experience and Chris Hall's practice is that relationships are transformative and that, without loving and caring one-to-one relationships, life goes very badly wrong. He likens boxing people to foster parents, 'great hearted people'. Mr Hall says: 'they give one-to-one quality time and attention to young people in a world that is generally very busy'.

Through one-to-one conversations, trust is established on a realistic basis with people who lack love and who can lecture Tom on the sexual rules of the street—'to take and not to give'. Without establishing relationships, a sense of trust, loyalty and common purpose between people, the aims and objectives tend to be lost and a culture of exaggeration takes over. That was certainly the trend over the last 20 years. There was not enough love in a system which was deeply unrelational and there has not been a transformation in the lives of the poor. This book indicates the possibilities that putting relationships at the centre of things can bring.

There are other lessons too.

One is the importance of local leaders such as Chris Hall, who are trusted and supported by parents and students, who can make informed judgments in difficult circumstances. Chris liked the students and they knew it, and that turned round many a tricky situation.

Boxing also provided a tradition of virtue through which the mayhem and violence, rivalry and aggression of the street could be mediated. The boxing gym, with the older boxers acting as mentors, provided an alternative world to that of the street while being part of it. It provided the platform for 'rules with relationships'. There were some girls in the academy and one of those who used the gym was the gold medalist Nicola Adams, but the overwhelming majority were boys, and boxing provided real examples of what it meant to be responsible, to have discipline, to be brave. As Tom Ogg says at the end: 'an ideal of what it means to be a grown-up'.

Anyone who saw Pete Townsend whirlwinding his arms at the Olympic closing ceremony will understand that there is a real problem of male infantilisation. Boxing offered a tradition of excellence and a definition of what it meant to be a man that gave a sense of belonging to a tradition that was upheld by an institution and underpinned by a set of relationships committed to a common ethos. It helped to give some idea of what it meant to be a grown-up.

Relationships, institutions, tradition. These should be the organising themes of welfare reform in the coming decade and Civitas should be praised for supporting and nurturing the writer, giving him the space to learn through doing, encouraging this book and indicating the direction in which we will all have to go to transform our country. Tom Ogg has made a significant contribution.

Lord Glasman

1

Boxing and Exclusion

Student: I'm looking for an alternative school.
Receptionist: This is an alternative.
Student: What... alternative, is?
Receptionist: What exactly are you asking me?
Student: Lady at my other school told me to come here. Hotel Theresa. Said it's an alternative school.
Receptionist: An alternative school? It's like, er... it's like a choice. It's a different way o' doin' things. So, I need your discharge papers sayin' that they discharged you...

From the film Precious *(Dir. Lee Daniels, Lionsgate, 2009),*
based on the novel Push *by Sapphire*

The London Boxing Academy Community Project (LBACP) was an 'alternative-provision' project in Tottenham, North London that existed from October 2006 until July 2010. The LBACP worked with young men and women who had been expelled, or were at risk of being expelled, from mainstream schools. The purpose of the project was to make use of the strong relationships that boxing coaches have traditionally held with wayward young men, in an educational setting. It specialised in dealing with young people of 14-16 years of age who had 'emotional and behavioural difficulties', and boys with aggression problems in particular. I was a teacher and co-ordinator at the LBACP. This book is about my experiences and the lessons I learnt during my time at the project.

Chris Hall, a professional boxing coach, initially founded the project and was the inspirational individual at its centre. Chris ran the London Boxing Academy (LBA), a boxing gym for professional and amateur boxers, and the LBACP was created as a subsidiary project of the LBA before it was registered as an independent charity. The school grew out of a successful placement programme at the LBA of students who had been expelled from mainstream

1

schools. The Pupil Referral Unit[1] (PRU) and Youth Offending Team (YOT) in Haringey referred some of their most difficult young people to the LBA in the hope that boxing training would help them to learn to control their aggression. One of the PRU's social workers who referred students to the LBA was so impressed by the improvement in the young people that she suggested to Chris that he should set up a project to help more young people. This led to the founding of what was initially known as the LBA 'Partnership Project', where Chris led a steering group composed of represent-atives from the Haringey PRU, YOT, Haringey Police and Gladesmore School (a comprehensive school in South Tottenham). The LBA and LBACP shared the same site and facilities in the Tottenham Community Sports Centre, where the rent was generously set at a very low level to support the project.

Civitas, the independent social policy think-tank, became involved in January 2007 after being approached by Simon Marcus who was an equal partner with Chris on the project. Simon was an aspiring Conservative politician whom Chris had previously coached. Civitas had just set up the first of its Civitas Schools,[2] which provided extra tuition to inner-city primary school children who were behind with their reading and arithmetic through after-school classes and Saturday schools. Civitas agreed to run the academic curriculum within the LBACP and provided a large amount of indirect funding to the LBACP by employing teachers— including me—to work on the project. Civitas raised money for the project from its supporters and secured funding from the Tom ap Rhys Pryce Memorial Fund for the salary of Chris Hall so that he could work full time on the project. Civitas's mission at the LBACP was to show that, with the right methods, it is possible to educate even the most difficult students to a high standard.

The project changed fundamentally in July 2010 following the departures of Chris Hall, Civitas and most of the staff members described in this book. It now operates under a different name and the observations in this book refer to the LBACP as it was during Chris Hall's time, and not to the new project. The departure of Chris Hall followed disagreements about how the project ought to be operated. These disagreements led the trustees of the LBACP to choose a new head for the school and made other changes that ultimately led to Chris Hall's resignation. Simon became a trustee of the LBACP for a time and is now an adviser, and later was one of the authors of the report produced by the Riots (Victims and Communities) Panel set up by the government to examine the causes of the summer 2011 riots.[3]

In September 2010, Chris set up a project called Footsteps, which was run on the same principles as the LBACP, but with football rather than boxing as the main sport. Civitas again provided support to Chris's project by employing a tutor at Footsteps, a role I fulfilled during 2012. Footsteps is now a very successful organisation and in June 2012 began running an additional full-time project in partnership with Tottenham Hotspur Football Club.

The book

This book is a narrative description of my experiences working with Chris Hall to better the lives of children who have been excluded from school. The book is almost exclusively about my experiences at the LBACP, although some of the things I describe in this book — especially concerning illiteracy amongst excluded teenagers — have been influenced by my teaching at Footsteps.

The main reason for writing this book was to document the work I did with Chris for the benefit of others who might wish to work with excluded children. I also hope that what I have written gives an insight into the lives of the children I taught. It is also a very personal book: it tells a little of 'my story'.

I kept a diary throughout my time teaching at the LBACP, and many of the exchanges set out in the book are based on those notes. I have also relied on written documents produced during my time at the school, and a number of interviews with students and staff at the project. Nevertheless, the views expressed in the book are mine alone, and may not reflect those of others who worked at the LBACP.

Readers should also be warned that the book contains a great deal of swearing, sexual innuendo and violence. In order for the account to be authentic, it was necessary to leave those elements unedited. I have created an 'urban dictionary' on a website that accompanies the book, which can be accessed at www.tomogg.net, if a slang word in the book defeats the reader.

Each chapter focuses upon a different aspect of the project, but there is a strong narrative thread running through the book. It is intended to be read from beginning to end rather than sampled. Chapter 2, 'We'll Always Have Devon', is an account of a school trip to Devon, where the staff and students first got to know each other. Chapter 3, 'A Bit of Background', describes experiences during my own education that influenced my work at the LBACP. Chapter 4, 'Teaching the Unteachable?', concentrates on the difficulties of teaching the students, some of whom were very behind academically, and explains the behaviour management system we used. Chapter 5, 'The Boxing Gym', is about the importance of boxing to the project and the influence that the boxers working in the project brought to bear on the students. Chapter 6, 'An Inspirational Individual', is about Chris Hall, and how his principles of honesty, realism and kindness guided his approach to working with the students. Chapter 7, 'The Classroom and the Street', examines the ways in which the lives of the students outside of the LBACP affected their behaviour within the school, with particular reference to gangs, drugs and the so-called 'postcode wars'. Chapter 8, 'Boxing Clever', asks: where are the students now? It includes an account of my work teaching illiterate students to read. The students themselves have the last say through a set of short essays about their dreams.

The book is structured to give the reader an idea of a 'year in the life' of a teacher at the LBACP. It is not an account of all the changes and improvements of the project, except where the differences provide wider lessons—such as the switch from teaching in a tutorial style to a classroom style. Consequently, the book is not chronological. Furthermore, some of the characters described in the book are composites of more than one student who attended the LBACP. Within each of the chapters there are sections in italics, which are accounts of trips, interviews or other specific experiences.

I have given pseudonyms to all of the students described in the book in order to protect their identity, although, for reasons that will become clear, one former student no longer requires that protection. Some of the details about the characteristics of the students have also been changed. All of the events described in the book, however, are true and accurate accounts. None of the descriptions in the book have been embellished for shock value—indeed, that was quite unnecessary.

Background: boxing and exclusion

Although the last decade has seen a surge in popularity and support for boxing, the sport faced considerable difficulties in the second half of the twentieth century. Boxing was removed from the curriculum of most schools after campaigns in the 1960s by the Labour MP Edith Summerskill, when safety standards were particularly poor. During the 1980s, the British Medical Association (BMA) campaigned for boxing to be banned.[4] Spurred on by tragedies in the ring such as the death of Johnny Owen in 1980 and the serious injuries suffered by Michael Watson in 1991, the BMA's campaign did considerable damage to the sport's reputation. The BMA's campaign, and litigation arising from Michael Watson's injuries, did however lead to great improvements in safety by making it mandatory to have ring-side medical equipment and doctors at fights.

Furthermore, the recent successes of both professional and amateur British boxers such as Lennox Lewis, Amir Khan, Joe Calzaghe, Ricky Hatton and David Haye have reinvigorated the British public's interest in boxing. The number of boxers registered with the Amateur Boxing Association of England has grown from 8,496 in 2005 to 12,390 in 2009, with a growth in the number of clubs from 619 to 822 over the same period.[5] The political reception for boxing has also markedly changed. Today there is near-universal support for boxing from the mainstream political parties. As the Labour Party's former Olympics Minister Tessa Jowell MP put it: 'We know it [boxing] can be a way of disengaging kids from gangs, carrying knives, from low-level crime and high-level antisocial behaviour... it reaches young people that other sports don't.'[6] Conservative politicians have supported the LBACP itself. London

5

Mayor Boris Johnson supported the LBACP financially from 2009 through funding allocated by his (Labour Party) sports adviser, Kate Hoey MP, and the current Sports Minister, Hugh Robertson MP, greeted students from the LBACP on a trip to Parliament in 2010. Finally, Prime Minister David Cameron, as leader of the opposition, praised the LBACP's 'great work with kids who have been expelled from school' at a Fresh Hope Trust awards ceremony in 2009.

The LBACP was the first project to combine boxing and schooling full-time in order to re-engage students who have been expelled from school or are at risk of being expelled. It is one of a growing number of projects in the 'alternative-provision' sector that are independently run but funded with public money from local authorities and mainstream schools. I wrote about the alternative-provision sector for Civitas in 'A New Secret Garden' which looks at the policy background to exclusion and alternative provision.[7] Recent government statistics suggest that there are in fact more students in alternative provision than in the traditional destination for disruptive pupils, PRUs, which are controlled by local authorities. There were 17,670 students of compulsory school age in alternative provision in January 2012, compared with 13,230 in PRUs; although there is a range of reasons why students are educated in alternative provision.[8] Alternative provision projects are not inspected by Ofsted[9] and they are not required to follow the national curriculum, although there are now government moves afoot to regulate the sector.[10] Alternative provision therefore offers unique freedoms within the UK education sector to experiment and, before the advent of Free Schools, perhaps the only feasible means of setting up new state schools without local authority support.

The London Boxing Academy Community Project

During the three-and-a-half years of the LBACP, around a hundred students passed through our doors. As Table 1:1 shows, the vast majority of the students were male (93 per cent). Only seven students were female. In 2009/10 the proportion of permanently excluded pupils in the UK who were boys was 78 per cent.[11] This over-representation of boys is likely to be explained by the focus upon sport at the LBACP, which led providers to refer more boys than girls to the project.

Table 1:1 LBACP students by gender and ethnicity

Students	Female	Male	Total
Black	4	46	50
Mixed Race	0	21	21
White	2	15	17
Mediterranean	1	11	12
Asian	0	1	1
Total	7	94	101

The preponderance of black, mixed-race and 'Mediterranean' students is accounted for by the large black and Turkish communities in North London, particularly in Tottenham. I have used the term 'Mediterranean' to very broadly cover Turkish, Kurdish and non-British white students from Europe (widely interpreted). There was only one student of Asian descent. Although black and mixed-race students have high rates of permanent exclusion nationally, it is geographical concentration that explains the bulk of the ethnic differences of students in the LBACP compared with the national picture. Of the 101 students who attended the LBACP, 34 did not complete the course.[12] The reasons for non-completion are set out in Table 1:2. Fifteen students were expelled from the course, and three students did not complete the course due to their imprisonment. Students placed in the 'social services' category withdrew from the project for reasons associated with their home life. Some of these students had irreconcilably fallen out with their parents which led to problems with school attendance, whilst other students were moved for their own benefit, sometimes abroad. Other students in this category were unable to attend the school due to gang-related problems that meant they were unable to travel to school, often for fear of their lives. Those in the 'withdrew' category, however, more straightforwardly decided to leave the project because they preferred to be educated elsewhere. Many of those were timid boys who often simply did not enjoy sport, and so withdrew because they were unsuited to the project. Some of the categories overlap, so the distinctions are meant as a rough guide only.

Table 1:2 Reason for non-completion of course by gender

	Female	Male	Total
Expelled	2	13	15
Imprisoned	0	3	3
Social Services	1	4	5
Withdrew	0	8	8
Total	3	28	31

Table1: 3 sets out the areas of London in which the students lived. The largest source of students for the project was Tottenham, where the LBACP was based. Closely following this was Hackney. There are excellent transport links between Hackney and Tottenham, on buses and trains, which made it possible (if not entirely safe) for students to travel each day from Hackney to the LBACP in Tottenham. A number of students were from areas to the north of Tottenham, such as Enfield and Edmonton. There was also a small number of students from other areas of Haringey and London.

Table 1: 3: Locations of the students' homes

Area	Number of Students
Tottenham	39
Hackney	30
Enfield and Edmonton	9
Wood Green	8
Other Haringey	8
Other London	7
Total	101

The project began with seven students in January 2007. Civitas teachers would go to Tottenham to teach for a few hours a week whilst administering the programme from the Civitas office in Westminster. In September 2007, I joined Civitas as the mathematics teacher for the LBACP and the project expanded to 18 students, with Civitas staff based permanently in Tottenham. An office was built at the LBACP in 2007/8 which allowed the administration to be carried out in Tottenham rather than Westminster.

In 2008/9 the school expanded from 18 students to 36 students, which remained the capacity of the school until July 2010. The majority of the students spent two years at the LBACP, joining us at 14 years of age (the start of Year 10), and leaving at 16 years of age after they had sat their GCSEs[13] at the end of Year 11. From those students I selected 26 characters to write about in this book.

2

We'll Always Have Devon

Mr Chipping, I am willing to forget the incident, but will those boys forget it? You are going to have to face them again. That will take courage, moral courage... Our profession is not an easy one, Mr Chipping. It calls for something more than a university degree. Our business is to mould men, it demands character and courage, and above all it demands the ability to exercise authority. Without that, I think any young man should ask himself seriously whether he has not, perhaps, mistaken his vocation. However, if you care to meet the trial, I shall watch your progress with interest.

Goodbye, Mr Chips, *Dir. Sam Wood, MGM, 1939*

When I arrived for my first day of work at the Civitas office in Westminster, I learned that in little over a week we would be leaving for a summer camp in Devon with the new LBACP students. I was introduced to my two colleagues who were organising the camp, Will Hodson and Pete Quentin, who had been working on the LBACP project at Civitas for about six months.

Will was a tall, calm Yorkshireman who was a couple of years older than me, and mad about cricket. Every weekend during the summer months he would drive from London up to Wakefield to play for his county cricket team. Will had come to the project after working with drug addicts whilst he was at university. He enjoyed a good joke and he showed a lot of care—always sharing his biscuits in the office, for example. When I first met him I thought he was a bit posh, as he dwelt upon his Rs when he spoke and wore Marylebone Cricket Club ties to work. But his generosity in buying drinks in The Speaker, the pub across the road from Civitas, quickly won me over.

In The Speaker I learnt a lot about Felix, a star student from the previous year's course. Felix was 16, and in the normal course of his school career should have left the LBACP before I arrived. But because he could still barely read or add up, everyone was keen for

Felix to stay on a further year at the LBACP, where he could be given more attention than he would likely receive at a college. Felix's concern at the time, though, was whether he would receive the Education Maintenance Allowance (EMA), like his friends at college.[1] The EMA was a weekly payment made to low-income students who were 16 or above and attended state-funded colleges or sixth forms. Felix was keen to stay at the LBACP, but equally, he wanted the EMA. Since the LBACP was not a directly state-funded institution, Felix would not be eligible for the EMA if he stayed with us. So a donor was found through Civitas who was willing to privately fund Felix's 'EMA' of £30 a week, in exchange for full attendance and Felix being a 'model student'. Will was going to discuss this contract with Felix at a student induction day later in the week. As part of the day, I would have some time to meet the students individually in order to get some idea of their level in mathematics. It was also my first visit to Tottenham, where I would meet the staff at the LBACP.

As the induction day approached, I became increasingly nervous about the students I was going to teach. I thought about the students who had been expelled from my secondary school, Tamworth Manor High School, a working-class comprehensive school in South London. One particular incident recurred in my thoughts, involving a friend of mine called Berek, who often got into scraps and arguments with other pupils.

Berek once said 'your mum' to another boy at Tamworth named Ashley. Unfortunately, unbeknownst to Berek, Ashley's mum had recently passed away. Ashley took great offence at Berek's taunt, but it was his friends, and particularly a boy called David, who decided to take action. David marched across the school towards where Berek and my friends hung out, shouting about what he was going to do, and other boys joined him as he walked. A large group of boys converged on Berek, with David at the front. Berek ran away as best he could, but David caught him and smashed his fist into the top of Berek's head. The mob gave him a beating as he lay in the prone position, taking blow after blow. Most of the group gave Berek a cheap kick before running away, but a small group made a sustained attack on Berek that caused him to be wheelchair-bound for days after the attack. Half-a-dozen or so students were expelled from the school. It was a chilling experience. I wondered how many of the students I would soon be teaching at the LBACP had been responsible for incidents like this at their own schools. I looked up the number of Tottenham police station and stored it in my mobile, just in case.

The induction day soon arrived. On the underground train to Seven Sisters station in Tottenham, I took the opportunity to ask Pete about the students. Pete was shorter, stockier and less reserved than Will, but he shared Will's love of sport—rugby, in Pete's case. He had an officer's commission in the London Regiment of the Territorial Army, and at the time had a black eye from the weekend's rugby match. Pete had an infectious enthusiasm and a good sense of humour. He was my predecessor in teaching mathematics to the students at the LBACP, but was going to work on another project for Civitas after the camp. He told me that 'the job is extremely satisfying: just very rarely. Most of the time it's just really tough trying to get the students to do anything, but when they do, the buzz is great.'

We got out at Seven Sisters and took a bus up Tottenham High Road. I only knew of Tottenham because of its football club, Tottenham Hotspur FC, and so I assumed that the Tottenham area would be wealthy like the areas that host the other Premiership clubs in London (Arsenal, Chelsea, Queen's Park Rangers and Fulham). I did not know about the racial tensions in Tottenham during the 1980s that led to Police Constable Keith Blakelock's murder in Broadwater Farm riots of 1985. It never crossed my mind that riots on a larger, more damaging scale in the summer of 2011 would be sparked off on Tottenham High Road. It is perhaps indicative of the difference between the riots of 1985 and 2011 that when I showed some LBACP students a BBC documentary about the Broadwater Farm riots and the quashing of Winston Silcott's conviction for Keith Blakelock's murder, the documentary did not resonate with them. They hated the police, of course, but theirs were individual grievances, rather than the cross-community anger seen in 1985. They also said that Broadwater Farm was not as rough as it used to be. By the end of my time in Tottenham, I have to say that I was not surprised that the worst of the riots occurred near the Ferry Lane estate and at the north of the High Road near Edmonton.

Certainly, riding the bus up the High Road in 2007, I remember thinking that the shops on the High Road did not reveal a wealthy area. There was a McDonalds with a large group of youths in school uniform outside and a large Tescos. But there was no Starbucks or Café Nero in sight, and certainly no M&S or Waitrose; instead there was an abundance of greasy spoon cafés, betting shops, hairdressers and multi-purpose shops offering international money transfers and 'mobile unlocking' services. Despite feeling quite tense about meeting the students, I allowed myself a wry smile at a sign on a funeral director's shop front, which said that 'pre-arranged funerals' were available.

We arrived at Tottenham Community Sports Centre (TCSC), which contained the boxing gym and classrooms that the school operated in. I read from a display near the entrance that the TCSC was a former Territorial Army centre, which had been left in trust to provide sports facilities for young people in Tottenham. I was led through to a large room at the rear of the centre which was to serve as our classroom. Its dark wooden floor had recently been polished, and was almost sticky. The brick walls were painted blue and there were wire mesh cages outside the windows. The room had a variety of chairs and tables stacked in the corner. I pulled out a table and two chairs, and waited for the students to arrive, whilst Will and Pete liaised with the LBACP staff.

The first students through the door looked young, timid and uncertain. Looking at them, I felt a sudden rush of relief: 'they are just kids', I thought, and my confidence returned a little. One by one they sat with me for an assessment. A few of the students gave disconcerting answers when I asked them why they had left their previous school. One tall light-skinned black boy called Desmond told me in a deep voice that he had 'been expelled because I punched a teacher'.

'Oh really?' I nervously chuckled. I rather pathetically joked that 'you won't be doing any more of that now, will you?' He gave me a puzzled look and said 'err, no'. Desmond was quite good at maths. He had a level six in mathematics, the same grade I had at his age. I wondered whether he could get a high grade, and I discussed the higher GCSE paper with him, which said he would try in a distant tone. By the end of the session I had a rough idea of each student's ability. The spread of abilities was wide, but the presence of clever students like Desmond gave me optimism for teaching during the year ahead.

Whilst I looked through my notes, Will was negotiating the EMA contract with Felix. Felix was not tall, but appeared athletic. He was wearing a grey hoodie with yellow stripes under a black jacket. For street clothes, he was well-dressed. Felix screwed up his face in scepticism at Will's condition that he should be a model student.

'Wot, d'ya mean I gotta be, like, a snitch or suttin? Naar man, I dunno about that.' Felix spoke in short, confident sentences that were often disarmingly direct, and sometimes rather wry. He had a high-pitched voice that was very clear, and had no problem with pauses or silences, unlike many of the other students. Will tried to reassure him:

'No snitching. I just want you to set an example to the other students, and show a bit of leadership. So if there's a fight brewing between a couple of students, I'd like to think that you'd try to calm things down if you could. And I certainly don't want to see you in any trouble yourself. And the other thing is that you're in every day, on time. What do you think?'

Reassured, Felix returned to business: 'so, how am I going to get the money den?'

'Well, we'll set you up a bank account and transfer the money there every week, depending on your attendance.'

Felix was annoyed. 'Bank account? Naar, that's long. Can't you just give me the cash, like?'

'Sorry Felix, it's got to be to a bank account for our records. I can help you set one up if you like?' After a long pause, Felix accepted Will's conditions, and left as the boxing staff came into the room for our introductory meeting prior to the camp.

Will encouraged everyone in the room to introduce themselves and describe briefly their role in the LBACP. Chris Hall introduced himself in a low-key manner as the course director. I had heard Will and Pete talking about Chris a lot in the days running up to the meeting. Whenever I had a question that Will or Pete couldn't answer, they said 'ask Chris'. Chris was white, about average height, but broad, and a bit round. He was in his late forties, and the size of his arms suggested that he was still doing weight training. He was wearing a Spurs tracksuit with shorts and trainers, had very short hair and wore a short beard of similar length. He certainly looked the part of the ex-boxer, with facial features that were tightly packed around the centre of his face, and deep-set eyes protected by a low-slung forehead.

Chris spoke in short, forceful sentences that were considered and sometimes blunt. He did not speak in the monotone you might expect, though. Rather, he varied the pitch and tone of his voice in little cadences that suggested he was willing to co-operate and engage. Chris said that he was really looking forward to a breakthrough year at the LBACP. He told us that he was in charge of student discipline, and that if anything happened he would deal with it. Chris also emphasised that if we caught wind of a conflict brewing between the students, or heard any news about a student's home life, then this information must make its way back to him. He pointed out that he tends to know the history of the students better than anyone else on the project, and that every scrap of information that reached him helped him to prevent looming problems, especially fights.

'I spend a lot of my time just keeping the peace,' he said, 'but it's harder if I don't know what's going on.' He told us not to try to deal with difficult situations ourselves: 'I'm responsible for what happens here, so please allow me to do my job. Don't try to solve conflicts on your own, because if it goes wrong then it will be my fault.'

Simon Marcus, Chris's partner in running the LBACP, was a tall, broad, man entering his thirties with a full beard. He fully fulfilled the rugby playing, heavyweight boxer image with his massive frame adorned with masses of muscle. He welcomed the new staff members and talked about his ambition to have an entire network of schools like the LBACP. The two other teachers employed by Civitas, for whom I was responsible, were Carmel Cadden and Caroline Jarrett. Carmel Cadden was the English teacher, and was a small, middle-aged white lady with short hair who possessed a winning smile. Caroline Jarrett was the sports teacher, a black woman in her early thirties. Caroline was a fitness trainer and boxing coach, and had worked with Chris previously.

Finally three boxers introduced themselves, who were employed to act as 'pod leaders': Peter Haymer, a very tall white boxer with a shaved head and a very defined goatee; Richard Ross, a quick-talking black boxer with a big smile, who was relatively small compared to everyone else, but much more 'street'; and Ervis Jegeni, who was a heavyweight boxer. Ervis was so big and broad that he looked short, despite being over six foot in height. They all looked tough and formidable, and had tattoos on their arms and necks. I later met Terri Kelly, who acted as a match-maker,[2] and light-welterweight boxer Michael Grant, both of whom served as pod leaders on the project.[3] Finally, always in the centre of the boxing ring was Paulo Muphungo. Paulo was the main boxing coach in Chris's gym, but had relatively little to do with the students.

Will handed out a list of the students at the LBACP that year, which identified the students who were joining us on the camp:

Table 2.1: Students attending camp

Year 10s	Year 11s
Craig	Alex
Emre (not attending)	Darren
Hunter	Collette
Jamie (not attending)	Darius
Laura (not attending)	Desmond
Lennox (not attending)	Felix
Russell	George
Marcel (not attending)	Lucas
Mohammed	Mehmet (not attending)
Ricky	Mitchell (not attending)
Robert	Tyrone
Suma	William

Will then explained the plans for the trip to Devon. The meeting was very positive, and afterwards I said to Will and Pete 'they're alright, aren't they?'

'Let's see how you feel at the end of the year, mate,' Pete quipped, and Will laughed. 'See you bright and early on Monday!'

****

We met at the gym to travel to Devon. It was the first time I had been in a boxing gym. In the middle of the main room there was a ring which had a springy base raised up from the ground by around a foot-and-a-half, and which was covered in blue felt. The ropes around the ring were covered in grubby white tape. The room had a high pitched ceiling whose black steel girders were exposed. It had once served as the garage for the Territorial Army's trucks. One wall was devoted to pictures of the fighters who used the gym, and the rest were covered in mirrors. A large banner hanging from the ceiling sported the slogan 'the right to remain violent' (for the kickboxing club), and another more elegant banner displayed the logo of the Haringey Police and Community Boxing Gym (the amateur boxing club). Punch bags lined the edge of the ring and there were ramshackle wooden benches lining two of the walls. Chris had a tiny office in the corner of the gym by the entrance, with enough space for a small desk, chair, fridge and not a great deal else. A menagerie of boxing gloves, pads, skipping ropes, footballs, head guards, groin cups and plastic spoons (for making tea) lined the shelving above Chris's desk.

The students shuffled in and sat with their Nike branded luggage on the benches. They were all fairly quiet and compliant, but I suspected that this would not last, and was soon proven right. Civitas had paid for a large number of black t-shirts with 'LBACP Summer Camp 2007' emblazoned across the chest. Will and Pete insisted that every student take one and wear it on the journey to camp, and began handing them out to the students. One student, however, refused point-blank to wear the t-shirt. He was a very small boy called Tyrone, who the students called 'Littles' (or littlz as they wrote it) on account of his height. He wore a wicked, slightly smug smile that exposed a perfect set of teeth. Chris and Will conferred about what could be done, whilst Tyrone basked in the glory of the confusion he had created. Will obviously felt, as I did at the time, that winning the early battles was important in establishing our authority. This was all the more important on smaller issues, we reasoned, because being tough on those issues would help us when it came to more serious matters. Chris however was very sanguine about the problem, because his analysis was precisely the opposite: flexibility about unimportant issues bought leverage when important matters arose. However, at our behest, Chris had a word with Tyrone. He grudgingly put the t-shirt on underneath his jacket; although he kept his jacket tightly zipped up, hiding the t-shirt, despite the glaring September sun.

During the long coach journey down to Devon it became clear that there was a divide between the new students (including Tyrone and Desmond), most of whom had previously attended Gladesmore School in South Tottenham, and the students from the previous year's course. The new students were considerably rowdier than the old and formed a loud gaggle at the back of the bus.

Felix was sitting at the front of the bus with Pete, Will and I. He pointed out the window at one stage and said 'what's that?' as he pointed to a field full of cattle.

'Felix, that's a cow' said Pete, who had a close relationship with Felix, but struggled to avoid a smile at his ignorance.

'Is it? Whrarr. Never seen one-o dem before you know. What about that white t'ing, that a cow too?'

'No Felix, that's a sheep,' said Pete, who was now a little shocked.

'Hm, seen. They don't have no sheep in Kingston y'know,' said Felix, referring to his upbringing in Jamaica. Felix came to the UK when he was 11 years of age, but obviously had not spent a lot of time in the countryside since arriving. Pete and I looked at each other in amazement as Felix continued: 'so, do we eat these cows then, Pete?'

'Yes Felix, from cows you get beef. You know, beefburgers from McDonalds, steaks, beef!'

'Aw, yeah, but when you get chicken from Chic-King[4] it ain't actually chicken, right? It's some other shit in there, I swear. That ain't no chicken.'

I interjected: 'so what do you think it actually is, Felix, if it's not chicken?'

'I dunno. It ain't chicken though,' insisted Felix in a matter-of-fact tone. As we passed another field, a wave of uproar filled the bus as the students caught sight of a cow mounting another in a field.

'Doggy style!' one of the students yelled, amidst general muttering amongst the students.

'Damn, that cow was really going for it!' another student contributed. Later, a further wave of opprobrium filled the bus as we passed through an area that, as Pete put it, 'smelled of the countryside'. The students insistently asked whether our camp at Devon would smell like this, and we reassured them that it would not (whilst crossing our fingers).

A few of the students had not seen the sea before—some had never left London, let alone Britain—and so as we twisted through the hills near Torquay, their excitement grew. It was a brilliant summer's day, with a clear blue sky, and when the sea emerged it was a glittering blue. Will told me that Felix had only been to the coast once before, but that he didn't enjoy it because, as Felix put it, 'something funny happened to the sea'. The tide had gone out, apparently, but Felix had no idea about tides and was somewhat disturbed by this.

The plan for our first evening was that we would brief the students, search their luggage for prohibited items, then allow the students to play sport and socialise until bedtime. The students filed off the coach into the building in which we were to hold the briefing. Chris addressed the gathered students.

'Welcome to the first camp of the London Boxing Academy Community Project. I'm really happy that...' Chris stopped because of sniggers by the students, particularly Tyrone and Desmond. 'Could you be quiet please?' asked Chris.

'Yeah, sorry' answered Tyrone, still mirthful.

'As I was saying...' Chris started, but he was interrupted by further sniggering. Chris ignored them and continued speaking, whilst Will and Pete quietly tried to hush them, without success. I found it painful watching indiscipline rule the first session at the camp—I was very glad when it was over with and we took the students to their rooms.

The students kicked up a great fuss to ensure they were roomed with their friends, a problem Chris had to solve with tactful diplomacy. The students' bags were then searched. Chris insisted on doing this himself, for reasons that I did not fully understand—I suppose he thought it was quite a serious breach of the student's dignity, and so it should be done by someone with authority. Nothing alarming was found, but since we had warned them before the camp that this would happen, we were not surprised.

We had laid on sport for the remainder of the evening in the hope that it would help them sleep. During the summer holidays, though, most of the students had grown used to going to sleep in the small hours of the morning and getting up after midday. So when we sent them to bed at 10pm, most of them were still wide awake. Chris, Richard and I took charge of one of the corridors and sat outside playing a word game called 'donkey' that Chris told us he played at moments like this, which Chris was incredibly good at. Will and Pete covered the corridor below, and Peter Haymer and Ervis went to the bar, much to my consternation, although I didn't say anything. We discussed corporal punishment —Chris in favour, Richard and I against—and played donkey until 2 a.m., at which point Chris told me to go to bed. 'I've got this under control,' he said, 'you get some sleep'.

The next morning the effort required to drag the students out of bed was tremendous. Ervis took to singing to the students, including a rendition of 'rocka-my-donkey' to Darius, whom Ervis had given the nickname 'donkey' on account of the characteristics he shared with the donkey in the film Shrek: prominent front teeth and extreme talkativeness. Darius was totally unresponsive, with his duvet tucked determinedly over his head. Tyrone periodically yelled at Ervis 'shut the *fuck* up, man. It's too *fucking* early!' Richard was pulling sheets off students' beds and teasing them for being weak-willed, and I joined in.

The morning's activities began with the high ropes. It was hilarious watching these previously threatening, rude and macho children kick up such a fuss over so minor a challenge. The best activity was centred around a fifteen-metre-high telegraph pole, which had to be scaled and then entailed a horizontal jump to a trapeze a metre or so away. The students would get to the top of the pole easily enough, but then became very nervous about standing up on the pole, and even more so about jumping to the trapeze. The pole swayed slightly with a person at its peak, which made the foothold at the top of the pole seem alarmingly small. Felix bravely went up first, whilst the rest of the students shouted encouragements tinged with ridicule.

'Look he's shaking!' said one student, as Felix nervously rose to his feet on the top of the pole.

'I'm going to tell your girl that you flopped, if you don't do it y'know!' declared another student.

'Do I have to jump?' squealed Felix. 'Yes!' came the reply from everyone below. The students chanted a count-down, 'three, two, one, go!' but Felix stayed put.

'Why you scared blood?' asked one of the students.

'I'm gonna die!' responded Felix wildly. Eventually, he jumped and caught the trapeze, to the cheers of the other students. Once lowered to the ground he stumbled towards us in a slight daze, before realising himself, adjusting his clothing and walking calmly back to the group.

Pete quizzed Felix: 'How was that?'

'That was hard, man,' said Felix.

'Why?' enquired Pete, deadpan.

'That pole felt like it was going to break, blood, swear down!'

'Why did it take you so long to do it then, were you scared?' taunted Pete.

'That wasn't long', retorted Felix with feigned disgust, 'that was less than a second!'

'You were up there for an hour-and-a-half!' joked Pete.

'Nah man,' Felix calmly responded, looking away, realising that Pete was ribbing him.

That afternoon we had a session on quad bikes. It was only a small track, but the opportunity to drive real motorised vehicles was a real draw for the students. Some of them were more experienced than we expected on the bikes. Robert, a muscled mixed-race boy who wore braids and was very polite to the staff, was one of them. He appeared timid, except when he felt something was amiss or not being done right, when he became quite assertive. He was amazingly quick on the quad bikes. He had clearly spent a few years riding them around Hackney, the borough he was from and which seemed to define his entire identity now that he was amongst the Tottenham boys. The other boys even took to calling him 'Hackney'.

We went to dinner in good spirits, but the students complained relentlessly about the quality of the food. In reality, for canteen food, it wasn't bad. I had heated arguments with the students about why mass produced food suffers in quality compared to home-cooking. Collette, our only girl on the course at that point, refused to eat anything for several meals, and responded badly to the staff's enjoinders to eat. Collette appeared sweet at first encounter, with her hair tied up in a fuzzy ball behind her head. But she could be ruthless and did not tolerate any of the boy's attempts to flirt with her. When they tried to play around, she punched them with force, and they would recoil in painful surprise.

We were sharing the camp that week with a group of primary school children. Whilst queuing up for their food they appeared very wary of our students, and were very quiet as they passed our table. They were clearly intimidated. Felix joked that they were 'behaving like they ain't never seen a black person before'. Richard, the pod leader, lectured the students, telling them 'don't give them any excuse' to have any racist feelings. 'You just gotta behave. Else they're gonna think that all black people are punks. You hear what I'm saying?'

Darius, responded: 'Well if they're going to take us for a dickhead then fuck them cuz, fuck them.' Darius then grinned broadly, exposing his brilliant white teeth.

'Donkey!' Ervis boomed. 'You're chatting shit again. Whassure problem, eh? Donkey? Wha' you always chattin' shit for, eh? You're like one of those shit-spraying trackers, everyone gets splashed, innit?' Darius giggled, and Tyrone burst out laughing.

'Don't chat shit...' said Darius, not wanting a confrontation, but looking to have the last word. Richard was very passionate about racial issues like these and had been getting increasingly irritated with Darius. Richard always spoke rapidly, sounding slightly cross. Peter had told me earlier that Richard was a rapper, but was 'a bit different to most rappers 'cos he ain't talking about shooting people all the time—he sings about some sad stuff man'. Richard performed under the name 'Dubble R', his initials. Richard took Darius to task.

'Why you always got to play dumb for, huh? How old are you, what, 14? You wanna start acting your age rather than your shoe size.' Tyrone and Darius giggled again, although slightly more quietly. 'Damn son, you don't listen,' Richard lamented.

Darius became serious suddenly: 'Nah cuz, just 'cos those dumb kids don't like us. It don't mean shit. I'm gonna just do ma ting innit?'

The next day we had an activity on a giant swing. Those who were not on the swing, played football. The swing was about 25 metres high, and was made of wood. Its seat was like a cocoon, with straps from the waist up to the shoulders tying the inhabitants of the seats into the capsule, from which the inhabitants' feet dangled. There were two seats in the swing, and the students had all paired off, except for Craig. Craig was habitually very grubby, greasy and was a bit fat. He was also a fanatical Tottenham supporter, and wore a variety of different Spurs strips throughout the week. Craig was also extremely competitive—he would never lose a prodding face-off or let any argument just lie, he would always go back for more, pushing, punching and running around like a large, over-excited puppy. He loved playing football, and looked a bit like a tubby Wayne Rooney chasing after the ball.

I admired Craig's spirit, so I volunteered to go on the swing with him. He was not keen on heights, and had a terrible time on the high ropes course earlier in the day. But he was determined to try, and so we got in line. Once tied into the seat of the giant swing, we were slowly winched up, and as we gained height Craig became increasingly nervous and talkative.

'I'm not sure about this you know. Will the rope snap?' asked Craig.

'No of course it won't. It'll be fine. You'll enjoy it!' I said.

'Look, here's what we're going to do,' Craig resolved. 'You're going to count down from ten and then pull the cord, so that we'll drop. Count slowly though, alright, slowly.' He looked down and made a funny squeak-like noise.

'OK, ten, nine, eight, 'I began.

'You're counting bare fast! Why you counting so fast?'

'I'm not counting fast Craig, what are you talking about? Seven, six, five, four, three'—'Tom!' screeched Craig—'two one'. I pulled the cord which released us at the peak of the swing's oscillation and Craig screamed with a mixture of joy and terror. We swung back and forth, with Craig dramatically saying that he was going to be sick. He had a lot of vitriol for me immediately afterwards, but always grinned whilst he complained about 'how fast you counted down. Way too fast!'

Once we were off the swing, we returned to the football match, which was getting a bit violent. The students had been wrestling with each other on and off all day, and much of the discussion at the high ropes had been about whether any student would dare to take on Ervis, the humungous heavyweight boxer. As the light began to fade, the students, pack-like, began to gun for the boxers. Eventually Darius decided to run up to Ervis and give him a cheeky punch in the ribs, before running off, giggling madly. Ervis roared and chased after him, but before he got far Tyrone had jumped on his back, and Robert was playfully attacking Richard.

It soon turned into a sort of brawl in the middle of the football pitch, with the students attempting to attack Richard and Ervis, whilst the boxers defended themselves by using their strength to throw the students off. The students were having a great time, giggling, shouting, 'getting brave' by running in towards Ervis before getting a thrown off and running away giddy with adrenalin. At one point Ervis had two students pinned down under his legs and one of his arms, whilst he fended off two more students with his spare arm. This went on for five or ten minutes until the violence died down, and staff and students walked back up the hill together having let off some steam.

On the walk back to the rooms, two students—Russell and Lucas—joined the rear of the group in fits of exaggerated giggles. They were doubled over in ever-longer laughing fits. Apparently they had spotted two of the camp staff having sex in their cabin, and they had knocked against the window, to the horror of the inhabitants.

'Did you see that bitch's face!' yelled Lucas. 'Oh my God, that was jokes.' Lucas loved to exaggerate. His voice became increasingly high-pitched as he again described the encounter. 'And then when the man came over to close the curtain! Hahahaa.' The two of them descended into another giggling fit.

Russell repeated banalities in trance of disbelief—'They were having sex bruv! Whrarr! Did you see that bruv? They were naked and everything bruv. Whrarr!' Russell was not the cleverest student. He had never shaved and so had a thick baby-moustache. But what he lacked in intelligence in made up for determination and brawn, as will become clear.

The most successful activity of the week was the kayaking. The activity was based in a small lake that was surrounded by trees on all sides, except for one corner which provided a view of the sparking blue sea. It was beautiful. The students had mixed feelings about getting in the water, though. Tyrone and Desmond stood back, aloof, muttering about not 'getting shit all over my swag'.

The instructors handed us all life jackets. They were about to begin explaining the tasks that they wanted us to complete when a student pushed Ervis into the water. He emerged, smiling, but demanding to know 'who did that? Eh?' Pete took it upon himself to jump in with a front-flip. The instructors gave up trying to instruct, and indulgently handed out paddles and kayaks for us to use. I too jumped into the lake. The water was pleasantly warm in the late afternoon sunshine.

Felix was doggedly determined not to go anywhere near the water. 'I'm phobic, innit? Wassa name for hatin' water, Tom? Wassit called?'

'Aquaphobic, Felix. You're saying you're aquaphobic,' I informed him.

'Yeah man, I'm aquaphobic. I ain't going anywhere near the water. I never been swimming in my life and ain't going to now.' Pete was in the water at the time and shouted to Felix.

'Look Felix, the lifejacket does the swimming for you. Look'—he stopped moving and let the jacket take his weight—'you're perfectly safe'. Felix gave us one of his shrewd, I-don't-believe-you looks with one of his eyebrows raised.

'Naar man, s'long. I'll do it later. S'not something you just... run into, you know?' Pete continued to remonstrate with him and, together with Will and one of the instructors, set about coaxing him into the water for his first ever swimming lesson.

Soon five boats were roaming around the small lake, each holding three people. The students hugely enjoyed being free to mess around in the water. Whenever one boat approached another an almighty splashing competition would ensue.

Once Felix had gained a little confidence in the water, I joined him in a kayak along with Hunter. After paddling around for a bit, we decided to attack Darius, Desmond and Russell's boat, success-fully capsizing it to the horror of its inhabitants. Padding away fast, we headed for the shore. To avoid retaliations from the students whose boat we had just sunk, I decided to capsize our boat, despite Felix and Hunter's protests. Once in the water Felix initially thrashed around shouting 'you bastard!', but once he had calmed down he floated around the pool in his life-jacket and said 's'alright y'know, this water stuff,' adding with a smile, 'you bastard'.

The instructors tolerated this glorious chaos for 20 minutes before calling us back in for a challenge. We were to build two rafts, using only some rope, six airtight plastic barrels and four wooden poles. We divided into two groups, the first following Pete after he declared his intention to build, as Felix put it, 'some army raft', and the rest joined me for a rival raft. My team was composed of William, a small boy of Portuguese origin; Darren, a tall muscular light-skinned black boy, who was very articulate; Lucas; Russell; and Mohammed, a quiet black boy. The remainder of the students went back to the rooms for an early shower.

We spent 20 minutes or so constructing our crafts. Russell became very over-excited at one point. He was trying to push a pole into its correct position using another pole as a battering ram. As he worked, he shouted 'die, motherfucker, die!' Russell received a few funny looks before he managed to get the pole where he wanted it. Once completed, both crafts looked sturdy, and naturally my team attacked the other team's raft as soon as we had the chance. To our surprise, our simple technique of ramming their boat managed to loosen the knots tying their boat together so much so that it disintegrated, plunging its passengers into the lake. We did a lap of honour of the lake whilst noisily declaring victory.

It felt like we had finally made real progress towards the objective that we had set ourselves for the camp: to bond with the students. Everyone had a fabulous time, and I felt the experience would stand me in good stead when it came to my teaching. As the sun set, the air cooled, sending shivers through a few of the soaked students. Exhausted, hungry, but full of spirit, the students gingerly trudged up the hill in their bare feet, chatting about the various outrages that had played out on the boating lake.

An hour or so later, I arrived at dinner ready for a good meal and eager to chew over the events of the afternoon with the other staff. Strangely, though, Will looked very worried, for reasons I did not understand, and was walking in and out of the dinner hall talking animatedly to Chris. At the end of dinner it was announced that the evening activity had been cancelled, and the staff were asked to escort the students to a hall in the complex that we had not used before. As we walked over to the hall, the students shot excited looks between them as they tried to work out what was going on.

Upon arrival Chris and Will explained to the staff individually, away from the students, that a number of items had been stolen from the primary school children who we were sharing the campsite with. Apparently their rooms were never locked, and when the children had returned to their rooms prior to dinner they had complained of missing ipods, portable playstation games, and small amounts of cash and sweets. It was probably our students; most likely the ones who had left the lake before the raft-building for an early shower.

The plan was to bring the students together to explain the seriousness of the situation to them. We would then search the students' rooms, and Chris would speak to each student individually to try to glean information from them. In this fraught situation, we were hoping that Chris's relationships with the students would bear fruit.

Will, Pete and I left to search the students' rooms, leaving the boxers and Chris with the students. Given that Chris did not want us to search the students' bags at the start of the camp, the fact he acquiesced to it now told me that the situation was serious. We checked each room in turn, looking through clothes, behind wardrobes, around toilets, under beds; every possible hiding place. But we found nothing, and returned to the hall to a volley of jeers from the students, who were sitting together on benches arranged in a horseshoe shape. On the way back from the rooms I overheard Will talking to various people from the camp and to our Civitas co-ordinators in London about what was going on. It all sounded rather grave. Darius looked at us mirthfully and said 'you didn't find shit, did you boss?'

Then Tyrone shouted out at Will, in his best mocking and belittling tone: 'Oi Will, what you so red for?'

'I'm embarrassed', Will exploded, 'that's why I'm red, I'm embarrassed at your behaviour that has led to our probably having to go home sooner than we should be.' The students 'oooohhh'-ed in response. Will ignored them and went to speak to Chris about whether his interviews had gleaned any useful information. Apparently they had not, yet. I asked Will if he was OK and he said he was, but that he was under a lot of pressure. I did not realise at the time how stressful taking responsibility for all of those students on a residential trip could be.

The next stage of Chris's plan was to give the students half-an-hour of free time, in order to allow for an amnesty. Chris explained that whenever the boys steal anything, they never hold it on their person or with their belongings, but hide it somewhere else for safekeeping and later collection. It seemed a far-fetched notion to me (later, I found Chris was absolutely right), but at that time we were willing to give anything a go. So the students were allowed to leave, after being given a stern talk from Chris which emphasised how new everyone was to the school, how damaging this episode was, and how much he trusted in them to return the items, else—he said in a deadly serious tone—the police would be called.

'You don't want to meet the police in Devon,' Chris said to the students. 'Bring back the items to the front desk and we can continue with the camp.'

The staff retreated, somewhat shattered, to the rooms. The students noisily argued with each other several doors down.

To my surprise, almost all of the items were returned during the amnesty. Two items—portable playstation ('PSP') games—were still missing. Chris and Will told the students that they must be returned, then sent the students to bed at 9.30pm with the message that if the items were not returned, the police would arrive in the morning. Things were starting to get out of control a little; students were being ruder, and more aggressive. Darren began staring down staff members in the corridor. Whenever any staff member tried to talk to him, he had a huge outburst—'what you talkin' to me for bruv?' I walked past one room and Darius ran out, giggling moronically, and handed one of the missing portable playstation games to me. I stood there, gobsmacked at Darius's audacity. He had just handed stolen goods to a teacher! Darius ran back into the room, where he was received by the other students with a chorus of laughter. I gave the game to Will and told him the story, who shook his head whilst he listened, clearly shattered.

'Police will be here in the morning,' Will said. 'Let's see if that has any effect on them.'

Supervising the students that night was hard. Once again Chris told everyone to go to bed, but this time I refused, noting the bulging blood vessels in Chris's left eye. We stayed up together and played the donkey game, finally sensing that things were quiet at about 3 a.m., when we went to bed.

In the morning at breakfast the students were all hushed voices and tense conversations. Apparently a window near the students' rooms had been broken during the night, and we were taking the blame for the damage. Will was standing with Chris by the door when a female police sergeant walked into the hall. She began speaking with Chris, with Richard and Ervis listening to the conversation. I sat with the students in the centre of the hall, which was empty apart from our small group. The students saw the police and discussed the development in colourful terms.

Darren said he 'don't care about the feds. They can do what they like, whatever.' The occasional loud insult rose over the top of the hubbub that could have been aimed either at one of the students or at the police.

Without warning, Richard strode over and spoke to the students. 'The police are sayin' that if the stuff don't come back, then you're all gonna be arrested and held overnight in cells.'

The effect of his words was instantaneous. The students suddenly ran in all directions, as if someone had tossed a grenade towards the breakfast table. 'This is long' muttered Darren as he dashed past me.

'Wow shit!' shouted another. The students ran crouched low, as if avoiding bullet fire.

'Bollocks,' I muttered to myself, and began to follow the students to make sure they did no further damage to the centre. I panicked, for the first time since arriving at camp, because I realised that we had just lost control. The police were the only effective sanction now.

I started walking through the hall towards the students' rooms, where most of the students seemed to have been heading. I spotted two students dart through a side door in another direction, which I saw as a sign of trouble, so I followed them. Once outside, I could not see the two boys, but I heard someone shouting nearby, so I followed the noise. I found Mohammed in a sloped driveway leading under the complex that took the deliveries for the kitchen, which also held several tall cylindrical rubbish bins. Mohammed was in tears, inconsolable with rage, kicking the bins with all his might whilst on his mobile to someone who I soon learned was his mother.

'I'm going to get fucking arrested... I know, I can't get fucking arrested because they'll fucking put me in jail, I fucking know mum. This fucking tag, and these stupid fucking cunts at this stupid fucking camp!' He lowered the mobile and booted the rubbish bins again before speaking to his mother. I knew that Mohammed had to acquire special permission from his youth offending team to attend the camp because he was wearing a tag, but I didn't realise that if he was arrested he would end up in jail. I suppose someone—a judge, the youth offending team perhaps—had warned him as much. I left

30

Mohammed and searched for Chris, figuring that Chris would be the only one who might be able to calm Mohammed down. I called Chris's mobile but unsurprisingly it was engaged, before luckily running into him giving a dressing down to Darren, who had apparently been threatening Will. Chris came immediately and his presence alone was enough to stop Mohammed booting the bins. Chris tried to reassure him and spoke to his mum on the phone.

I walked back towards the rooms in a bit of a daze. I came across several students dragging their suitcases along the main path towards the complex's exit. Craig was in a huge panic, shouting 'I'm going to get a taxi, fuck this shit, I'm going to get a taxi. I ain't getting arrested for no bullshit at camp.' I tried to talk to him but he would not listen. He started climbing on top of a small hut that straddled the perimeter fence of the camp, and looked out on to a wooded area.

'Craig, where are you going to get a fucking taxi?' I asked.

'I don't care, I don't give a shit, I'll walk all the way if I have to. Those cunts who stole the shit, I ain't getting arrested for them, oh no.' Craig had dragged his suitcase up to the top of the hut. If it were not for the seriousness of the situation it would have been hilarious, and I couldn't help being sarcastic.

'So Craig, what money have you got to get you home? Do you know how much a rail ticket from Devon to London costs? About 80 quid, mate. Have you got that money? No. So what are you doing?'

'I'm not getting arrested, that's what,' responded Craig.

'Look Craig, will you just stay there for a minute whilst I try to sort this out, please?'

'OK, alright, you've got two minutes. But if I see any feds I'm gone'.

I strode back into the hall with a growing head of steam. I spotted Darren running out the front gate, with Richard in hot pursuit shouting 'where you gonna go bruv? Huh? Where you gonna go?' and shook my head in disbelief. I don't often get angry, but this strategy to get the goods back that was based on anarchy, as I saw it, was mad. I came across the police sergeant and I asked her whether the item had been returned yet.

'No it has not' she responded.

'You do realise that you're creating absolute chaos in this camp right now? I've got students crying their eyes out, and others making mad escape attempts, it's not doing anyone any good so far as I can tell. Do you understand what I'm saying?'

'Yes, I do understand what you're saying. Just take it from me that this has got results in the past, and hopefully it will this time' she said firmly. I walked away with my head swimming with expletives.

Will then caught me and gave me some good news. 'They found the item at the front desk. Someone must have left it there. Go tell the students, and Craig!'

'Thank God, will do' I said, with tremendous relief. My first thought was with Mohammed, so I went for the bins. I found Mohammed still sobbing and shouting, which I found quite disconcerting because I'd never seen him anything but cool and calm. I said to Mohammed and Chris: 'It's been found. The police are going. You're not going to get arrested, Mohammed.' He didn't respond directly to me, but slowly stopped crying, and reached for his phone.

'I'm not geddin arrested' he said to his mum, the gunge from his nose causing his voice to sound extremely deep. He spat out his phlegm towards the bins with contempt. I walked back towards the students' rooms and spotted Craig, marooned on the top of his little building with his suitcase, vigorously fending off Pete and Ervis' entreaties for him to come down.

'Craig,' I shouted, 'no arrests, get down you pillock.'

'Fuck you' Craig replied, before he threw his suitcase off the building back towards the rooms, and gingerly started his descent from the building. Pete asked me what we would do next.

'I dunno mate,' I said, 'I suppose we should try to get everyone back to their rooms and work it out from there,' adrenalin still pumping through my system.

We regrouped, and with the students back in their rooms, Will briefed us. 'The camp are happy for us to carry on, but they want the perpetrators off the site. Do we know who they are, Chris?'

'We can only guess. I've got theories, but no proof. But we can't send anyone home and blame them without proof. We just can't do it.'

'But can't we just send a few home to save the rest of the camp for the other students?' Will asked insistently.

'Will, we can't do that. If they want the perpetrators off site, then everyone will have to go home.'

'OK well we better get ready to go home, I'll call the coach company' said Will, resignedly. Will had already called the coach company the night before to prepare the ground, so we would only have to wait four hours for a coach to drive down from London, which would then take us home. It was decided that we would keep the students in the youth club-type building until then, allowing them to pack their suitcases in their rooms in small groups. This gave the staff time to pack, which I was allowed to do first.

I returned to my room through the bar area, which was reserved for adults only, and found Darren skulking around the room.

'Darren, you know that you're not supposed to be in here. Can you go over to the youth club please?' I asked.

'Fuck you,' replied Darren, ignoring me. I replied calmly.

'Darren listen, you can't be…'

'Fuck you,' Darren repeated. He turned suddenly and moved towards me, with his head dipped and eyes bulging, staring right into my eyes.

'You gonna make me leave, Tom? Huh?' he said with more than a hint of menace. He stood in front of me, holding my gaze and with his right fist clenched behind his back. I stood my ground, staring right back. I spoke as plainly as I could.

'No Darren, I'm not going to make you. But please could you leave and go back to where you are supposed to be?'

Darren continued to stare at me for a moment, before chuckling in a short, amused manner. Then he walked off towards the youth club. It was the most threatened I had felt all camp. I honestly wondered if he was going to hit me, but I thought it was important to stand my ground. I was also surprised that this articulate, considerate boy, who seemed able to understand so many things that the other students could not, was such a tiger.

I packed my bags, and returned to the youth club area, where things were increasingly chaotic. Students were running around wildly, wrestling in corners and disregarding what the staff were telling them to do. Even Felix and Hunter were 'off the hook', as the students might have put it. Will was red-faced again, so I knew something else was up.

'The students have been trashing their rooms,' Will said, 'we've got to have better supervision of the students in their rooms. And Darren is going crazy, he won't listen to a word I say.' In one room a lot of damage had been caused by a student blocking the plughole with tissue and leaving the shower on. Although we had organised regular patrols of the rooms, this clearly was not sufficient. We wondered, in paranoia, whether the students had been using lookouts.

Darren had also been trying to threaten Richard, who as the smallest of the boxers had to put up with this frequently. He was particularly small at the time because he was keeping his weight down for fights. Peter Haymer and Ervis had to intervene and face down Darren, who quickly backed down in the face of the two heavyweights.

When Chris heard about all this, he decided that as the main troublemaker, Darren should return to Tottenham in Chris's own car, along with Will and two other troublesome students, rather than taking the coach. Darren's behaviour had been a big surprise to us all, given his previously polite and courteous demeanour.

Chris told me that when he approached Darren and told him of his decision, Darren exploded. 'It's over between us. That's it. I ain't going in the car and that's it. It's over' asserted Darren.

'What do you mean it's over, Darren? What are you talking about? Listen, you're coming in the car with me, or one of your parents is coming down to Devon to collect you, and that's it.' Darren fumed at Chris, walking around in circles. Chris said that he had not previously had to tell Darren to do anything—up to then everything was optional. Darren's reaction, full of malice and aggression, surprised Chris. Eventually Darren relented. I had not been looking forward to sharing the bus home with him.

When the bus arrived, the students piled on whilst moaning about having to go home early. They went out of their way to lay the blame on Will. They were not interested in the obvious point that it was the stealing that caused the camp to end early.

The bad feeling amongst the students towards the staff did not last long. They were soon back to joking around. For example, Darius and Lucas had taken to screaming 'Jennifer!' in orgasmic tones, because they had discovered that Ervis' girlfriend's name was tattooed on his neck. Periodically Ervis would get up and squeeze the students, who would cry out with a mixture of pain and humour, although this was usually followed by someone else on the bus shouting 'yes, Jennifer, yes!'

After half a week of no sleep and endless antics, the students were very tired. Stopping at a service station on the way home, some of them were slumped over tables, dozing. For some reason, though, Suma looked forlorn. This was despite having the Burger King meal we had just bought him in his hand. I walked up to his table, where he was sitting with Hunter, Craig and Felix, who were jabbering away, ignoring Suma, and sat down. Suma was a black boy with very dark skin, which led the other students to label him as 'the African' (to my dismay). Suma was silly in a giggly, girly way, which was relatively unusual amongst our wannabe-masculine students. He was usually disruptive only in a low-level way, but sometimes, like at that Burger King, he could be very withdrawn.

'What's up?' I asked Suma, quietly sitting next to him.

'Mmmbbbmm,' he mumbled, looking at his feet. 'I don't want to go home,' he said, before raising his head to stare towards the large green field that lay beyond the window of the service station.

'Oh... I'm sorry to hear that. Why don't you want to go home?' I asked gently.

'Home's rubbish. Devon was fun. I can't wait to leave home so that I can go on my own trips like that. Mmmmbbbmm...' he mumbled again.

I felt sorry for him. I knew from his file that he'd been in care at various points, but that his mother, father and grandfather were still involved with him.

'There'll be another trip, I promise,' I told him. I then tried to persuade him that the quickest way to leave home and earn his independence was to go to university.

'That's how I left home, and it was great,' I said. 'Loads of people I knew where I grew up were still living with their mums when they were like 20, but I was gone at 18. If you can do it, Suma, that's the best way, trust me.' Suma considered what I said for a moment, then looked down at his feet again.

'Yeah well I'll be one of those guys living with my mum,' he said miserably. At that moment Craig threw a chip at Suma, who responded by throwing an opened sachet of tomato ketchup at Craig, which narrowly missed his white t-shirt. I sternly told them to cease hostilities, which they reluctantly did, and leant over to speak to Suma.

'Just don't rule university out, alright?' Suma grunted in a non-committal way and took a bite out of his burger.

Later on, Chris and Will told me that during their journey back to London in Chris's car, they were able to have a long and productive talk with Darren. Darren was reflective about his aggressive behaviour and something of an accord was reached. Chris had been minded to expel Darren, but that car journey home convinced both Chris and Will that there might be something to salvage from the situation. Furthermore, Darren was very bright, and it would have been a shame to lose someone with potential.

Darren told them about his life in Tottenham and about gangs. Darren said that if you came across a rival gang in a chicken shop, for example, you might not want to beat them up or cause any trouble, but 'sometimes you just got to'.

When they approached Tottenham, Darren became tense, and circumspect. He asked not to be dropped on the busy High Road in Tottenham. 'Why not the High Road?' asked Will.

'There might be people that I don't want to see, who'll cause trouble. Nowhere on the High Road, please, I beg you.' They dropped Darren off on a side street.

I returned home, absolutely shattered and in shock that the camp had ended a day early. I wondered what teaching, starting on Monday, would bring.

3

A Bit of Background

Why the fuck would you want to work in a shit-hole like this if you was at Oxford? You is mugging you'self sir, swear down.

Laura, LBACP student, 2010

In August 2007, a month before I began teaching at the LBACP, I was a graduate student at the University of Oxford studying sociology. I stayed on at university to investigate a theory: that schools in working-class areas achieve poor examination results because they cannot attract enough good teachers. Only teachers with the deepest commitment to social justice would teach in really challenging schools, according to my theory. If the money were the same, most teachers would eventually choose to teach in schools where there are fewer discipline problems.

This would be true even for teachers who, like me, enjoy teaching very basic material to students who are behind, simply because the resources available to deal with the challenges presented by those students are often insufficient to do the job properly. If this theory were correct, then it follows that it would be possible to radically improve education for the poorest if some means could be found to encourage more highly qualified, enthusiastic teachers to work in the most difficult schools.

But would the schools really be that much better? Isn't it because of the upbringing of working class children that they tend to have trouble in school? And what makes a 'good' teacher anyway? From my sociology classes I knew that the biggest determinant of how well students do in school was their social background, by some margin. But I was certain that this was not the whole story.

That certainty was based upon my own personal experience of education. I went to two secondary schools, both in the state sector, but quite different in their intakes and in the characteristics of their teaching staff. The first was Tamworth Manor High School, where I studied until I was 16 years of age. Tamworth was the school where the incident mentioned in the last chapter involving Berek occurred.

Tamworth was a working-class school with relatively poor examination results: less than a third of the students achieved five A*-C grades at GCSE, the most basic academic benchmark required to move on to A-Levels, whereas around half of students achieved this nationally. It had no sixth form, and closed in 2006 as part of the then Labour government's City Academy programme. Harris Academy Merton now stands on the same site.

Tamworth was a ten-minute walk away from where I grew up in Mitcham, South London, near to the rough Pollards Hill estate. Mitcham is a suburban area in South London. It is not wealthy, but by no means has the worst concentrations of poverty in London. There were few exciting things going on for young people in Mitcham. My friends and I used to jokingly imagine that if a set of Japanese tourists ever mistakenly visited Mitcham, they would be forced to take photos of the McDonalds in the town centre, for want of anything else interesting to photograph.

One of Tamworth's problems was its infrastructure. The main teaching block was designed with a series of fire-escape style stairwells with classrooms either side of each landing, which created a cacophony of noise whenever students used them. The headteacher once wistfully told me she would demolish that teaching block if she had the chance. A horrendous red grit football pitch dominated the front of the school, where I played football at lunchtimes and often got very muddy. Tamworth was however based in a relatively large, green site with generous playing fields. The major rebuilding work accompanying the school's transition to becoming Harris Academy appears to have improved its facilities markedly.

The school's biggest problem when I was a student, however, was the low morale of its staff. Some of the staff blamed the parents for the low standards of the pupils—'you know who I blame' was a constant refrain of one of the older teachers (he blamed the parents). Other staff complained bitterly about the management of the school. One of my teachers boasted to us in class that by threatening to leave he had extorted a lighter teaching schedule and higher pay from the management. Impressive as this extortion was, it did not give me great confidence in Tamworth. I remember feeling vindicated in this belief when at the start of year nine we were allocated a mathematics teacher who was new to the school and whose grasp of English was extremely poor—worse, in fact, than a newly arrived student from Ethiopia who had just joined the class and later became a friend of mine.

'You know who I blame' did have a point though—we did not make it easy for the teachers. The large loud-mouthed boys who dominated the playground bullied our religious education teacher so much that, by Year 11, she simply wrote the chapter number on the board in each lesson and left us to mess around. The only students more fearsome than the lads were the gold-hooped-earring wearing, fringe-sporting female students. I was always impressed by their ability to keep the lads in check. Though decidedly nerdy, I played my part in those difficulties, making a point of going out my way to disagree wherever possible with the headmistress who taught me business studies. The poor mathematics teacher who appeared not to speak much English did not stand much of a chance in her first lesson with us. After 20 minutes of paper aeroplanes and abuse, she showed us that she knew enough English to declare that she was 'going for a cigarette' and we never saw her again.

There were good teachers at Tamworth, two of whom came to mind when I began teaching at the LBACP. The teacher who made the biggest impact upon me was Mr Twitchell, who was my head of year and physical education teacher. He was a tough, rugged man who told us he was in the Parachute Regiment before he became a teacher. His hair was short, jet-black with streaks of grey. He had an earring in one ear, and an angular face that often wore a sardonic smile. He was not tall, but he compensated for that with abundant anger. If a student stepped out of line he would be in their face without hesitation. The other teachers often threatened to 'have a word with Mr Twitchell about you' in order to maintain control of a class. All the students in the school respected him, and many feared him. His humour, and the quiet authority that stemmed from his obvious life experience, gave him the tools to work with students that the other staff found extremely difficult.

Mr Dunn was a very different proposition. He was a science teacher, and one of the few who we knew had studied at one of the top universities in the UK—Durham, in his case. Mr Dunn was young, tall, charismatic and attractive in a swashbuckling, gentlemanly kind of way. He used to wear loose un-ironed cotton shirts with brown shoes, and was something of a hit with the girls, who appreciated his self-deprecating confidence and willingness to banter. Once, he was explaining the concept of a 'moment', which determines how much force you can create using leverage, and he told us a story about actor Martine McCutcheon. McCutcheon famously played the sweet working-class girl Tiffany in the BBC soap Eastenders, and had just launched her pop career with the single 'Perfect Moment'. Mr Dunn explained that a few weeks previously he had been driving down the M1, whereupon he spotted a pretty woman on the side of the road whose Mercedes had a flat tyre. Mr Dunn, ever the gentleman, pulled over and changed her tyre for her, using a very long pole to loosen the screws on the wheels. McCutcheon asked Mr Dunn whether it was his big muscles that allowed him to remove the wheel screws so easily, but Mr Dunn explained 'no, it's the moment created by this long pole I'm using that allows me to remove the tyre so easily'. McCutcheon allegedly replied 'this is my perfect moment'. This amusing pack of lies received a very sceptical reception in my science class, but Mr Dunn insisted over the groans—'you'll always remember what a moment is though, won't you?' Well, he was right.

The reason that I found the weaknesses of Tamworth so frustrating was that I was very academically ambitious. For me, school was the obvious route out of Mitcham and towards a better life. The house I grew up in was a two-up, two-down Victorian semi-detached house where I shared a small room with my younger brother, Harry. Both of my parents worked in modestly paid jobs, my mother as a qualified nurse, and my father in a variety of jobs related to mortgage advice. At the time, I thought my family was poor, and I wanted to be as successful in my career as I possibly could be, in order to have a better material standard of living than I had when I was growing up. I know now that compared with some of my students at the LBACP I was not really poor at all—but at that stage it was my impressions that were important, rather than the reality.

The big complication in my family, though, was that my father was a manic-depressive, which is a form of mental illness that is also known as bipolar disorder. Manic depression causes long-term, and severe swings in a person's mental state. At one extreme is depression, a relatively common condition, which sucks the energy and optimism out of a person. The other extreme is mania, or being 'high'. When a person is high they behave impulsively, sometimes aggressively, sleep very little, and tend to have irrational, unfounded beliefs. A wave from its manic peak to its depressive trough generally took between one and three years for my father. For the majority of the time, manic-depressives are neither depressed nor manic; they are in a normal state, like any other person. However the next swing, either up or down, is never far away.

This fact about my father had one important effect on me that is relevant to my work at the LBACP: it helped me develop a number of ways of coping with challenging situations, the most useful of which was humour. When my father was high, for example, he variously believed that he was the long-lost brother of the famous pianist Vladimir Ashkenazy, that Princess Diana was in love with him, but also, somewhat contradictorily, that he was a member of the royal family himself—'Prince Ken'. I found that the best way to deal with these kinds of things was to laugh at them, when the time was right. So when my mother received a phone call from Vladimir Ashkenazy's secretary, after my dad had written to him explaining that he was indeed his long-lost brother, what else could you do but laugh? These coping mechanisms, I am sure, were of immense value in dealing with the challenges that the students at the LBACP threw at me.

I was, however, privileged in a number of ways. Most importantly, my mother held the family together even at the most difficult of times when my father was unwell. She prioritised the family's well-being above her own. My parents also had relatives who would help them financially when the need arose, and they owned the house that I grew up in. More, our house was at the edge of Mitcham Common, a wonderfully wild green space which I was able to wander freely over without fear of bumping into any other group of young people, friendly or otherwise. The situation is quite different for the students of mine who lived near Hackney Fields or Bruce Castle Park, which were surrounded by high density housing.

My parents also had a reasonable amount of what sociologists call 'cultural capital'. Although neither had a degree, my mother keenly followed political programmes like *Newsnight* and my father was passionate about classical music. A baby-grand piano dominated one of the few rooms in the house, and my father loved to play the Rachmaninov second and third piano concertos (albeit badly, he would emphasise) and for several years listened to nothing other than a particular recording of the third on his stereo. Their working arrangements also meant that they were able to spend a great deal of their time with me when I was growing up, so I was very privileged in the amount of attention I received from my parents.

Not being highly educated, my parents were not much help on questions I had about how university worked, which local sixth-forms were better than others, or exactly how good your grades had to be in order to get into a top university. One unusual opportunity available at Tamworth changed much of that. Tamworth was in the London Borough of Merton, which contains Wimbledon, famous for its tennis tournament. 'The Championships', as it somewhat pompously referred to itself, recruited ball girls and ball boys from all the schools in Merton, including Tamworth. Each school had a set number of individuals it could nominate for further training at Wimbledon, so schools tended to have a training programme and selection process to decide who would be sent on to Wimbledon. At Tamworth, there were eight places, and dozens of eager students put themselves forward for selection each year.

Competition for places was intense. The training was run by Mr Twitchell, and it was a very serious business, involving punishing circuit training, running and 'ball skills'. I put myself forward for the training slightly hesitantly, because although I enjoyed sport I had never taken it that seriously before. As Mr Twitchell predicted at the time, I have never been physically fitter than when I was competing with the other students at Tamworth for a place at Wimbledon. We trained three times a week for six weeks, and at home did further sit-ups, push-ups, running and studied the rules of tennis.

Mr Twitchell used the training as a form of control over the more badly behaved boys. Given the value of the prize, his threats to dismiss them from the training really had bite. For my part, I really wanted to win a place. As the announcement of the selection process neared, rumours about who was in and who was not flew about the school. Mr Twitchell told us that he would give a written explanation in a card of his decision to every person who undertook the training. I vividly remember a great sense of anticipation as I waited amongst the other students for our cards. Despite my desire not to offend any of my rivals who had not been offered a place, when I read my card informing me I was going to train at Wimbledon I jumped for joy, shouting 'YES!'

The Wimbledon Tennis Championships in 2000 were a life-changing experience for me. The training at Tamworth was so tough that once at Wimbledon, even under the control of the redoubtable Wally Wonfor, a former RAF physical training instructor, the training was easy. I was soon a 'Captain of Court' ball boy, leading a team of 'bases' (who supply the balls to the players from the back of the court) and 'nets' (who crouch either side of the net ready to collect balls from the centre of the court). In my first year as a ball boy, Pete Sampras went on to win his last Wimbledon title. I was one of the ball boys in the 'Guard of Honour' that form lines across the court after the singles final, and as the light faded we witnessed Sampras's emotional climb into the stands to hug his father. My relatives all spotted me on television as my legs shivered in the cool evening breeze and we chatted with royalty. I was awestruck by that great public spectacle and the blizzard of camera flashes from the spectators as Sue Barker interviewed Sampras. What was life-changing for me, though, was nothing to do with the glamour of Wimbledon or the training. It was the unusual social experience of being forced to socialise with other young people from much more privileged backgrounds, whose aspirations and plans were so much better formed than mine.

The ball boys and girls were based in a brightly lit and modern basement underneath Centre Court, where we were fed regularly and relaxed during our hour off, before we went back on to court for another hour. This 'hour-on, hour-off' schedule continued for the two weeks of the Championships. During our hours off, we had a great deal of time on our hands to talk about our aspirations for the future, as young people spend much of their time doing, whilst playing card games such as 'speed' and 'blackjack'. This was probably my first encounter with young people who had been privately educated, and I remember particularly vividly the girls from Wimbledon High School, a private girls day-school located a short walk from the All England Club. There were some stunning young women amongst those girls and I took enormous pleasure in chatting with them. They were beautiful and they were clever. The more I spoke with them, though, the more I realised that there was something of a gap between the way they thought about their futures and the way I did. Their expectations of themselves were simply greater, and they were much better informed about the various options available to an ambitious young person like me. I remember once asking a girl what she expected to get for her GCSEs. 'Twelve A*s', she said, matter of factly. 'And then I want to go to Oxford to study either politics or law.'

Christ, I thought. I was ambitious, to be sure, and I was hoping to pick up a few A*s and go to university. But at 14 years of age I was really quite ignorant, and when that girl told me about her grand plan it was something of a wake-up call. Perhaps it is not very surprising that I found her rather attractive. She ended up being my first girlfriend, and I learnt a great deal from spending time with her and her privileged friends, who were equally ambitious and articulate.

One thing was clear to me from my Wimbledon experience: that I needed to take the initiative and up the ante academically. I started buying newspapers and revision guides for my exams. I tried to read more books, but did not manage many, the local library at Pollards Hill being more like a play-centre, and my house being just a little too small easily to find a quiet space to read undisturbed by either my younger brother, my parents or our three cats. I had to banish my brother downstairs, where he played the piano incessantly, lock the cats out and exercise great self-restraint in avoiding playing computer games to get any academic work done at all.

I also became increasingly frustrated with Tamworth. It seemed that as far as the school—as an institution—was concerned, if you were going to get a grade C or above in a subject, then that was all that really mattered. I know now that this is because the statistics for GCSE examination results are based upon the proportion of the students in a school that achieve five GCSEs at grade C or above (or their vocational equivalent). State schools such as Tamworth therefore put a wholly disproportionate amount of effort and resources into students who were marginal between the C/D grades, for example by laying on special after-school classes for students at that level. Individual teachers made great efforts to support the clever students, of course—my maths teacher, for example, taught us GCSE statistics after school. But their efforts all too often went against the grain of the institution.

I digress, perhaps, but my experiences at Tamworth and at the LBACP have convinced me that there is no good justification for the examinations system incentivising schools to put all those resources into the C/D marginal ability bracket. It is simply arbitrary. Some make a case for putting extra resources towards the education of the most talented students. In my view there are stronger reasons put scarce resources towards educating the least able students, not least because a lack of academic confidence is an important contributor to poor behaviour in and exclusions from mainstream schools. But putting resources into the C/D marginal students, at the expense of everyone else, makes no sense at all.

Another problem at Tamworth was numerical, and not the fault of any of the teachers. It was that there were at best around half-a-dozen students who were seriously academically orientated in my year. This meant that, even when classes were streamed by ability, in a standard class of 30 students there was an extremely wide range of abilities that the teachers had to cater for. Even really good teachers like Mr Dunn struggled to provide for both the students who were aiming for D grades and those, like me, who were hoping for A*s. This problem was compounded when the teacher was not much good, and the worst teachers didn't take any notice of us at all. My ICT teacher, for example, did not teach us any of the higher level material necessary to get grades above C, despite putting several of us forward for the higher exam. Infuriatingly I only found this out in the examination, when I faced a whole paper full of questions that I had never had the opportunity to study for.

No doubt there were and are worse schools than Tamworth. Indeed, the half-dozen academic students with whom I kept in contact did very well after leaving Tamworth: one studied at Oxford in the same year as me (although we were not aware of any other Tamworth alumni who had reached Oxbridge), and several others attended prestigious academic institutions. Nonetheless, I spent a lot of time thinking about what would have been had I gone to a better school, and in particular had I attended a private school. I was somewhat annoyed that my parents had not known about the scholarships available at private schools or where might be a strategic place to live to get in order to get a place at a good state school. I was even more annoyed at an education system that seemed to allow parental know-how to determine the extent to which children received a decent education. When looking at sixth-forms I therefore acquired a steely determination, now that I was more in control of my own destiny, to go to the best possible institution I could.

That institution was Graveney School in Tooting, South London, as advised by Mr Twitchell. Graveney is a former grammar school with a variety of government statuses which increase its funding and autonomy. At one time it was allowed to select around a fifth of its intake, with the remainder of the places going to pupils who lived locally. Graveney was a different experience to Tamworth from the very start. I had my induction interview with a teacher called Dr Magreola, who was a stern Nigerian with a wiry moustache. I told him that I wanted to get As in my A-Levels and that I wanted to go to Oxford or Cambridge. He looked at my GCSE results, which were pretty good, although not the perfect set of A*s the Wimbledon girls talked about.

'Well,' he said, 'we can cater for that, if you're willing to put the work in. We send a few to Oxford and Cambridge every year, and if you're serious, then you could be one of them.'

It is impossible to overstate how much I loved that school. I am still in awe of it. My law teacher, Mr Quinty-Williams, a rotund African lay preacher, declared a few weeks after meeting me that I would be a barrister and told me that I should not go into politics, which he regarded as bankrupt, having resigned his Labour Party membership in bitterness over the Iraq war. My economics teacher, Mr Corcoran, was a huge man, with a ginger goatee and a gruff, acerbic wit. He would march into the room, and hold court on the economic matters of the day. He would teach whilst on his feet, drawing graphs on the board, the lesson being a sort of interactive lecture. We would take notes of what he was saying, bringing up anything we wanted to, in a relaxed and intellectually stimulating atmosphere. I admired his ability to ad-lib effortlessly, constantly jumping back and forth between the theoretical and historical, which brought to life causal links between economic phenomena with a flourish. Mr Corcoran had friends in the City of London from his own time at university and kindly organised a week of work experience at the foreign exchange sales desk at Citibank, where I marvelled at the millions passing nonchalantly through the bank's desks and learnt that I did not want to be a banker.

Mr Abraham, teaching philosophy, would talk endlessly about China, Russia and Cuba, and was obviously some kind of socialist. He looked a bit like Lenin would have appeared if he'd survived a few more decades. 'Abes', as he was reverentially known, had read history at Cambridge and sang in the school's Community Choir. Ms Hamill, another philosophy teacher, carefully introduced me to J.P. Sartre, J.S. Mill and the philosophy of religion. Finally there was Mr Perks, who ran the debating society, and who was indirectly responsible for my landing a job at the LBACP. Mr Perks, now a prominent writer on science education in addition to his teaching, would argue with us every Friday lunchtime about the topic of the day, and took us to political conferences run by his friends in the Institute of Ideas.

What was astonishing to me about the teachers at Graveney was that they were quirky, stimulating and had links to the real world that they invited me to interact with. There were teachers who had been to Oxford and Cambridge, and even some with doctorates. There were parallels with life in Tamworth—Mr Corcoran, my economics teacher, was rumoured to have been a policeman before becoming a teacher (when I asked him about it, he grinned widely and said 'I wouldn't want to quash a useful rumour now, would I?'). And there were plenty of rough types at Graveney. They just weren't in charge, partly because the children of the middle classes that I had first met at Wimbledon were there en masse—complete with dope, Glastonbury visits and pashminas. The school was also extremely ethnically diverse—very roughly a third white, a third black and a third Asian. The critical mass of academic students— enough to make a top set or two—was present, but there were also plenty of less academic students at the school, which made for a good mix.

The following example probably best exemplifies the difference between Tamworth and Graveney. The leaving ceremonies at Graveney always seemed to be extremely emotional affairs where tears flowed freely and the demonstrations of gratitude never seemed to end. The few students who had travelled with me from Tamworth to Graveney regarded this middle-class over-expressive-ness with some scepticism. The feelings were genuine, though. The same could be said of Tamworth's leaving ceremony, where instead of tears of gratitude, we had refused to allow our head teacher to address us. We booed her off the stage and walked off without hearing her in what I took to be an act of cruel revenge for what we felt was a substandard education. Mr Twitchell had left the school the term before our leaving ceremony, and we suspected that the blame for his departure lay with the head. In the local pub afterwards with the teachers, we learnt more about their feelings about Tamworth's management. I learnt for the first time about the importance of leadership in schools—the head was too academic, they complained, and suffered from her poor rapport with both the teachers and the students. I learnt that most of the teachers were either planning to leave Tamworth or were counting the years until retirement. Even 'you know who I blame' was adamant that things could have been much better.

During my time at Graveney, I began to form some political opinions. What was clear to me was that there was something quite wrong in the differences I had encountered during my educational career at Tamworth and Graveney. Surely, I thought, things would have been better for me if I had been at Graveney for my GCSE years or at some private school? Would I have been more likely to get that perfect set of A*s, and perhaps a proper liberal education — maybe even some Latin or Greek, which seemed so useful to the other philosophy students in my class? Soon, though, I realised that these desires to 'get out' were rather selfish. What about all the other students at Tamworth? My anger at being unable to go to a better school soon morphed into questions about why it was that I went to a poor school, whilst my new middle-class friends went to Graveney? What exactly could be done to change the situation?

I was later lucky enough to be granted a place to read PPE (philosophy, politics and economics) at Corpus Christi College, University of Oxford. Before embarking on the graduate study programme mentioned at the start of this chapter, I worked for a summer in the United States of America. I worked for the Fresh Air Fund, a charity which provided summer-camps for poor, inner-city children in New York City. My experiences there informed what I did at the LBACP, so it is worth describing them briefly.

Only children with a parental income of less than the equivalent of about £10,000 were offered places at the Fresh Air Fund's camp. My section of the camp was called Camp Tommy (after donor Tommy Hilfiger), and it catered for 12-15 year old boys, almost all of whom were black or Latino. Most of the staff, and all of the students, would have described themselves as being from 'the ghetto'. It was an enormous contrast to Oxford. I found the street language used to be almost impenetrable when I first arrived. What was really shocking was almost everyone on camp referred to each other as 'nigger'. They used the 'N-bomb' in the same way I used 'mate' in London, which took some getting used to.

The students were very similar to those I met at the LBACP. One of the older students was called De-Bo, and he was very serious. He once told me in a low voice that his family had 'a lot of links with the Haitian mafia'. I am still not quite sure whether to laugh or cry at that statement. De-Bo explained to me that the use of the term 'nigger' was just a habit, and that people used it without thinking. No one meant any disrespect, or to exclude whites from the conversation. In time, even I was called a nigger.

What stuck with me about the Fresh Air Fund was the way they tried to broaden the horizons of the city boys they catered for. For example, one of the staff members was blind. I doubt any of the campers had ever interacted with a blind man before the camp. To take another example, every mealtime the campers were expected to sit at a table, sharing their food, and to eat with a knife and fork. They had to stand listening quietly to a blessing before eating. They found this very difficult, because few of them had space for a dinner table in their homes. Little things like that stuck in my mind when I began work at the LBACP.

At the Fresh Air Fund, they were used to dealing with the problems associated with bringing 'the hood to the wood'. For example, when students arrived at camp, we searched their bags. This was for two purposes. First, to make sure the campers had actually packed enough clothes and toiletries to last a week at camp. If a boy only had two pairs of underpants for the week, for example, we would resolve that problem for them. The second purpose was to sure that nothing illegal had been packed. De-Bo, for example, had brought an eight-inch knife that we confiscated. Searching the students' bags was one idea I borrowed for the LBACP's trip to Devon.

The director of camp Tommy was a man called Richard Williams. He was a tall, strict, African-American man. What Richard lacked in ghetto-style charisma, he made up for in commitment to the cause of improving his campers. He told the campers upon arrival that 'there are more males than men amongst you. We're here to change that. We have a lot, and we give a lot'. There are parallels between him and the way Chris worked at the LBACP.

When I returned from America, I was finally able to look in detail at the research into 'teacher effectiveness', as it is called in the academic literature. In those academic papers I looked for evidence for the theory outlined at the start of this chapter. What I found was that schooling accounts for between five and 18 per cent of the variance in pupil attainment.[1] In other words, very generally, if a child moved from a bad school to a good school this could result in a five to 18 per cent improvement in their educational performance.

Satisfied that I had found some academic answers to my questions, I wanted to know more about the practicalities of running a school. If I really wanted to know about education, I reasoned, there was no alternative but to become a teacher. That is what I did at the LBACP.

4

Teaching the Unteachable?

'Yo, he new and white. We got it made!'

> *Randy Wagstaff,* The Wire, *Season Four, Episode Three*

Recovering from Devon

Our loss of control over the students' behaviour in Devon after the police threatened them with the cells set a very unhelpful precedent, because the students got away with a lot of rudeness, disobedience and disrespectful behaviour during the chaotic last 24 hours of the camp. I suppose from the students' point of view, once the police were involved, school rules didn't seem important any more. In any event, back in Tottenham we had a job on our hands to redraw the lines of acceptable conduct. Chris said we had 'lost ground that's going to take a while to make up'.

It is useful to compare Devon with a similar adventure week I organised a year later in the Highlands of Scotland. Both Will and Pete had moved on to other projects, so I was in charge of the trip. I did my best to learn from our experiences in Devon. I was convinced that, in fact, it was possible to take the students on a residential trip without the kind of difficulties we had faced in Devon. The first lesson I learnt from Devon was to make sure that we were not sharing facilities with any other groups of children. I also devised as systematic a schedule for supervising the students as I could.

But, perhaps inevitably, the Scotland trip turned out to be a further learning experience for me. Although the supervision schedule helped (one of the students complained it was 'like prison'), the reality was that the students were always going to misbehave. So the real issue was how the trouble was dealt with, rather than how to eliminate it entirely. In the circumstances, in

Scotland we were able to avoid cutting short the trip by sending home five of the worst behaved students. If I organised another trip like Devon or Scotland, I would hold it closer to London, and take extra staff for the purpose of escorting home the few students who would inevitably cause trouble.

Generally, I found that the fewer students taken on a particular trip, the more those students got out of it. Although this rationing approach limited the opportunities for students to go on trips, it gave us a useful lever with which to persuade students to improve. The ideal scenario on a trip was to have more staff than students! Where we managed that, an adult atmosphere would reign, rather than a silly teenage one, and we were able to build strong relationships with the students who did attend. In retrospect, then, the 15 students we took to Devon, and the 23 we took to Scotland, were just far too many. It would have been better to take ten students away in the spring as a reward for good behaviour. On smaller trips, I would take no more than five students.

But both Devon and Scotland were far from being disasters. The objectives that we had set ourselves before the camps were met. We gave the students an enjoyable summer camp that they would probably not otherwise have had the chance to experience. We took the students out of their comfort zone, and challenged their conceptions of what it means to be brave and tough. And most importantly, we created bonds and shared experiences with the students that were useful in the year ahead. For example, although Craig never ceased complaining that I had released the giant swing far earlier than he was happy with, he clearly enjoyed talking about the drama of the camp. I often used those shared experiences to get a smile out of students who found mathematics decidedly unfunny. Chris told me after I had left the project that 'however extreme the behaviour was from all of the students, it was a bonding experience, and that's the most important thing... I mean we had some tough characters down there, and I do feel it would have been a lot worse that year [at the school], as tough as Devon was at times, had we not gone down there.'

Some of the difficulties created by the camps were very personal. For example, after Devon, the students went for Will, deciding to blame him for ending the camp early. Similarly, after Scotland, the students who were sent home early decided to blame me for cutting short their time at the camp, and made my teaching very difficult for quite some time after the camp. Taking responsibility for removing privileges from the students was no easy thing to do, and I admired Chris all the more for doing this on a day-to-day basis. I remember Will telling me, much later after the camp, that once he got home from Devon, he burst into tears from the strain the camp had put him under. Similarly, when I got back from Scotland, I found myself in a shell-shocked daze for a full week. But it was worth it. Ricky regularly encouraged me to organise another 'big trip', joking that he 'needed a holiday'.

It took one of the more articulate students, in this case Darren, to explain why students like Ricky and Darren really did need a 'holiday'. He once told me: 'it'd be really good to go away again. No one gives us the opportunity to go somewhere where there's no beef, no trouble.' Although in my darkest moments on the trip to Scotland I felt I had sponsored a group of feral criminals to invade an unsuspecting rural village, the reality was that by removing all the normal pressures and influences of gangs, estates, parents and the like from the students, we had allowed them to breathe a little and be themselves for the first time, often, in years.

Nonetheless, the damage to student discipline had to be repaired. We were able to reassert control only because the students liked being at the LBACP. Most of the students liked the school in a way that they hadn't liked any other institution. They liked, for example, the mix of sport and academics in the timetable, which meant that they did not sit in a classroom all day long; they liked not having to wear school uniform and the fact that staff and students were all on first name terms; they liked starting school at 10a.m.; they liked the large amount of personal attention they received, owing to their organisation into 'pods' or classes of a maximum of six students; they liked spending time with hard-nosed, but kind, boxers to whom they felt they could relate; and importantly, they liked Chris and the way he ran the school. The fact that they liked the LBACP meant that we had a lever over the students when it mattered most. Students who were in crisis (for whatever reason) considered the

LBACP a positive part of their lives. They were usually sufficiently keen to preserve their place that if we had to threaten to kick them out, they would grudgingly adhere to the demands that we made of them and behave. In their previous school, by contrast, they were often only too happy to leave.

A behaviour management system

One of the key tools we used to control the students' behaviour was the points system. This helped to improve behaviour by giving parents a wealth of information about a student's performance. It also harnessed the students' competitive spirit by incentivising good behaviour. Each staff member leading a session (sports, academic or otherwise) would award a certain number of points to each student for every session they attended. In their academic lessons, three points were awarded for a lesson in which the student did a good amount of academic work without any bad behaviour (or not much, at any rate). One point was awarded for a poor effort in their work or behaviour. Two points were awarded when the student's performance was somewhere inbetween. If the student were absent, no points would be awarded. A similar logic applied in sports sessions, where the pod leader would award points based upon the student's participation and behaviour.

We did two things with this data. First, we created detailed 'conduct reports' which we put in the post to the students' parents every week. The conduct report was a copy of each student's timetable with each period colour-coded according the student's performance in that session. We used a 'traffic lights' system, whereby three points meant the session was coloured green, two points was yellow, one point was red and a blank session meant the student was absent. The conduct reports allowed parents to see how their son or daughter had performed during the week, and in exactly what periods they were doing badly or were absent. In this weekly 'mail-out' Chris would also write an individualised report for each student, included in a letter which made all the announcements about trips, exams, rule changes and so on that the parents needed to know about. The point of the conduct report was to help the students' parents to hold their children to account. I often heard stories of parents screaming at their children, e.g., 'what the hell happened on Wednesday, huh, Tyrone?' It taught the students that poor behaviour has consequences.

The second use to which we put the data from the points system was to rank the students according to their total weekly score, and to incentivise students to do well in those rankings. The total weekly score was composed of all the points accrued in each of their lessons during the week, and like the conduct reports, a copy of the weekly rankings was sent home to the student's parents. Over time, Chris tinkered with the points system so that points were also awarded to students for a number of other behaviours we wanted to encourage. For example, Chris had given LBACP-branded sports clothes to students who behaved well. The clothing was relatively smart—navy blue jackets, t-shirts and jogging bottoms—and was similar to the uniform the LBACP staff wore. Two points a day were available for wearing this 'uniform', although it was not compulsory to wear it. The fact that the older and more mature students wore this uniform was a symbolic way of making new students feel they had to work for a membership of a club, and counter-intuitively, wearing uniform became almost cool.

A small cash incentive of ten pounds was given to the student who 'came top' of the rankings, which concentrated their minds. We often used the rankings to decide who ought to be given privileges, such as being offered a place on a trip, and Chris devised a way to send implicit messages to the students by describing the student who came top as the 'alpha student'. The point of this labelling exercise was to associate the idea of being the dominant individual with trying hard at school. This did not mean that they had done well academically; only that they had turned up and done their best.

Chris explicitly wanted the students to 'play the points game', because it would make the students more aware of how well (or badly) they were behaving. Over time, in each individual lesson the students became more concerned about whether they were awarded 'a three' or 'a one' because they realised that their scores would affect their ranking, privileges and that their parents would be told of their score. It also provided a means of highlighting the consequences of the student's bad behaviour over time. Normally a student who has a bad day soon forgets about it. The weekly rhythm of the points system however meant that when the next week's rankings were announced, students who loudly complained that their score was lower than it ought to have been could be reminded about their day of poor behaviour.

We also used a more flexible slip system whereby a student would receive a 'green slip' for good behaviour and a 'red slip' for bad behaviour. This was very useful for dealing with Darius's irritating habit of entering a room and shouting an insult at full volume at no one in particular (although I strongly suspected that it was usually directed at me). So when he entered a room, shouting '*dick*head' and making me spill my tea, I could threaten him with a red slip. Students would gain three additional points for a green slip, lose three points for a red slip, and we sent copies of the slips home to the students' parents.

However, whilst the points system and the slips were useful, the real work with the students was personal. Good relationships with the students were just as important as the behaviour management system, but were much harder to maintain. The staff had to be scrupulously fair, and resolutely tough, but most importantly, they had to show the students that they cared.

Learning to teach

The topic I chose to teach in my first mathematics lesson was fractions. In that lesson, though, I learnt a great deal more about teaching than Tyrone learnt about fractions.

Tyrone entered the room with a big grin on his face, and I beckoned for him to sit down at the desk in front of me. I started to explain what fractions are, why they might be useful, and how to add them together. I put to him a first question:

$1/3 + 1/4 = ?$

Tyrone considered my mangled explanation of how to choose one of the common denominators required to answer the question, before looking up and blurting in irritation:

'What?'

'You have to choose a number that both bottom numbers can multiply to, Tyrone' I said. A grin spread across Tyrone's face.

'Look, that's too many fractions...' he began. He said the word fractions with peculiar venom, as if he were naming an old enemy. He continued:

'Two fractions 's a bit much to start off with. How about, what is it, a third of ten?' His question threw me. I hesitated.

'Errr...' I mumbled, not wanting to get into recurring decimals just at that moment. Tyrone leaped upon my uncertainty.

'Come on!' said Tyrone, taunting me.

'Look, if you'll just concentrate on the problem I've given you...' I began. Tyrone loudly interrupted me with exaggerated exasperation.

'I swear you're not a maths teacher, sir' he goaded. Hearing this, the students at the other end of the room studying English laughed rowdily at Tyrone's taunt. With a flush of embarrassment, I privately acknowledged that he was right—for now. I manoeuvred him back on to the safe ground of finding common denominators, feeling somewhat shaken, and I resolved to be better prepared for our next bout.

Why didn't I want to talk about recurring decimals? In part, because it was off-topic, and I didn't want Tyrone to succeed in deflecting me. But I umm-ed and err-ed because I was inexperienced. Today, I would brusquely tell him the answer to his question and then politely but firmly tell him that he had to engage with my question. Another problem was that, when I began teaching, I lacked confidence in my own understanding of the material I was supposed to be teaching. I had not studied basic number since Tamworth. All of the applied maths I had used at university was algebraic or conceptual and did not involve written calculations. Like most teachers when they start teaching, I had simply to re-learn the material. Then, once I had learnt the material, I had to learn the best way to deliver it. Both the academic and pedagogical knowledge came with time, and I think it's fair to say that my first year teaching was not my best.

What this episode with Tyrone illustrates is one of the problems of allowing teachers to teach without being trained.[1] Untrained teachers were once the preserve of the independent sector, but were also permitted in alternative-provision projects such as the LBACP, and in a moderated form through 'learn-on-the-job' programmes like TeachFirst. As of 27 July 2012, all state funded academies—which are now the majority of secondary schools in the UK[2]—can now hire untrained teachers.[3] In my case, I did not even have an A-level in maths, although I did complete the A-level whilst teaching at the LBACP, and had used advanced mathematics in other academic disciplines prior to joining the school. On the other hand, I had a lot of experience working with young people, and I was adaptable, which in the experimental situation of the LBACP was important. More generally, I don't think I would have considered going into teaching at all if I had to train for a year, because when I started I was not sure how long I wanted to stay in teaching.

In my view, the benefits of recruiting teachers who might not have otherwise considered the profession are large. It is one way of encouraging the kind of cross-class contact that I benefitted from at Wimbledon. It also brings a different set of experiences and contacts to a school—for example, it is unlikely that we would have chosen to take the students on a trip to Oxford University (documented below) but for the fact that I had studied there. However, for poorly performing schools like Tamworth, having trained teachers was at least some guarantee of quality. So I do fear that more students in England and Wales will have similar experiences to the one documented in the previous chapter, where my mathematics teacher's grasp of English was very poor. The more important issue, though, is not the requirements potential teachers have to fulfil before starting teaching, but the quality of the individuals choosing teaching careers. That is determined, as I suggested in the last chapter, by rates of pay relative to other professions.

In any event, I was eased into my teaching career, because in my first year I taught the students in very small groups, in what might be called a 'tutorial style'. Teaching in the 'classroom style' (discussed below), which is the normal way to teach, came later for me at the LBACP. The arrangements in the tutorial style were as follows. Both English and mathematics were taught in a single classroom, which the students would enter in their pods of up to six students. They would then split, with up to three students going to Carmel for 30 minutes of English, and the remainder joining me for 30 minutes of maths. The students would swap over after 30 minutes to study the other subject. This completed the hour-long 'maths and English' lesson. I arranged two tables in a V-shape, with the students sat around the longer edges of the V, facing me. A mobile whiteboard served as a screen between the two sides of the classroom. A pod leader would sit by the whiteboard to supervise both classes.

As the students' attendance was patchy, we were often able to teach students in twos or alone. This allowed us to provide a real 'personalised' education to each student, because I could (and often did) change the subject and difficulty of what I had planned depending on which student, or combination of students, I had sitting in front of me. Although the reasons for the students' patchy attendance were what you might expect of our cohort (illness, truanting and lateness), a surprisingly large proportion of absences were for court appearances. Nevertheless, it must be emphasised, attending school at all was a big jump for some of the students. Ricky, for example, had not been in school for two years, since year seven. Alex had been out of school for a similar period after being expelled from his PRU. Darren told me he had missed the whole of year ten. So the fact they attended at all was an enormous achievement in itself.

The fact that we taught students in such small groups was a way of forcing the students to concentrate on their work. However, as far as the students were concerned, that was a drag, so they would try to distract me from the work that I had set. For example, Lucas was a particularly rowdy student, but born of sheer energy rather than spite. He would often look suddenly across the room, like a cat which had heard an alarming sound. He also was in the habit of muttering rap lyrics under his breath. Both of his eyebrows had diagonal lines shaved through them, a little like David Beckham had some years previously, and he had lots of little scars on his face, making him look as if he had once plunged face-first into a thorny bush.

Lucas sought to distract me by mounting a campaign for me to give him ten pence, allegedly to allow him to buy a drink. I had made the mistake of answering one of his questions about how much I was paid by saying 'enough', to which Lucas, quick as a flash, had replied 'then you can give me 10p then innit?' Lucas was persistent, but I was unwilling, for fear of a flood of '10p' requests once I had accepted one of them. I tried another tactic. I had been going through some of my academic materials from my degree in order to look for a statistic on how much money, over the course of a lifetime, a person could expect to earn if they passed their GCSEs rather than not. The answer was around £100,000. I told him so.

'That's like, an extra house, Lucas. Would you like to have two houses when you're older? Yes? Then please do your work.' This didn't fox him for long. Soon he was asking for some of my share of the £100,000 that I would likely earn as a result of passing my GCSEs.

I was saved from this particular argument by one of the other students. Darius shouted from the other side of the classroom.

'So let me get this straight', cackled Darius from behind the whiteboard, 'you're sacrificing a GCSE in mathematics for 10p? You must be really cheap *and* dumb blud!'

Darius laughed triumphantly at his elegant double put-down. This ended Lucas's '10p' campaign.

Some students were more than just rowdy; they were hostile. There was a group of boys from South Tottenham who spent a lot of time together and could be very difficult. The group was primarily made up of Tyrone, Desmond, Mitchell and Jamie (Mitchell and Jamie had not attended the camp). William and Darren were associate members, William out of timidity and Darren on account of his alpha-male status.

I found Mitchell to be the most difficult of the South Tottenham students. He was a light-skinned black boy with large lips, a baby-moustache, short hair and narrow eyes. He wore a slightly pained and distant expression most of the time, and when he laughed, I often detected a note of bitterness. Mitchell was actively confront-ational: he would frequently sit down at my table, call me a 'dickhead' then get up without a word and walk off again. I found this extremely annoying and at that early stage of my teaching I had little idea of how to deal with him.

Jamie was not as malevolent as Mitchell, but he was silly and hyperactive. He was tall, white with a Mediterranean complexion, sporting a thin, mousy moustache, and extremely scruffy. He wore a yellow coat, which reached down to his knees, but was very dirty, with rips in the cloth. Unlike Mitchell, Jamie would attempt to do the work I set him, and was willing to hold a serious conversation with me. But he always seemed to be propelled along by a kind of group-think towards ridiculousness.

One afternoon I happened to be leaving the school around home-time in order to go to a meeting. I came across Mitchell, Tyrone and Desmond at the bus stop. I'd had a torrid day, especially with Mitchell, and I was, frankly, sick of him. Mitchell muttered to his friends that I was 'that dumb maths teacher'. He came quite close to me with what I thought was malevolent intent, so I pushed him away, hard enough to show some strength, but not that hard. Realising this was silly, if not possibly dangerous, I backed away and got on a bus that had just pulled up. The group didn't seem that bothered about the incident, laughing whilst they got on a bus behind mine. I thoroughly regretted getting physical. It was quickly forgotten, but I never connected with Mitchell in the way I did with most of the other students.

Marcel was another student who seemed impossible to reach. He was a small black boy whose eyes darted around, it seemed to me, for opportunities to create mischief and to stare in a challenging manner at teachers. In Marcel's first lesson I had an alarming conversation with him. I should perhaps have expected him to be difficult, because even the boys from South Tottenham appeared to revere how naughty he was.

'D'you mind if I have a fag, boss?' he asked.

'No Marcel, you can't, this is a classroom,' I responded.

'Go on boss, just out the window, like.' I shook my head, but he continued: 'no one will mind, blud! What's the problem?' He suddenly smirked in an odd way, before standing up and heading over to the window.

'Marcel, sit down please' I told him. 'You can't smoke in a classroom. You know that.' He sat down, but took a lighter from his pocket and began fiddling with it, flicking it alight occasionally.

'Put that away please Marcel' I said. He put it away, before getting it out again.

'Put the lighter away please...' I repeated slightly more firmly, and he put it in his trouser pocket. Slightly exasperated, I thought it was clear that he was not interested in doing maths work, so I tried to learn a little more about him. 'What do you want to do with your life, Marcel?'

'Drug dealer' he said. I was not sure whether he was being serious or not, but I decided to take him at his word.

'Well that's a shame,' I said, 'and dangerous. But anyway, we're here now. So are you interested in getting a qualification in maths, or just to improve your level a little?'

He smirked at me again. I continued, mildly mockingly: 'Or if you want I could concentrate on drug related mathematics, imperial and metric measures and the like?'

'Nah blud,' he said, 'I'll do the GCSE innit. The propa ting. Can I ask you a question?' I nodded, surprised at his apparent seriousness. 'Have you ever smoked, like?'

'Weed?' He nodded. Clearly he still wanted to mess around. 'No I've not,' I said. 'To be honest with you, although half the people at my sixth form and university did, I'm worried about what it might do to my mental health. It might be alright for some people, but I don't fancy taking the risk.'

He listened intently, occasionally pausing to turn around and smirk at Richard, his pod leader. I told him about recent research[4] that showed that skunk and weed were quite different drugs. Weed, the traditional 'hippy' form of cannabis known to my parents' generation, has both a psychotic and depressive element, but skunk is bred to concentrate the psychotic element (THC) and remove the depressive element (CBD). I asked him whether he smoked weed or skunk.

'Skunk blud. No one smokes weed no more round the way.'

'Does what I'm saying about skunk make any sense?' I asked.

'Yeah blud,' he agreed, 'the time I'm most likely to get nicked is when I'm high, innit? When am on da road, like, and all aggressive like cos I'm high, that's when I get nicked most often. I'm a crazy motherfucker when I'm high.' He gave me another of his odd smirks, and I wondered whether he was trying to disconcert me. He then got his mobile phone out and insisted upon showing me a picture of his brother in prison.

'He's hench innit?' Marcel commented. Then he played a rap song on his mobile phone which he told me mentions his brother. I decided that our bonding session had run its course, and I was about to ask him to do some work.

'Do you think I'm high now?' he asked. His eyes were a little red, but I didn't know him well enough to know whether that was normal or not. I was beginning to wonder whether he was a bit crazier than the rest of the students. Marcel's pod leader, Richard, noticed what was going on and intervened at this point. This was quite a relief. Later that day, though, on my way out to lunch, I came across Marcel on his own. He moved towards me and suddenly made a punching motion, before withdrawing once I had tried to move out the way—his little joke, apparently.

Surprisingly, it was not Mitchell or Marcel who I had the most serious confrontation with. It was William, the timid Portuguese boy. It was becoming clear at the time that it did not work to hold two classes in the same room. The pretext for the confrontation was a dispute about whether the students did mathematics or English first, and in what groups. Unexpectedly, the students in general preferred maths to English. Although maths was seen as a bit boring, it was at least short and to the point. Maths lessons tend to involve looking at a narrow concept that I had chosen to ensure that it was appropriate to a student's level of understanding. I then asked the student to complete a set amount of work on the concept. The subject was easily broken down into small, manageable chunks which I could feed to the students.

English, by contrast, was a never-ending painful experience of misspelt words, incorrect grammar and books that needed reading. You could never get a question right in English, the students felt— there was always some niggling improvement that could be suggested. Worse, it often involved talking or writing about feelings and relationships—something few boys are willing to do with their friends nearby, let alone the insecure, unhappy bunch we were dealing with. English as a subject also requires experience of the world: you need something to write about. But most of the students appeared to have a shocking paucity of experiences outside of their patch of north London, being unaware even of relatively local sights such as Hampstead Heath. Carmel despaired of this lack of imagination that resulted in students glumly saying 'I dunno' to most of her questions. So limited were their horizons that Carmel's first descriptive writing task had to be a description of the boxing gym.[5]

Furthermore, on average, the students were noticeably worse at English on arrival at the school than they were at mathematics. Most of the students could read, but had very poor spelling, grammar and vocabulary. Carmel told me that William had once spelt poem as 'powem', best as 'beast', and I once overheard Hunter once asking Carmel how to spell 'fact'. Writing by the students was strewn with such errors; i.e. every sentence would have one, if not two or three basic spelling mistakes. Their vocabularies were little better. I once told a student to put her 'possessions' away, but she replied that she had no drugs on her: she had not heard the word 'possession' outside the criminal context. Their reading ages were simply shocking. Hunter had a reading age of a seven-year-old, but was in fact twice as old. William had a reading age of an eight-year-old, but was 15. Felix and Ricky's reading ages were so poor they fell off the scale—it would have been 6.5 years of age (at 17 and 15 respectively), but if it were possible to have a lower reading age than this, those two would certainly have had it. Only a small number of the students had reading ages that approximated their real age—boys like Darren, Tyrone, George and Darius. Everyone else was behind.[6]

This preference for maths would result in four or five students piling into the classroom insisting on 'doing maths first'. Obviously Carmel and I would prefer to split the students up, in order to give each student more attention, but who 'did maths first' was a serious bone of contention. A further complication was the extreme variation in the students' ability levels. Carmel and I would have to tortuously negotiate the right combinations of students, academically, to form two appropriate groups at either end of the classroom.

William was a low ability student, like Hunter, Felix and Ricky, and he was most easily taught with students of a similar ability. But he hated being seen to be part of the low ability group. We were consequently very sensitive about embarrassing him in front the other students. But when we took him aside individually to explain the reasons why we moved students within the class, he hated hearing the explanation. Over the course of a week or so of these difficult negotiations, William's attitude became increasingly prickly. I had moved William twice that week to get the right academic combinations, but due to his stubborn, whiney responses I also once deliberately moved Tyrone instead of William to keep him happy. On the Friday afternoon in question I was due to teach William, Felix and Tyrone. The best combination was to teach William and Felix together, and for Tyrone to be taught alone. But William had sat next to Tyrone at my desk. So I asked him to do English first.

'It's always me you pick on, innit Tom?' said William, outraged.

'No William, I'm just trying to make it so that we can teach everyone properly, and it'd be easier if you could do English first with Felix please.'

'Nah man', interrupted Tyrone, who always stirred up a conflict if he could, 'he's trying to bump you William. Jamm.' William became steamed up.

'I wanna do maths first,' he insisted.

'Look William it would be a lot easier if...'

'Fuck you then' interrupted William as he got up and ran towards the door. It was a heavy wooden door, painted blue, which swung freely and made a huge thumping sound when it was (frequently) slammed shut by students leaving the classroom. As William reached the door it swung violently open towards him, and the corner of the door caught William squarely in the cheek. One of the other students had been messing around, trying to make a big entrance to the classroom by kicking the door inwards. William squealed with pain before running out the classroom. It looked like it must have hurt a lot.

I tried to get on with the lesson with Tyrone, who was hyped up by all the drama. He seemed to be brimming with pride at William's defiance, and grinned at me as if to let me know that this lesson wasn't going to be easy. I had barely begun to re-start the lesson when William suddenly re-entered the room and sat down at the desk in front of me, with Richard, his pod-leader, following behind him. I began to ask him if he was OK but he interrupted.

'*Don't look at me*,' he demanded, breathing heavily and looking very upset. I didn't respond, wondering what I should do. I decided that I couldn't very well not look at a student I was supposed to be teaching. I began explaining the work.

'So please if you could do this worksheet...' I began, and glanced up at William, who had tears in his eyes. When I caught William's eye he suddenly jumped up out of his chair, moved rapidly towards me and tried to punch me. I moved out the way and he caught me in the shoulder before Richard grabbed him and dragged him out the classroom. William was sobbing and overwrought with anger.

'*Fucking dickhead*' he screamed. I was in shock, but Tyrone was jubilant.

'William banged Tom! Wrah!' beamed Tyrone. Carmel stopped what she was doing and came over to my side of the classroom to see if I was OK. I could not really believe that it had come to this after only a few weeks. But I didn't feel too shaken. If anything I was more irritated by Tyrone's jeering, and asked Carmel to get rid of him. I knew that William was just a silly kid who had lost control. Quite soon I felt sorry for him.

Chris arrived in the classroom and came over to ask if I was OK and removed the remaining students. I briefly told him what happened. Someone brought us some tea. Then, a group of us discussed what we should do in the car park outside the gym. Simon, Chris's business partner, had been talking to William and he told me William wanted to apologise. Up to that point the issue had been whether William ought to be expelled or not. William was sheepishly walking up the driveway to the school and we all agreed I should hear him out.

'I just wanted to say,' William began in a high pitched voice, 'I'm sorry. It's just that I get really upset when I'm crying and hurting. When that door banged me in my face...' he halted, sniffing loudly, then said simply 'I'm sorry.' I looked into his eyes once more and saw remorse rather than anger. I felt for him. I thanked him for his apology and told him that we would try to work something out.

I told Chris that I thought his apology was heartfelt. I said I didn't want to see him expelled, there was work that could be done with him. Chris said that was his feeling too—he was never one to give up on a student—but that William would definitely be suspended for a long time and his return would be on stringent conditions. Although I endured taunts that someone might 'do a William' for the rest of the year, particularly from Tyrone, it was the right decision. Every student had to be dealt with on their own terms, and we were not ready to give up on William.

The 'Thursday problem'

Each Thursday, the Tottenham Community Sports Centre hosted a market. Our students were banned from the market, because they could not resist the temptation of stealing from the stalls and arguing with the stall owners. It was a strange weekly event that we had to work around, and symbolised some of Tottenham's most intractable problems.

Each week the poorest of Tottenham came to the market to find bargains, and the wheeler-dealers of North London came to sell their wares. One stall sold fake Gucci and D&G watches retailing at a tenner each, and another sold trainers at knockdown prices. Women's underwear dangled dangerously at head height on the left of the main path, and jeans were sold on the right. There was always a large removal van near to the entrance of the sports centre auctioning a variety of goods, from televisions to children's toys, which I were presumed were acquired at house clearances. The white skin-headed man who owned the van wore a single-strap bag across his front, in which he put the dribbles of cash given to him by the crowd of bidders arranged before him.

At the front of the sports centre, a haggard old black man sold various clothes that looked as if they might have been obtained from a clothes-recycling bank, and were displayed on a tartan rug laid on the grass at the *front of the centre. When Barack Obama was elected President of the United States of America in late 2008, a jagged piece of cardboard declared his 'Obama sale: all £1'.*

Despite appearing penniless (for the most part), the stall-holders and punters had their pride. For example, I once saw a man ask a stall owner for the price of a pair of jeans.

'Twenty pound', said the stall owner.

'Twenty fuckin' pound?' replied the man incredulously, 'I'm on benefit o' £50 a week, I can't afford prices like that, you cunt.' The stall owner turned red and contorted his face at this throwaway insult.

'What? Don't you call me a fucking cunt!' The stall owner launched himself forward, arms blazing, shoving the punter to the ground. The stall owner easily overpowered the man, and climbed over him with his fist raised in the air ready to pound him.

'I apologise!... I'm sorry I called you... a cunt,' screeched the man. The stall owner, wretched with rage, spluttered a reply with his fist still aloft over the buyers head.

'OK' said the stall owner. 'Just,' he began, 'don't, call me a fucking... cunt' he spat out. The stall owner lowered his fist, his face still red as beetroot, and stomped back behind his stall. The buyer scuttled off.

To avoid the pitfalls of the market, every Thursday we moved the entire school off-site and paid to use the facilities of Tottenham Hotspur Football Club. Spurs, as they are known, are one of the richest clubs in the world and their stadium was directly opposite the gym. Spurs have a charitable arm called the Spurs Foundation, based in the stadium, in which there is a computer suite that the Foundation uses for its projects.

So each Thursday I taught ICT at Spurs, which was a strange privilege. On our way into the computer suite we walked by the conference centre where Spurs managers and players gave interviews, and we got to know the security guards who over time appeared less alarmed by the group of hooded students who traipsed into the stadium each Thursday.

Our tenure at Spurs did not last long. This was primarily because the Foundation charged us for the use of their facilities, and so I sought and found an alternative venue at Bruce Grove Youth Club, which Haringey Youth Service allowed us to use for free. The need to find a new site was hastened, however, by one session at Spurs during which Mitchell set off the fire alarm. This caused the staff of the entire stadium, including Spurs's administrative staff, to pour into the chilly car park as the fire brigade arrived. Whilst waiting to be re-admitted to the building, one of our students leant against the bonnet of the Spurs chairman Daniel Levy's Range Rover, which we only realised when one of Spurs's staff asked us to remove him.

Mitchell had set off the fire alarm after being sent out of the class. He had been rude and confrontational towards me because I would not let him spend the lesson browsing the social networking website MySpace and the video website YouTube. Later in the same session he managed to expose the weaknesses in our communication systems by blagging his way back into the class after he was sent out. Mitchell had lied to Peter Haymer, telling him that Chris had allowed him back into the class, which Mitchell knew would annoy me. He cackled at me when he entered the class: 'Ahh, Chris is your boss innit? You have to do what he says!'

I only discovered Mitchell's deception once I had irately rang Chris to complain about his re-admittance. This incident led us to develop a strict rule that if a student was dismissed from a class then they would not be re-admitted during that session. Experience showed that no matter how positive a student's intentions, they were always disruptive if they were permitted to return.

The second consequence of the fire-alarm incident was that we made ICT, and all subjects apart from maths, English and BTEC sport, non-compulsory. Chris believed that it was better if students had to earn their place in a lesson, because they would behave better once there. It was a sort of 'envy strategy': 'look,' explained Chris after the fire alarm incident, 'if you tell these kids to do something, they don't want to do it. You take something away from them, then suddenly they want to do it. That's the way it is with this lot.'

Starting from scratch

The first challenge the students presented was their behaviour. But the shockingly wide range of abilities amongst the students presented at least as large a challenge. I had to purchase books intended for four-year-olds, as well as advanced books intended for 16 year-olds, and spent many evenings in London bookshops[7] looking for appropriate books.

All the students had gaps in 'pure number'. Most of them didn't know how to multiply and divide by ten, knew no formal written methods of multiplication, division, subtraction or addition, and they did not know the names or order of the numbers beyond the thousands. No one really understood that the numbers to the right of the decimal place were worth tenths, hundredths, then thousandths. Without understanding those things, they were always going to be extremely limited in their capacity to do applied work, like finding the areas of shapes or making statistical calculations. So I spent much of my time on these basics, even for the higher ability students who could move through it at a pace.

My most shocking discoveries were at the bottom end of the ability scale. The less able students fell broadly into two camps. The first group, made up of Ricky, Felix and to a lesser extent Hunter, had difficulty with the most basic tasks. They were effectively innumerate. They needed to use their fingers for single-digit addition and sometimes even then got the answer wrong. For example, I might ask Ricky to subtract three from seven. He would count:

'Seven, six, five. Is it five?' he would ask, plaintively. What Ricky did not understand was that the number you are subtracting by tells you how many times you move from seven.

Although they often got their subtraction and addition wrong, the most behind students did not understand the concept of what multiplication or division is. Unbelievably, Ricky claimed not even to have heard of the words 'multiply' and 'divide'—at 15 years of age. I had to teach the concepts to him as 'lots' (as in, so many 'lots' of three, for example) and 'splitting' respectively. He did not recognise the signs for multiplication or division either, despite wanting desperately to improve. It was heartbreaking to hear him say things like:

'I need to learn these times and, what was it, divide signs man. Got to get good for my GCSEs... but I jus' don't get this, this, division business. What is it, Tom? I don't get it.' Ricky had labelled himself a 'dunce', and although he did make painfully slow progress during the year, it was distressingly difficult to dissuade him from using this label.

Just as shocking was the students' lack of basic mathematical knowledge. Ricky thought that degrees were a length (like metres or feet), rather than a measure of an angle. Felix had no idea what a centimetre was, let alone what length it represented. I spent a lot of time gesticulating with thirty-centimetre rulers, reminding them of basic measurements of lengths. They were generally more interested in imperial measures, since penises are conventionally measured in inches, and height is generally measured in feet and inches.

I could understand ignorance about relatively technical matters. What I did not understand was ignorance about practical, real-world matters. For example, my predecessor Pete Quentin once asked a student to calculate the number of days until Christmas. Mathematically, the student was capable of completing the task. The problem was that he did not know the date of Christmas day. Of the students I worked with, Suma was the worst in this respect. For example, Suma understood the technical aspects of fractions reasonably well. But he was tripped up by real-world questions about 'a quarter-of-an-hour' and 'half-an-hour'. So I asked him, 'how many minutes are there in an hour?'

'Err, dunno,' he said.

'OK, what about half-an-hour. If I said that I'd see you in half-an-hour, how many minutes would that be?'

'Don't know' he said quietly, miserably looking at his feet once again. I wondered whether he was messing around, but his demeanour suggested that he was not.

'What about a quarter of an hour? How many minutes would that be?'

'I don't even know you know,' he said, sitting up in frank confession. Bloody hell, I thought. How could Suma possibly have got through 14 years of life without knowing how many minutes there were in an hour? It was flabbergasting.

Felix was by no means ignorant of practical matters—he once offered his 'pimping services' to me—but he was a massive challenge because his reading was so bad. Mathematical questions would often defeat him simply because he could not read the words in the question; whereas if I read it to him, he might be able to tackle it. He could reliably add, slowly, and with fingers, numbers

72

resulting in an answer of less than ten. But unless the answer could be expressed in banknotes, anything higher was guesswork. Felix had never learnt by heart the most simple addition facts that most people take for granted. For example, if you asked a person in the street what three add two was, they would without thinking about it just say the word 'five'. They do not work anything out, there would be no *calculation*, they just know from learning by rote that the answer is the word 'five'. They have memorised the basic facts of addition. Felix, Ricky and to a less extent Hunter and William, had never been forced to learn those facts, so were hugely slowed in any mathematical exercise by having to calculate the answer to every such question.

I resolved that Felix and Ricky had to fix their basic addition before we could move on to anything else, because there was not much we could study without it. I resolved to make them complete lots of mental arithmetic sheets, and painstakingly explained multiplication using special plastic blocks and other tools. But there were two problems with this approach.

First, Felix and Ricky were understandably embarrassed by how bad their mathematics was. It was very difficult to give them work appropriate to their level without other students cottoning on to how behind they were. Most of the material appropriate for their level was quite childish, with cartoons scattered across the worksheets because it was intended for primary school children. Consequently, neither Felix or Ricky would study with other students in the room—which, incidentally, was probably why they were removed from their mainstream school in the first place. It was simply more important, as far as Ricky and Felix were concerned, to hide their low ability than to risk being ridiculed, even if it meant not completing any work at all. For example, each year we brought a special literacy assessor into the school for the purposes of working out who was entitled to special help in the GCSE examinations such as extra time or (in non-English exams) a reader. The literacy assessor was a very pleasant middle-aged lady. But at the start of his assessment, Ricky was as obnoxious as I have ever seen a student, because Russell was also in the room. Ricky swore endlessly, drew large hairy penises on the work in front of him, talked loudly about 'pussy' and masturbation, and made a point of saying to the female assessor that he could 'smell fish'. But when Russell left, Ricky was perfectly charming, even angelic. All the disgusting bile he came up with was to ensure that Russell did not catch wind of Ricky's extremely low ability level.

The second problem was that even when I was able to teach them alone, they would often get bored with doing addition and subtraction over and over again.

'I wanna do some proper work man', Felix would say, 'let me do the proper work.' Eventually, I relented, and attempted to teach algebra to Felix and Ricky. To my surprise, they were good at it. Ricky took great joy at being able to compete 'with dem big mandem' on a real mathematical topic. After a few lessons, Felix remarked that he 'didn't even know that letters could be numbers, and all that shit. It's crazy, innit?' Unfortunately, Felix and Ricky were good at algebra because it involved very limited mental arithmetic. Felix, in particular, was perfectly competent at following rules and instructions—it was numbers and written words that stumped him.

For the majority of the students who were not as disastrously behind as Felix and Ricky, but who were merely very behind indeed, I had a different strategy. I relied upon their competitiveness. For example, to help them learn their times tables, I printed out multiplication grids (starting just with the 1s, 2s, 3s and 10s) which I required the students to complete under timed conditions.[8] I kept a record of their times on a rankings list on a whiteboard in the classroom. The students really cared about beating their peers in this rankings list, and would complete the grid repeatedly to try to improve on their time. Robert once spent an entire lesson doing these sheets, determined to take the top spot on the rankings. It was a relatively short and intense task, so it was well suited to students with concentration problems (which was most of them), and led to great improvements in the students' mental arithmetic.

It often took the students a very long time to complete the grid the first time around. William's first attempt, for example, took over seven minutes. It was a struggle to get him to complete it, because he was embarrassed that it was taking so long. But I had found that if I let a student get away with giving up the first time around, he was unlikely to ever attempt it again—he 'knew' it was beyond his capacities. So it was important that students completed it first time around, even if it was a battle and took a long time. There was, however, a balance to be struck. It was just as important, if not more so, not to push them too hard. When I did push them too hard, and irritated them with my earnestness, they would take a 'principled' stance against attempting the grid again. For weeks afterwards they would resist it, saying 'I don't like that thing, I don't want to do it, leave it' and so on. Some of them were so stubborn that I was never able to get them to do it again after blowing it the first time.

Another technique I used that relied on the students' competitiveness was the game I offered them at the end of the lesson. The game was mathematical noughts and crosses: I drew a grid on the whiteboard in which each square had a mathematics question that the students had to answer in order for them to be allowed to put their cross or nought in the square. If they got the question wrong, it was the other team's turn, which made for some very competitive and rowdy games of noughts and crosses.

I also recorded the quantity of work that each student had completed and put this information on the wall in the form of 'tick sheets' that I affixed to the wall. To get a tick on the sheet, a student had to complete a piece of work. Each student had a snake-like record of red ticks next to their name, which the students avidly monitored. One of the students once observed that he had the fourth greatest number of ticks, and asked me 'am I fourth in the race, then?' Often the students would compare their position in the 'race' with other students, exclaim 'that dumb fool is ahead of me? Naar man, that's peak!', then sit down to do a load of work.

Who's in charge?

The main sanction in my power to combat poor behaviour was to send students out of the class. We did not have detentions, and did not shout at the students, because these were punishments that had already failed for our students in mainstream schools. What we insisted on, however, was positive participation in all activities. If a student did not positively participate, then something else would be found for them to do. As Chris later put it to me, bad behaviour would quickly spread around a pod if we did not nip it in the bud; 'they're all vulnerable in one way or another, which is why they're here. It's better to have one student lose half his English lesson, rather than the whole lesson go to pot.'

In the second year of the project we decided to change the format of the teaching into a classroom style, where I would teach six students at a time without the disruption of having another smaller class at the other end of the room. The primary reason for the change was to allow the school to expand in size, in order to increase the overall funding for the project. Fortunately, the students preferred the classroom style to the tutorial style. This was because they felt their personal space was invaded in the tutorial style, because they had to sit so close to a teacher. The classroom style was also much less pressured for the students because it was possible to hide somewhat in the classes, as they did in mainstream, whereas a tutorial demanded a great deal of concentration from the students. To my surprise, therefore, although the tutorial style was better in theory, and crucial for the students who were most behind, in practice I got more done with the students in the classroom style.

I found the classroom style of teaching to be much more demanding that the tutorial style. The teaching was much more formalised—I taught standing up with a whiteboard—and required much more planning. This formalisation was helpful in de-personalising some of my battles with the students, but in general, student discipline became more challenging to manage. Although overall it was a better style of teaching, I found I had to send many more students out of the class in order to keep order.

The decision to send a student out was normally one for the teacher. The pod leader in the class could remove a student if they thought it was necessary—e.g. if they saw a fight brewing—but generally it was up to me to maintain discipline. Deciding where to the draw line of unacceptable behaviour, and being consistent in applying that standard, was a perennial problem. For example, Lucas once pointed to his desk with a wide grin and told the class that there was some graffiti on his desk that read 'fuck Tom'. The class laughed and waited for my reaction. I checked the desk, and of course there was no such graffiti. Should I chuck him out for that? No, I thought at the time. I chose to make him apologise instead, which he did, reluctantly. His glee at having gotten away with it changed my mind, but by then it was too late. Darius even accused me of being 'weak'.

Those two boys, Darius and Lucas, were the most difficult to deal with in the classroom style. They found it difficult to listen whilst sitting quietly, and were always interrupting me with rude comments. The next lesson with Darius and Lucas, for instance, saw Lucas repeatedly muttering under his breath whilst I was trying to teach. He would time his muttering so that he began just as I was about to start talking myself. After a few minutes of asking Lucas to be quiet, and false promises from him to stop, I lost my rag.

'Lucas, shut up for goodness sake, this is ridiculous!'

'What, blud?' he responded, clearly not taking well to my outburst. 'Shut up yourself fam,' he said. I gave him a lecture about how his misbehaviour would only harm himself, and that given how clever this was, that was a shame. He apologised again. But as I turned to the whiteboard to continue my explanation of the work Lucas loudly muttered about 'how cheeky Tom is getting...' Exasperated, I asked to him to leave the class. It's a bad idea to tell any student to shut up, no matter how sorely provoked.

Mobile phones were a particularly difficult issue. The rule was that if a mobile was seen by a member of staff, or it rang, then it had to be confiscated by the pod leader until the end of the school day. The general rule was that the students were allowed to keep their mobiles with them, because a ban would simply have been ignored. But the phones were supposed to be set on silent so that they did not disturb the lessons. When a mobile did appear or went off in class, the students would go to some lengths to try to retain their phone. They repeatedly tested the standard for confiscation.

For example, one afternoon I was teaching Ricky and Mehmet. Mehmet was a muscular Turkish boy who loved boxing and weight lifting. Ricky got his phone out to look at a text message, so I asked his pod leader, Ervis, to confiscate it, to Ricky's great annoyance. Then soon after Mehmet asked me with great seriousness whether he could get his mobile out in order to put it on silent. Experience subsequently taught me that I should have told him that it ought to have been put on silent before the lesson. Often getting a phone out to 'put it on silent' was merely a way of 'legitimately' checking a text message. But this time, I allowed Mehmet to check his phone. Ervis, his pod leader, did not hear me say this and promptly demanded Mehmet's phone. In his maturely outraged manner, Mehmet appealed to me to be allowed to keep his phone, and I had to explain to Ervis what had happened. Ricky was then outraged that I had allowed Mehmet to keep his phone, and the rancour he created went on for some time.

At their most disruptive, I was driven by the students to demanding silence with a threat to send out the next student who spoke. This was usually followed by a student testing my by asking a semi-serious question: 'erm, so sir, do we have to do the work set on the board?' I then had a difficult call as to whether to dismiss them or not. Normally, I did.

The procedure once I had asked for a student to be removed was well-defined. All staff members had portable radios which were mainly used for removing students from lessons. The pod leader in the classroom would radio for the senior pod leader, Peter Haymer, who would come to the class and take the student away. Calling for Peter was such a frequent occurrence that the students often imitated their pod leaders in a deep voice: 'Peter can you come to maths please.' Whilst we waited for Peter I would write down what happened on a piece of paper called a 'red slip', which would be given to Peter and then to Chris so they both knew what had occurred from my perspective.

Peter spent much of his day patrolling the school for students who had wandered off from their activity, or who were coming in late, until he was called to a session to collect a student who had been sent out. The fact that it was Peter, rather than me, who asked the student to leave the class was important because the student had little reason to be angry with Peter. By contrast, they were usually very irritated with me by the time I had sent them from the class. Often the student would initially refuse to leave the class on the grounds that their dismissal was unfair, but I often thought they were refusing to leave in order to spite me by ruining the rest of the lesson.

In the vast majority of cases Peter was able to persuade the student to join him. When they refused to leave with Peter, Chris would collect the student himself. During my three years at the academy, no student ever refused to leave the room when Chris asked them to. But if a student did refuse to leave, I know that Chris would have sooner called the police to remove the student than for the student to get their own way. It was important for me to know that Chris and Peter would back me up if I had taken a decision that a student needed to leave, and not try to second guess what had occurred. Chris and Peter's support in this way helped me establish my authority in the classroom. It is an approach that is in marked contrast to the practice in some mainstream schools, where colleagues of mine have been asked 'what was so wrong with your teaching that the students misbehaved so? Why didn't it interest the students?' We had the opposite attitude at the LBACP: it was for the student to conform with what was required in the classroom, not for the classroom to conform to the wishes of the students.

Once the student was out of the classroom, however, the attitude was much less hard-headed. Chris described it in the following way: 'when they're sent out, initially you find out what went on. The first big advantage of this is that it gives them a chance to get something off their chest. They get a chance to explain what happened from their perspective, and how they feel aggrieved. They normally always feel aggrieved, which is why they responded in an unacceptable way [in the classroom]... but at least this way they get a chance to say to someone of authority: "Well this is what happened and this is why it happened", and once we get that information we can actually say to them: "Well that wasn't perhaps the best response, the better way to go about this was to do this or to do that", and then we talk it through with them. Nine times out of ten we can get them calmed down and thinking rationally enough that they can go back to their next lesson. So we don't send them home, and they lose their whole day, they just lose half of one lesson.'

Chris emphasised that listening to the students was very important: 'they really feel that they want someone to listen... this cohort generally do not have anybody to listen to them, so if they get someone of authority who is actually listening to them, that's half the battle... Just go through it with them, and it nearly always works. It's just a question of one-to-one quality time. Talking.'

In a way, therefore, Chris and the teachers ran a classic 'good cop/bad cop' routine, and as teachers we had to be very careful to avoid feeling that Chris was too soft on the students just because he had greater scope to play 'good cop'. Chris's attitude would change if a pattern of disruptive behaviour in the classroom emerged: 'If someone keeps getting sent out of a lesson, it's monitored, but then if it becomes a problem, we actually take it to different level and we stop being so accommodating and start looking at what the problem is. Instead of managing their issue, we then start looking for a solution. That solution could be a meeting with them and their parents, it could be a meeting with them and their referring school, it could be that they're just told that if it happens again there's going to be a suspension, because some people will chance their arm and just do it for the sake of causing an issue or to avoid a certain lesson they don't like.'

Once the student had been sent out, they would have an informal mentoring session with Chris or Peter, before being put into a different session. The idea was that the students should do something useful if they were not going to do their academic lesson: 'we had a dilemma, once we'd got them out of a lesson. We couldn't just put them into anybody else's academic lesson. So one of the good things we did was to try and get them doing something physical, to get rid of a little bit of that adrenalin. So we'd do one of two things, either the boxing, or we'd take them to the fitness room. The reason we didn't take them to football or table tennis was because we were a bit concerned that they might choose to go play football or table tennis [by getting sent out deliberately]. So we'd always take them from a lesson and actually put them somewhere they're going to work hard, so they didn't see that as a better option. And at the same time it released this pent up energy they were feeling.'

Moreover, we knew full well that sometimes the students had bad days. As Chris we put it, we 'accepted the right of the students to say: "Look I actually can't cope with maths today", and provided it wasn't habitual, we would deal with it and accept it. Bearing in mind the cohort, and the things they had going on in their personal lives, sometimes it would be better that they didn't go to the maths lesson if it was going to have a negative effect on the running of the class.'

All we asked from the students was their positive participation in the activity. We provided all the materials: pens, pencils, calculators, exercise books and textbooks. They just had to take part. When they failed to do so in my lesson, I occasionally was forced slowly to empty the room by sending students out one by one. Chris was perfectly happy with this: 'sometimes you just need to do that', he would say.

However, to return to the point made at the start of this chapter, the students would only accept the rules because they liked the LBACP. Although I had to get comfortable with playing 'bad cop', making the students like me as a teacher was just as important as making them respect me as a disciplinarian. Depending upon the situation, sometimes it was just as important to know when to 'allow it', as the students put it, as it was to hold the line. As I learnt over time, I might well have done better to give Lucas the 10p he was after, or once in a while, to let Ricky had his mobile phone back. It was a question of judgement. The most important thing was that the students accepted that they were in the classroom to learn, and made an effort to do so.

The 'Blood Brothers' Theatre Trip

One of my responsibilities at the LBACP was to organise educational trips intended to broaden the horizons of the students. The first of these trips was to the musical Blood Brothers *at the Phoenix Theatre, London. Chris was keen that we should feed the students as part of the trip, both as a treat and to ensure they actually did eat prior to the show, so we decided to go to a restaurant in Chinatown. I undertook a reconnaissance exercise prior to the trip to find an appropriate restaurant, and carefully planned the route that we would take around London.*

On the evening of the trip, Darius and Lucas were late. When they arrived, they told us they had been stopped and searched by the police on their way to the meeting point. They regarded being searched by the police as a routine occurrence. Darius told me that he had been stopped and searched three times in a single day earlier that the year at the Notting Hill Carnival.

We took six students and four staff members on the trip. Looking around our staff whilst we travelled to central London on the tube, I was reminded of a similar journey I was reading about at the time. The novel To Sir With Love, *by E.R. Braithwaite, was serialised on Radio 4 when I began teaching in 2007.* To Sir With Love *is an autobiographical novel about Braithwaite's experiences teaching challenging students in the East End during the 1950s. Braithwaite was a highly educated black teacher attempting to teach some very rough white and Jewish youths. He eventually won over the students through a consistent display of personal integrity and love of learning. I, on the other hand, was an educated white man trying to win over a group of (mostly) young black students. The book was a something of an inspiration for me.*

One of Braithwaite's key breakthroughs with his students was when he took them to the Victoria and Albert Museum. Few of Braithwaite's students had ever ventured to the cultural treasures that central London offered, and the students were inspired by what they saw in the museum. On the tube journey to the V&A, Braithwaite suffers a racial slur from an old woman also travelling on the tube. To Braithwaite's great surprise, one of his female students stuck up for her teacher, humiliating the old woman and in turn challenging some of the racist attitudes of her classmates. From then on the bond between Braithwaite and his students went from strength to strength.[9]

Unfortunately, although I had my bonding experiences with the students on occasion, this tube journey was not one of them. As with the experience in Devon, taking the students away from the academy allowed them to stretch the boundaries of acceptable behaviour. Desmond and Darius were captivated by a young light-skinned black woman who got on to our carriage half-way through the journey. They giggled and hollered at her, only quietening down when Chris chastised them. The girl got off the tube at the next stop, but Desmond could not resist thumping his fist loudly on the tube window as the woman walked past. Astonished and shocked that young girls had to put up with such behaviour, I asked Desmond whether he thought that any girl would actually be attracted by his foolish antics. He just shrugged his shoulders, saying 'allow it, man'.

Like Braithwaite's students, most of the students attending the trip had never been to the theatre. George, however, said that his mum and dad had taken him to see We Will Rock You *just a few weeks before. George was unusual in coming from a relatively wealthy background compared with the other boys.*

We got off the tube at Leicester Square and walked to the Chinese restaurant. The set menu I had chosen for the students included shredded duck as a starter, followed by individual platters which had portions of chicken chow mein, sweet and sour chicken, fried rice, fried vegetables and dumplings. The students did not like the look of the dumplings but took well to the rest of the meal. Although some of the students decided to play hide and seek in the empty downstairs area of the restaurant, they rose to occasion and behaved well during the meal.

Blood Brothers *opened with a bang, and we had front row seats. The volume of the show largely banished my worries about keeping the students quiet. As the story progressed, they were captivated by the humour, brashness and poignancy of the theatrical display. When a bailiff took the toy bear of a poor child in the play, they joined the audience in outrage, crying of 'that's deep' and 'aww, peak'. When Mickey, the poorer of the blood brothers, chaotically rolled on to the stage with his new girlfriend, they cheered.*

There were a few difficult moments. Darius was listening to music on his mobile for the first ten minutes of the show. Later on, his mobile rang, and he answered the call. He said, just a little too loudly, 'call me back later innit!', such that the children in the row behind us frowned. A painful moment occurred when, as one of the ballads began, Russell loudly opened a packet of crisps. When Chris sharply told him to put them away, Chris was shocked by the wide eyed incomprehension and protestations of innocence from the boy. Theatre etiquette clearly was something new for Russell. The conductor of the orchestra looked around at us as this was going on. Darius responded by saying to the conductor: 'What? What?'.

Those minor difficulties aside, the play successfully captured the imagination of the students. It portrayed in lively fashion many of the themes that affected their lives: close male friendships, however destructive, were often all the students had; single parenthood and adoption were not uncommon; and the themes of poverty, dealing with the police, mental illness, and class were daily challenges. When I asked them what they thought of Blood Brothers, *George said 'yeah it was blessed man, I'd do it again, still'.*

Some of the most inspiring times working with the students were when they voluntarily chose to do extra lessons. We ran classes during the holidays, especially for coursework, which the likes of Darius, Darren, Lucas, George, Suma and William attended regularly. We called the extra after-school classes ABC classes, to suggest that by attending them they should be aiming for As, Bs and Cs in their GCSEs. The most frequent attendee of the ABC classes was Darren. He always dragged another student along with him, which was usually Desmond, but was often required to implore them to 'stay, blud, stay!'

Usually I had help in the ABC lessons from Peter or Richard, but one afternoon Chris came into the classroom to cover for a staff member who had to leave. This was very unusual as he only usually came to the classroom if there was a serious disciplinary problem. When he entered the room Chris sat in the corner in shock at the studiousness of the three students in the classroom at the time; Darren, Desmond, and William. They sat in total silence, beavering away at their mathematics sheets and English essays, for a good 20 minutes after Chris had joined the class.

When we had finished, Chris approached the students and said: 'It's really inspiring to see you work like that,' before shaking their hands. Darren stood up straight and said in a deep voice: 'I appreciate that, Chris.' William and Desmond stood up too, and Darren strode over to shake my hand, then Carmel's. After the boys had left I walked over to Carmel's desk and broke a big smile, and she laughed in pleasure. It was rather emotional, given all the drama those boys had put us through up to that point. Outside the door, Chris spontaneously gave the boys ten pounds each, and told them to go and enjoy themselves.

5

The Boxing Gym[*]

Don't let reformers of any sort think that they are going really to lay hold of the working boys and young men of England by any educational grapnel whatever, which hasn't some bona fide equivalent for the games of the old country 'veast' in it; something to put in the place of the backswording and wrestling and racing; something to try the muscles of men's bodies and the endurance of their hearts.

Thomas Hughes, Tom Brown's Schooldays *(1857)*

A new student's first experience of the gym

A student enters the boxing gym for the first time, followed by a parent or teacher from his previous school. He gingerly closes the door behind him and looks around. He sees half-a-dozen or so large men with bulging muscles aggressively pounding the punch-bags that line the edge of the ring. Each blow causes the chains holding up the punch-bags to emit a soft jangle which floats above the rhythmic thuds that echo around the room.

'Come on! Thirty seconds to go!' yells Paulo, the boxing coach, and the boxers lean forwards in determination. Mirroring the standard three-minute rounds of a fight, every bout of exercise in the boxing gym is three minutes in length. The new student looks at the ring, where one of the boxers is dancing around on the blue felt in front of the coach. Paulo has red practice pads on his hands that he holds up facing the boxer as they begin a series of different punch combinations. The student hears the cries of the boxer as he works

---

[*] This chapter is indebted to Loic Waquant's *Body and Soul: Notebooks of an Apprentice Boxer*, OUP, 2004. Loic's ethnography of boxing strongly influenced the way I saw the gym in which I worked, and some of the abstract ideas in this chapter are Loic's.

the pads: 'ack, ack…' after the coach demands a one-two jab combination, then a more rapid 'ack-ack-ack' when he motions for a more complex double-jab-hook move. The boxer suddenly moves over to a dirty black bucket labelled 'spit only' and unloads a mouthful before returning to the pads. A few boxers are warming up in front of the mirrors, including a short but formidable female boxer. They adjust the wraps on their hands and their eyes flash like steel as they psych themselves up for the physical exertions ahead.

The new student takes all this in with a deep breath. He inhales the underlying musty odour of sweat that pervades the gym. It smells as if the paint on the walls was intentionally mixed with the pugilists' sweat, so as to mark their ownership of the space; a smell only partially masked by the cheap air freshener that is sprayed around every morning. The student looks up towards the ceiling, taking in the exposed metal pipes and water tanks that line the walls. A part of him is arrogant and dismisses the significance of what he sees before him. But he also feels drawn to the obvious camaraderie between the boxers and their raw physical power.

The new student is also intimidated by what he sees. Even the strictest of the teachers in his old school, the only ones for whom he had any respect at all, seem just at this moment to be wimpy stuffed-shirts. The student looks at his companion for reassurance, and studiously avoids looking any of the boxers in the eye. He cuts out all his normal strutting and bravado. He is sheepish and withdrawn.

Just as the student and his companion are starting to feel a little lost, Chris pops his head out his office, which is located by the door to the gym, and enquires whether the student is the one he is expecting. He says in simple, melodic terms: 'welcome to the boxing academy', introduces himself, and shakes hands with the visitors before taking them on a tour of the gym. If both student and Chris are happy, then the new student will join the academy in the coming weeks.

The pugilist garrison

The fact that a new student found his first experience of the boxing gym to be intimidating was important. It meant that the student at least started his or her time at the LBACP behaving at somewhere near their best. And starting off on the right foot made it much easier to maintain a high standard of behaviour for the rest of their time at the school.

Equally important was that, as the student experienced the gym for the first time, they met Chris, the head boxing coach, who was kind to the student. Being welcoming was just as important as appearing tough. We wanted the students to take us seriously, but we also wanted them to know that we cared, and that we were offering them a chance to reform themselves for the better.

Running the school in a boxing gym had a further benefit. The physical superiority the boxers enjoyed over the students meant that the students felt safe. Almost all the young people we worked with had used violence in the past and many would have done so again with little hesitation. But students knew that if they were near a boxer, they were fairly secure from attacks from other students and even from malign influences outside the gym.

This was true, for example, for Lennox. Lennox was both very vulnerable and very aggressive, and this unfortunate combination caused him to suffer a great deal. He always wore a white Nike woolly hat, black gloves and one of the impractically small Nike backpacks that were fashionable at the time, which measured about 20cm by 20cm. His manner was quiet and almost stuttering. He would often make a noise at the back of his throat, followed by a pause and a tilt of his head, before he began any sentence.

Lennox's problem was that he talked like a tough guy, but never matched his words with deeds: so he was often in fights that he had caused and which he always lost. Worse, he did not learn by his mistakes, repeatedly going out of his way to create confrontations by threatening other boys with violence, sometimes for no apparent reason. I once witnessed a bizarre confrontation between Lennox and Mehmet. Mehmet was a new student, and so I suppose that Lennox, who was generally bottom of the pecking order, wanted to see whether he could dominate the new boy. Lennox was sitting at a desk in front of me whilst this verbal confrontation occurred, and during the argument Lennox snapped one of my pencils in what was for him a typical faux-dramatic display of rage. Lennox and

Mehmet's anger boiled over into a shouting match, with each threatening that they would 'do' the other after school.

When home time arrived, Mehmet was hanging around outside with some of the other boys who were eager to see a fight. The pod leaders and I had told Chris what occurred in the classroom, so he was ready to keep the peace. Chris told Lennox to stay behind for an extra English lesson, and then told the other boys to go home. Outside, in the group of hopeful voyeurs, Tyrone was withering in his assessment of Lennox: 'he's always makin' threats wen he's standin' behind a teacher blud. Then on da road, he's nothin'... Wasteman.'

What was significant was the fact that the boys did, in fact, go home. They did not try to invade the classroom, because they knew that it was no good trying to get in. They knew that if there was a boxer between them and the person they wanted to beat up then the game was up. This pattern of events—confrontation, followed by protection by the boxing staff—occurred repeatedly during my time at the LBACP. Given the cohort we had, confrontation was inevitable. But one of the reasons the boys kept coming back, day after day, was because they could be sure of protection when they needed it.

This protection also extended to threats from the outside world. Marcel had quickly established himself in our minds as one of the wildest boys we ever worked with. More than any other student I met, he seemed completely out of control. A few days after my conversation with him about skunk, Marcel punched Emre in the face in the sports hall for some trivial reason. Emre, naturally for him, went completely bonkers, but since there were lots of pod leaders in the hall at the time, there was not a lot he could personally do to settle the score. 'Alright then,' he said as a threat to Marcel, after being restrained by the pod leaders. Emre got on his mobile to his Turkish mates on Tottenham High Road, and summoned them to the academy with the intention of getting revenge on Marcel. Shortly after that a car zoomed up our drive with three Turkish guys inside who were a lot older than Emre and who meant business. I was in my classroom at the time and I remember the cries of the students: 'shut the door, shut the door!' Our heavyweight boxer,

Ervis, was luckily on the scene and faced down the intruders as they tried to enter.

'Whass going on?' he demanded, looking as intimidating as that 250 pound, 6'2" bulge of muscle could, with Peter, Richard and Michael backing him up. The gang of Turkish lads suddenly turned very polite at the sight of Ervis and the boxers, saying essentially that they couldn't have their Emre being hit like that in school, and that they were just there to make sure Emre was OK.

Ervis said to the gang: 'Listen. I can't deal with this right now. I'm at work.' Ervis turned to Emre, in a serious, and strangely professional tone: 'Emre, tell your friends to fuck off. I'll fight them after school if I have to. This ain't the time or place.'

Emre had always responded well to Ervis's muscular brashness, and grinned at this latest command. Satisfied, perhaps, that he had made his point to Marcel, Emre did as he was asked.

If it were not for Ervis and the rest of the boxers, who knows what might have occurred that day? Marcel might have been seriously hurt (perhaps sparking a long-running feud in Tottenham), I expect we would have had to call the police, and the incident might even have made the local papers. But thanks to the pod leaders, there was no trouble.

After the incident, Marcel was searched, and we found a Roman candle firework in his possession. This is a type of firework that can be held in a person's hand and fired like a gun. Bringing a weapon into the school was one of the few disciplinary offences that was likely to result in permanent exclusion from the school. Given all the trouble that Marcel had already caused in the short time he was with us, this was the last straw, and he was excluded. But whenever a student was expelled, it was always with great regret, because we knew that after leaving us, the only institution that was likely to be able to cope with students like Marcel was a prison. This was not, however, the last that I would hear of Marcel.

Boxers and pod leaders

'Pod leader' was the label that Chris gave to the boxers who worked most closely with the students. The pod leaders led a 'pod' of up to six students, and they ran the students' sports sessions, escorted the students from session to session, and acted as teaching assistants in the academic lessons. Chris selected the pod leaders from professional boxers whom he had trained (Peter Haymer and Ervis Jegeni), boxing trainers he employed in the gym (Caroline Jarrett) and contacts of his in the amateur Haringey Police and Community Boxing Club (boxer Richard Ross and match-maker[1] Terri Kelly).

Many of the pod leaders were male and black, reflecting the characteristics of the students. They were there to serve as positive male role models for the students, and crucially, they were people *whom the students felt they could relate to*. We needed staff who were a little bit rough around the edges, who would 'tell it how it is' in the same way the students did. It was important that at least some of the pod leaders were black so that the students who were black were able to see a little bit of themselves in the pod leaders who took care of them. It was important that some of the pod leaders were male, because it was *male* role models that most of the students lacked, both because their fathers were often not around and because the opportunities for contact with good male role models in their area was limited.

Chris sought pod leaders who were charismatic, whom he knew well, and whom he could trust. He told me that in his experience, the students would show up primarily to see their pod leader: 'to see Spicy or Dubble' (the nicknames for Michael Grant and Richard Ross respectively). But as well as being charismatic, they had to be moral role models as well. Chris told me he didn't employ just any boxer in the gym, he wanted 'family men' who set an example to the students and transmitted values of commitment to and respect for women. They were by no means just bodyguards for students and teachers, they were integral to the project and the development of the students.

Furthermore, it was important that the pod leaders were not 'role models' in the sense of being distant objects of admiration, like the captain of the England football team or a rapper-come-good like Ashley Waters. Rather, they were intended to have positive relationships with the students brought about by *being there* during the day-to-day development of those young men. This allowed the pod leaders to correct the students' mistakes, to set an example of how to behave, and to drum sensible, down-to-earth advice into the boys.

In the classroom, the pod leaders were intended to be able to communicate with the students in a way that the teachers could not, and to use their close relationships with the students to avoid conflict and promote academic success. The pod leaders helped to avoid conflict in at least three ways. First, having a second staff member in the classroom defused conflicts by de-personalising them, because although I took the decision about when a student left the classroom, I was not responsible for removing them. Second, the additional staff member in the classroom helped to avoid both false accusations being made against teachers and factual disputes about what occurred in a particular incident, because there would be two adult witnesses in the room at all times. Finally, the pod leaders' strong relationships with the students resulted in our being much better informed about the students' lives than we might otherwise have been. So, for example, if a student were suffering from some difficulty at home, his pod leader would normally hear about it and let me know before the lesson began. Based on that information, I could take a different approach with the student in the lesson, and thereby avoid a possible confrontation with a student in a bad mood.

A school of morality

Loic Wacquant's book about his experience boxing in a gym on the South Side of Chicago is a brilliant description of the culture and mechanics of boxing. He writes that a boxing gym is:

> a school of morality... a machinery designed to fabricate the spirit of discipline, group attachment, respect for other as for self, and autonomy of will that are indispensable to the blossoming of the pugilistic vocation... the boxing gym thus defines itself in and through a relation of symbiotic opposition to the ghetto that surrounds and enfolds it: at the same time that it recruits from among its youth and draws on its masculine culture of physical toughness, individual honour, and bodily performance, it stands opposed to the street as order is to disorder, as the individual and collective regulation of passions is to their private

and public anarchy, as the constructive—at least from the standpoint of the social life and sense of self of the fighter—and controlled violence of a strictly policed and clearly circumscribed antagonistic exchange is to the violence, seemingly devoid of rhyme or reason, of the unpredictable and unbounded confrontations symbolized by the rampant crime and drug trafficking that infest the [Chicago] neighbourhood.

I found the same implicit code of honour in the boxing gym in Tottenham. Though largely of the street, the gym was an institutional means of lifting its members above the street. The talk in the showers was concerned with self-improvement, getting ahead in life, and doing what was right by their families. The community of boxers and its leader, the boxing coach, deliberately set its moral values in opposition to the street. Those values seep downwards from the head coach, who sets the tone and becomes a father figure for many of the boxers within the club. The idea at the LBACP was that those values would be fed to the students through the pod leaders, and through Chris's relationship with the students.

The effects of the subtle communication of this moral code were rarely seen in dramatic, single incidents. The morals were drummed into the boys through repeated interactions between staff members and students. However, the following anecdote should, I hope, give a flavour of that process.

I was teaching a lesson in which Tyrone and Desmond were talking loudly about sex. Darren was sulky listening to Desmond and Tyrone. The reason this topic dominated their conversations was that the night before the boys had come into contact with a 13-year-old girl who was very 'up for it'. The previous day's lessons had been full of chatter about this girl, and half of the boys had skipped the last lesson of school to go to her house. When they all arrived, though, Russell was already ensconced inside with the girl. Darren, Desmond, Tyrone and the other boys hung around outside the house for hours, in the rain, hoping to get lucky. During my lesson, they were plotting how to get back at Russell for excluding them. Darren was particularly annoyed with Russell.

I had listened to this discussion on-and-off all day, and I found it very tiresome. Tyrone kept talking about girls who 'just want dick, they don't care'. I learnt that their slang term for sex is 'beat it', a nasty piece of imagery, but one that correctly portrayed Tyrone and Desmond's attitude to these girls ('it' refers to a girl). They advised me to never be sexually generous to a partner—'take it, but never give it'—and discussed driving around London to see other 'slags', a term which they told me they use in their presence. As usual they tried to make the conversation about me: was I as 'on it' when I was their age? Had I ever done it with a girl? I ignored them, so they asked Peter, the pod leader in the room, what he got up to with his girlfriend.

Sex was not something that Peter was shy to speak about, and he authoritatively held the boy's attention whilst he told them about the importance of commitment, partnership and maturity. Peter said to Tyrone, 'bruv, me and my woman been together for eight years now,' and he spoke about his daughter. Peter's words had a calming effect on the boys and I hope they also felt a tinge of shame for talking in the way that they did. Peter did not sound like a priest: his speech was punctuated with some outrageously dirty jokes. But they listened to him. And importantly, as far as my teaching was concerned, he had silenced them, which allowed me to get on with the lesson.

It was Peter's *informal* relationship with the students that allowed him to command their respect. Peter once told me that sometimes he squeezed the wrists of the most troublesome students, just to remind them that he was a real, serious person whom they shouldn't try to mess with. Peter went on: 'Really, I just enjoy working with these here boys, and telling 'em a bit about what's what to sort them out, 'cos I enjoy it.' He gave an example where he refused to let Darren through a door when Darren wanted to hit another boy for insulting him. 'The main reason I stopped big Darren trying to bang that boy was to teach him that, even though he's so big, he can't always get his way. 'Cos with him, if he keeps thinking like that, he's gonna go getting himself hurt sometime, hell, even stabbed up. And no one wants that shit to be brought down on them.'

Richard Ross was definitely the most 'street' of the boxers. In his spare time he was a rapper, and he was known around the gym by his stage name 'Dubble R', after his initials. Peter would often sing his stage name when Richard was around, mimicking the jingle at the start of each of Richard's songs—'dubble-aaarrr'. Richard was not a stereotypical rap-artist though, because he didn't glorify sex and violence, and did not swear in his songs. Richard's music tended to be about the tragedy in young people's lives rather than in the glorification of its negative aspects. Peter said to me once: 'Dubble's different to all them other rappers, he raps about some sad stuff, man.'

One of the most valuable talents Richard brought to the project was his ability to browbeat the students about their moral decisions. He would rarely lose an argument with a student because he had seen so much more of the street goings-on than the students could possibly claim to have seen. He once told me that one of his cousins had been shot in a nightclub in King's Cross and that another was in jail. If a fight was brewing for no good reason between the students, Richard would authoritatively and unhesitatingly tell the students: 'you gotta be the bigger man and walk away bruv, don't get involved.' Equally, though, he was not against standing up for yourself: 'If there's a whole bunch of them who are gonna rush you, and you can't get out of it, then you make sure you spark out the biggest guy there first before they get you. You gotta show some heart.'

Richard would scrutinise and ridicule the students according to the moral standards that permeated the boxing gym. The students put up with this because they respected Richard. He was funny, kind, honest and knew what he was talking about. He tended to be given the 'hard-case' students in the school, so Richard was at various points in charge of Tyrone, Lennox and Emre. Richard could match Tyrone's banter (just about—Tyrone set a high standard) and Richard made it his personal mission to sort out Lennox.

Emre's main problem was his aggression. He had a tendency to hit people with his gangly arms, sometimes without much justification. Richard called him the 'crackhead', which always made Emre grin, probably because he recognised the unhinged element in his behaviour. Emre was in three different fights in his first year, and he was often the instigator of the violence. Richard spent a lot of his time telling Emre about the errors of his ways.

For example, Emre was once telling the class that he didn't 'care if I go prison blud, I'm not bothered innit?' Richard was not impressed by this at all. He said: 'What about your family blud, don't they care if you go to jail?' Emre grinned as if to suggest that he knew he was being silly, but said it anyway: 'Fuck the family blud, they don't care.'

Richard lost his rag with Emre. 'What you don't realise is that if you're in prison, you *depend* on your family visiting you blud, just to get by. There ain't nothing else for you but those visits blud. You need those people outside; so don't be talking about no "fuck the family" bullshit, alright?' Emre looked a bit reticent, so Richard reduced the ferocity of his assault, but continued: 'I remember I went to see my cousin once, and there was this guy there waiting for his mum. He was expecting her to come, and he looked like he needed it. But she didn't turn up for some reason. He went beserk blud, he was going mad. Cos if you're expecting a visitor, you gotta sit there with everyone else and see them gettin' visited by their mum, or their wifey and daughter, and you gotta sit there watching for the whole time when you know no one's coming. It was tense, boy! He smashed the place up. So don't chat shit you don't mean Emre.'

During the first year of the school, the boxing gym and the school ran simultaneously. This meant that it was not just the pod leaders who had an influence on the students, but also the wider community associated with the boxing gym as well. As with most boxing gyms, there was a core group of regulars who used the gym regularly and a disparate group of other boxers who only attended occasionally. It was quite normal for a boxer to disappear from the gym for months at a time for whatever reason, then reappear.

The amateur and professional boxers around the gym knew each other well. The amateur club was called the Haringey Police and Community Boxing Club, which was founded by policeman Gerry Wilmott. Chris trained the professionals as part of the LBA. The Haringey club and Chris's LBA shared the gym and its equipment. Chris and Gerry were constantly going off to the café for cups of tea to sort out matters of gym business. There was a great deal of overlap between the two clubs. Many of the boxers in the Haringey club would come to the LBA during the day to train, and all of the professional boxers working for the LBACP had boxed for Haringey in the amateurs before turning 'pro' with Chris.

Many of the core group who trained during the day were boxers in the Haringey club who came for additional training for up-coming fights or to prepare to turn professional. I got to know this group over time and would exchange pleasantries with them. Others I knew only by sight. Chris of course knew all of them, and chatted to them vigorously.

The most famous boxer to who trained regularly at the gym in Tottenham was Nicola Adams, the gold medallist at flyweight at the London 2012 Olympic Games. Nicola grew up in Leeds but moved to London in 2008 because of the Haringey gym's reputation for excellence in coaching female boxers. Little did I know when I was teaching that one of the gym's 'lady boxers' would achieve Olympic greatness by winning the first ever gold medal awarded to a female boxer! The LBACP students would have seen her train in the gym, and I am sure many of them would have recognised her on TV after she won her gold medal.

The remainder of the gym's attendees were less auspicious, but no less memorable. An elderly white gentleman with ashen hair, who must have been in his seventies or eighties and was rather spindly, frequented the gym every few weeks to meekly punch the bags and use the skipping ropes. His correspondingly elderly kit of very small shorts, short-sleeved white t-shirt and brown leather boxing gloves contrasted magnificently with the baggy clothing fashionable today. Another attendee was a rather fat, aggressive looking white man in his late thirties who had the air of a mortuary attendant or slaughterhouse manager. He would hit the bags with great malicious swipes and sweat bucket-loads before abruptly leaving without speaking to anyone save for a nod to Chris at the door. There was also a group of four or five very large black guys who arrived in a Land Rover to train together, mostly using the weights gym, but kept themselves to themselves.

The most regular boxer that I saw was a young black man called Erick, who had a big smile and a huge appetite for training. One afternoon I got chatting to him and he attempted to convert me to evangelical Christianity by asking me to list my sins through the shorthand device of the ten commandments, which, obligingly, I did. Erick told me that he had been saved and taken up boxing around the same time, before then having been 'a bad boy, like one of those students you got; you know, mugging people, stealing, beating people up and all that'. Chris confirmed later on that if it were not for boxing and his faith, Erick would be someone you wouldn't want to meet in a dark alley. I declined to be converted by Erick, but took it as a sign that I was slowly being accepted into this strange boxing community I had been catapulted into. It was a good feeling; a feeling of security and camaraderie, which made Tottenham feel a lot safer, knowing that help would be there for me in the gym if I needed it.

The regular boxers like Erick and the pod leaders would often share a joke or anecdote in the gym within earshot of the students. The students did not always know who those boxers were, and this was a good thing. The solidarity between the boxers gave the students a sense that they were entering a different world, where mutual respect and camaraderie was the norm. In blunt terms, it also taught them to show a little more respect for strangers. Having extra pairs of eyes around the place was also very helpful in ensuring that fights and other nefarious activities such as smoking were deterred and quickly contained when they broke out. However, having random boxers wandering around the gym during the school's hours of operation did pose some difficult questions in relation to child safeguarding legislation, which ultimately led to the boxers' exclusion from the gym during school hours. But during the time that we worked that way it was a unique ingredient in making the culture of our gym come alive for the students. Unlike pupil referral units, we did not operate in a sanitised, professionalised environment. The boxing academy was a real, living, breathing community with its own characters, culture, and rules. When students came to the school, they were special guests in that boxing community.

The effect that the boxers had upon the LBACP students was analogous to the effect that the sixth form students have upon the students in its lower school in a mainstream school.[2] I noticed the

97

difference that having a sixth form makes to a school in my contrasting experiences at Tamworth (which did not have a sixth form) and Graveney (which had both a sixth form and lower school). The fact that the younger students could see how the sixth-formers behaved, and often had links and relationships with them, set an example that improved the younger students' behaviour and deportment. For example, simply by moving around the school calmly, rather than chasing each other around the playground as young children tend to do, the sixth formers set a standard. I remember discussing this with Mr Corcoran back at Graveney, in the light of the fact that Tamworth did not have a sixth form. 'You don't realise the influence you exert just by *being around the school*,' he said. The same was true for the relationship between the students and the boxers, who would have seemed far more credible future selves for the students than most sixth formers would have. At the LBACP, the students were slowly being exposed to the culture of mature masculinity that was the ethic and badge of the boxers in the gym.

Over time the students began to imitate the pod leaders and boxers around them. Some of the most enjoyable changes were the small ones. For example, the students would go out of their way to greet people — to say hello and to shake hands (or at least to 'spud' — a touching of fists). I am also sure that, in addition to the effects of puberty, the students deliberately tried to speak with a deeper voice when they greeted me with the phrase 'alright Tom?' They would make an effort, occasionally, to hold serious conversations with the staff, putting forward their point of view on some matter they felt was important. In my third year of teaching, for example, I came across Ricky in the local café, and he asked me what the effects of the 2010 hung Parliament following the general election would be: 'that guy, wassis name, Nick? Wassi got to do with it?' The maturity that the environment encouraged could be seen particularly in discussions about important boxing matches, such as the Hatton v. Mayweather fight in late 2007. It also could be seen when one of the pod leaders brought in a video of one of their fights. The students, pod leaders and teachers would gather round the small TV in the gym whilst our fighter talked us through the good and bad moments of the fight. It could be seen when the students calmly sat beside the ring and watched a sparring session between a set of boxers. Other moments of maturity were more domestic, however. Chris had converted a small cupboard into a kitchen, in which there was a kettle, toaster, fridge and microwave. Students and staff were frequently together in this cramped space, negotiating access to the facilities and politely organising refreshments during lunchtimes and in the mornings.

'What these young men lack, I've realised,' Chris once told me, 'is approval, from men they respect.' He gave the example of his youngest son, for whom he had just bought a leather jacket that matched the jackets worn by Chris and his eldest son. The boy walked around in the little jacket with great pride — the jacket was a sign of approval from his father, whom he loved and respected. But our students 'don't have many men they respect. But they do like to come into the gym and chat with Dubble R (Richard) and Peter. They love to get respect and approval from them.'

Interview with Richard and Felix

Around two years after Felix left the academy, I interviewed Richard and Felix together. Richard was Felix's pod leader, and often claimed responsibility for sorting out Felix. The purpose of the interview was to explore their relationship, and to illustrate the way they interacted.

Tom (T): So, what I'd like to talk to you guys about is that, Richard, you used to say that when Felix came to the academy he wasn't the upstanding, charming young man that he is now...

Richard (R): He was a little shit! [Laughter.]

T: But over time, through your relationship, things changed, right? Tell me, how was Richard when you first came to the academy, Felix?

Felix (F): I used to hate Richard, boy. [Felix smiles.] He thought he was a little know- it-all! I was thinking like, who is this guy?

R: No, no, you didn't hate me! He wanted to, but he couldn't, because he realised that everything that I said was right.

F: He was meant to be from the ghetto, but...

R: That's what he said when he saw me—he said, 'yeah, you're too road to have this job'.

T: Too what?

R: Too road, like, too street. That was just my appearance but, you know, [smiling] I was a down to earth sort of guy. Felix realised that the way he used to talk to people wasn't really the right way.

T: So what sort of stuff did you used to get up to, Felix?

F: Before I used, well... I used to be a little shit, boy!

T: Why?

F: I was on the road flex, very hard, and then I got kicked out of school, and I went to the Wood Green Unit [PRU]. I was behaving a little bit good and then they said, uh, 'I think we got a better project for you—at the London Boxing Academy', and that's how I met Richard and Tom and everyone.

T: When you first went to the academy, you had another teacher, named Lisa.

R: I was just about to say her name y'know!

F: Lisa never really liked me y'know [smiling].

R: What did you say to her Felix? You said something to her, and then she went red and then she started to cry!

F: Huh??

R: About three of you said the same thing, just to upset her, I can't remember what you said to her though. What was it?

F: Oh yeah, I think I said, oh, 'you're a stuck up cow' or something like that...

R: Yeah or something like that, all three of you said the same thing.

F: But she was, man! It's like, yeah, some Oxford student to try come teach in a ghetto school...

T: You remember that I'm from Oxford... [Laughter.]

F: Oh, sorry... take that bit out the recording!

R: Basically, someone from a different walk of life, with no understanding of what's going on. She wasn't used to people talking to her like that.

F: Yeah, like in a certain manner... but I like her now, innit, she's alright.

T: Anyway, we're getting off-topic...

R: Basically, what happened was bling [Felix] said to me 'hey Rich, you get all the women, how d'you get all the women?' I said 'look man, you gotta talk to them correctly'. You remember being at Spurs? [There were a number of attractive women who worked at Spurs.] You'd go in there and say [posh voice] 'hello, good afternoon' [laughter]. I taught him how to be a gentleman—a road gentleman.

T: So, what did boxing have to do with it?

R: He thought he could fight, yeah, on the street level, swinging and everything. I taught him how to turn his punches over and to fight properly. Then he realised the benefits—mental, and physical—of what I taught him. Then he became quite good! But then he got a bit chubby and stopped doing it [laughter]. Threw it down the drain!

F: Too much chicken and chips man!

T: Can you remember what it was like when you first started doing some boxing?

F: Yeah, I didn't really wanna do it, man.

T: Why?

F: I thought it was a bit silly, really. I didn't really wanna do it.

R: Just cos he didn't get on with Hunter, he hated that Hunter was good!

F: Nah! He wasn't good, he was just a little bit 'advanced' [laughter]. Nah at the start I never really liked it cos, there was too much technique, man. I tried to fling a little road in there, but Rich was like no, no, no... but boxing is good man. I met a lot of celebrities.

101

R: ... say my name then, go on, I'm a celebrity, innit? [laughter]

F: Nah I met that guy on the news, whassis name... anyway, whenever he's on the news, I'm like 'I know that guy, I met him'.

T: So was there a time when you thought, 'yeah, boxing is changing me'?

R: Yeah, it was physical. When he took his top off and his girl didn't laugh, right? [Laughter.]

F: I plead the fifth on that one...

T: Richard, why did Felix listen to you?

R: Cos otherwise I'd knock him out. [Laughter.]

F: I think personally, yeah, when I first met Lisa, she seemed a bit up-tight, yeah, like she come from a rich background.

R: What you trying to say I'm poor? [Laughter.]

T: What did you think when you first met me?

F: The same, y'know. I just think that about everyone who... until I get to know you and, yeah you're not that bad, y'know...

R: [Being serious] What is was, right, was a thing whereby I was more closer to his age group. I knew things that he was speaking about, I'd got knowledge of it, cos of where I grew up and cos of the things that I'd seen in my life. So I could give him good advice, I could tell him things that I'd seen, and he could relate to it, so... I think it's that.

T: Felix, did you respect Richard?

F: Yeah! If you don't respect someone you wouldn't talk to them, would you? And he was a good laugh...

R: A comedian, son, a comedian. [Laughter.]

T: That was important, was it, that he was a laugh?

F: Yeah! You don't wanna be around someone who's moaning at you and, like, taking life too serious, man.

T: Do you think that the students could benefit from a stronger hand, a more disciplined approach?

R: *Yeah well, certain people, no matter how much you give to them, or how much you talk to them, they're just doing what they're gonna do. Felix had a ray of hope because deep down, he didn't wanna be what he was getting up to.*

F: *Basically, I wasn't a follower. People like Lennox...*

R: *You try everything, everything, everything... Lennox... [shakes head] he got kicked out, came back, but got it wrong again because in his head, he wanted to be a badman.*

F: *Nah, he's just weak-minded, man. If you're a strong-minded person, you should never be brought down so low. That's just the way I see it. He's a wannabe, basically. Saw him the other day actually. Chat bare rubbish to me... [Laughter.]*

T: *How would you sum up the LBA, generally?*

R: *Look, we expected the kids to be bad. We expected that.*

F: *Cos they got kicked out of school.*

R: *But there's a ray of hope for like, all of them, if possible. Obviously I get a bit down when one of them gotta get kicked off—that contradicted what we were trying to do. Like, sending them out of class, and all of that, like. But the thing is that some people can't be helped, some people need to find out the hard way, can't be spoke to and realise 'oh yeah'... they need to find out the hard way.*

F: *I loved the LBA really. I loved it there. It was alright, still.*

T: *Why?*

F: *It was just nice man, just nice people, it was just nice, man.*

R: *Except when I always beat you at basketball.*

F: *Aw, what you lying for, man? [Laughter.] We went on trips, Devon—don't really do that in school. You have to work for that. Work your arse for that in school, cos you're bad now, they don't even see that you're trying to work... I liked the LBA.*

Practicing the manly art

One of the benefits for Chris of employing his own boxers was that he was able to provide them with an income, as well as being able to keep an eye on what they were doing from day to day. Boxers who are serious about their training face a perennial problem in finding appropriate employment for purely practical reasons. It is very difficult for a boxer to simultaneously complete all the training that is necessary to compete at the highest level and to hold down a normal job. This is both because of the quantity of time that training takes up and the huge amount of energy that boxing training consumes.

A serious boxer needs to be training at the gym at least four to five times a week, with the addition of 'road work' (running) which is usually done early in the morning. At the gym, training would be a mix of weight training for strength, circuit training for stamina, purer boxing training on the pads and bags for technique and power (and for those who liked to show off, the speed ball).

Boxing training is notorious for being the most 'hardcore' training of all the sports. I frequently wandered past Paulo conducting a circuit training session, and saw Erick thrusting forward a pole, which had weights on each end, in a horizontal punching motion. I think any normal man might be able to do that for a couple of minutes at the very most. But 15 or 20 minutes later, after having sorted something out in the classroom, I would walk past the boxing ring again and Erick would still be there, thrusting away with his pole, perhaps having disposed of his t-shirt to proudly expose his 'ripped' (muscled) physique, and certainly being much sweatier. Then, passing through the circuits room, John Vanner (another boxing coach) would be standing on top of a filing cabinet, throwing down a medicine ball to a boxer sitting on the floor. The boxer was expected to catch it, lie backwards and complete a sit up, and then in the same motion throw the medicine ball back up to John on the top of the filing cabinet. Just as the boxer was tiring John would say 'ten more mate!' to squeeze every last ounce of energy out of him.

Strangely juxtaposed to this almost mad level of exertion was each boxer's constant underlying worry about his weight. To be able to fight within a given weight category a boxer had to 'weigh in' the day before the fight under a certain number of kilograms. It is very strange seeing all these large, alpha-male boxers talking about dieting—or, more often, guilt-laden accounts of transgressions into booze or McDonalds. My conversations with Chris in his office were constantly interrupted by boxers asking for use of Chris's weighing scales. Often the required weight, a boxer's 'fighting weight', was well below the boxer's normal weight, to the extent that they were virtually only muscle and sinew come the day of the weigh-in. Sometimes, if mismanaged, the weight loss required shortly before a fight could be quite dramatic, and boxers have sometimes fail to make the weight, with disastrous consequences.[3] In the lead up to a fight, boxers would often train in plastic suits—the more expensive ones lined with foil, or for those on a budget, just plastic bin-bags—which they wore in order to make themselves sweat more, and thereby lose weight.

In addition to these normal training sessions, serious boxers were expected to participate in sparring. Sparring is essentially a mock fight, where the boxers hit each other and try out different moves for real in the ring, but where the intensity of the violence is carefully controlled by the boxing coach. Sparring allows boxers to gauge what a real fight is like, to hit and be hit, and to put into practice all the advice and training completed thus far in their boxing careers. Its purpose is to help boxers learn and practise for real boxing matches. Boxers tend to do a great deal more sparring than is normal in the lead-up to a fight in order to ensure they are well practised before they enter the ring. Sparring sessions often determine the hierarchy of prestige within the gym. It is the mechanism for fighters to see how good they are in relation to their peers.

To an outsider, sparring looks like a fight without an audience or judges. But there is a strong social logic to what takes place in the ring. In sparring, two boxers consent to hit each other, but without intending to do damage, as they might in a real fight. Depending on the circumstances of the spar, especially the experience of both the boxers, sparring sessions can pan out very differently. Wacquant's description, again, is the best. Wacquant writes that often two boxers who know each other well will slowly find their way, increasing their power and aggression a little, which is then matched by a response by the sparring partner. But both will usually be receptive to a slowing of pace or power, which would be taken as a signal that things are getting out of hand. Always at the end of a sparring session, however aggressive or one-sided, boxers hug or touch their gloves together in a show of mutual respect and thanks.

The boxing match

I saw first-hand the preparation for Peter Haymer's defence of his English Championship title at light heavy-weight against Tony Oakey. The fight was in early February 2008 and preparations were in full flow over the Christmas 2007 period. Chris organised sparring for Peter almost daily, and so he was frequently covered in bruises and cuts which the students admired and remarked upon.

One afternoon I saw Peter sparring several fighters, a different one each round, in order to simulate the freshness and aggression of an opponent in a real fight. Peter fought hard. Chris was watching slightly nonchalantly from the side of the ring, occasionally shouting encouragement and instructions to Peter. At the end of each round, Chris would call 'time' and then approach Peter in his corner, remove Peter's mouth guard, and pour some water into his mouth. Chris would then give Peter further advice—I saw him acting out an uppercut motion as he told Peter to get inside his opponent more. After the final gruelling round, Peter's legs turned to jelly and he collapsed over the ropes grinning, saying 'I'm fucking knackered!'

In the quiet period between Christmas Day and New Year's Eve it was just Peter and I in the gym, as it was closed to everyone who did not possess a key. I was preparing for my teaching during the next term. Peter would do some weights work, use the running machine and hit the bags. I remember asking Peter how his Christmas was.

'Well it weren't much of a Christmas for me, you know, with this fight coming up. Couldn't have any turkey really or relax like you'd want to on Christmas day. Gotta stay in shape for the fight y'know'. The sacrifice, I could see, was large. Peter did more and more sparring in the weeks leading up to the fight, battering his body day after day to prepare for the fight.

The weigh-in was the day before the fight, and Peter was frantically trying to lose a few additional pounds to make the weight. I remember walking into the male changing rooms in the sports centre looking for Chris, only to find Peter in the sauna-box, stark-naked, talking with Chris. He emerged and weighed himself to Chris's satisfaction, before Chris allowed Peter to have a quarter of an orange to sustain him. Peter looked very white and slightly gaunt, and sported dark rings under his eyes; but whether as a legacy of sparring, lack of sleep or food, I was not sure. After Peter had his orange they left for Leicester Square for the weigh-in and press conference.

Chris had decided to make a school trip out of the fight, so tickets were given to Darren, Lennox, Hunter and William. Chris gave the tickets as a reward to the students, with the exception of Lennox, who I suspect was given a ticket in an attempt by Chris to entice Lennox into good behaviour by showing him generosity.

Chris drove them all down to York Hall in Bethnal Green for the fight. It was a big event, broadcast live on television by Sky. It was also a controversial bout because Peter had won the last fight against Oakey on points in a tight match, but Oakey's team felt they should have won. Chris was wearing his boxing coach get-up, which included a shiny blue and white waistcoat bearing Peter's ring name, 'The Daddy'. I remember talking with Chris about the fight, and Chris remarked that he felt calmer than he usually did before a fight—'too calm, probably' he said. Many of the other pod leaders were there—including Richard and Ervis—and had bought expensive ring-side seats from which to watch the action.

I saw the fight from the balcony with the students. We had a job keeping them out of the bar area, and had a delicate problem to negotiate when Lennox asked us to buy alcohol for him. We compromised by buying them chocolate and crisps. I took the opportunity to talk with the students about their progress in boxing. Since William had hit me, he had been getting more involved in boxing. I had seen him doing pad work with Paulo after school, and William had exceptionally fluid, rapid movements on the pads. I thought he looked like a natural, being small, compact and athletic. Chris agreed. So I asked William how his boxing was going. He mumbled 'OK... I don't really like it', by which I think he meant that he did not really enjoy being hit. William was a bit of a softy—or a 'sweet-boy' as Ervis put it. In truth, despite his athleticism, boxing wasn't William's sport.

After the build-up fights, all of which finished a little earlier than anticipated due to knock-outs, the compere announced Peter's fight: 'And now the defending champion, Peter, The Dadyyyyy, Haaaayyyyyy-mmmmeeeerrrrrr!' Peter strutted out with Chris, bouncing on his toes and doing rolling punches to keep warm, and gave a nod to the other pod leaders who were on their feet by the ring cheering and punching the air for Peter. The students screamed their lungs out in support, albeit slightly mockingly, as if they didn't want to be seen to be taking it too seriously. Tony Oakey, the challenger, emerged to a similarly tuneful announcement by the compère, before his theme tune 'oh, the Hokey-Cokey' (sung 'Oakey-Cokey') came on, which his fans belted out with gusto. William and Darren looked at each other and agreed that it was 'a dickhead song'.

The fight started brightly, with strong exchanges from both boxers. Oakey was shorter and stockier than Peter, and also had a lot more hair on his chest and head than Peter did. Chris told me beforehand that Oakey was 'a real tough boxer, someone who's always looking to get inside and smash some upper-cuts'. Peter's advantage by contrast was his height and his reach, since his arms were a lot longer. Peter looked good during the first few rounds, keeping Oakey at a distance, landing his jabs and making Oakey work hard to stay in the fight. The students and I continued to yell our guts out, shouting 'C'mon Peter!' at regular intervals.

Several rounds later though Peter started to tire, and Oakey released a savage combination of punches that penetrated Peter's defences. Peter looked a bit long and gangly in contrast with Oakey's tough, tight stance. Peter told me after the fight that one of those punches had burst his eardrum, putting him off balance and making him feel out-of-sorts. Eventually Oakey unleashed a damaging combination that left Peter floundering against the ropes. I saw Peter look over at Chris and shake his head, at which point the referee lifted Oakey's hand to declare his victory.

The students looked annoyed that they had travelled all the way to East London to see their pod leader lose a fight. 'Nah man, he lost!' declared Darren, outraged. 'He's rubbish! My pod leader is rubbish!' I told Darren that actually, what Peter needed right now was his support, and that it wasn't any good behaving like that. Darren processed the idea carefully, but did not respond. It was a disappointing end to the evening, but the boys enjoyed their big night out nevertheless.

Learning to box

Boxing is an extremely physical sport in the way it is *learnt*, as well as being very demanding upon the body. It is not a sport that theory or reading will help much with, and even oral instructions are not particularly helpful in describing what is required of the boxer to complete a move. Loic Waquant put it this way: 'the rules of the pugilistic art boil down to bodily moves that can be fully apprehended only in action and place it at the very edge of that which can be intellectually grasped and communicated'. Like dance, boxing technique is too complex to fully describe verbally. The moves are learnt by trial and error, imitation and, ultimately, through endless practice. It is analogous to learning times tables, except that times tables require verbal memory recall whilst boxing moves require physical memory recall. Once a boxer starts thinking through the process of a move, he is radically slowed down and becomes ineffective, in the same way that a student cannot be said to have learnt his times tables if he has to make a calculation in order to get an answer. But for boxers it is not just a single answer that is required, but the weaving together of the entire performance: correct footwork; guarding against and anticipating attacks; executing one's own attacks; all a brutally intimate foot or so from an opponent.

In order to teach a stance or move, boxing coaches often must physically adjust the body of the boxer they are training to show them what is required. I often heard boxing coaches adjusting the hands or feet of a boxer, then grumpily saying 'right, now *keep them there*'. One can see perhaps why so-called 'kinaesthetic learners', who tend to learn best through movement and physicality—rather than visual or auditory inputs—would be attracted to boxing. I am sure that this is part of the explanation for Alex and Hunter's attraction to boxing.

Alex was a student who did well when he attended class, but whose attendance let him down. When I ask him about this, he said 'I just hate sitting down, sitting still. Hate it. I want to be up and 'bout, I want to be in the boxing gym, I can't stand all this sittin' about. Thas why, I suppose, it ain't gonna happen for me.' Before the joining the LBACP, Alex had been out of school for two years.

Alex personified, in an extreme way, a common problem: active, energetic boys in school who need plenty of sport to keep them happy. He was expelled from his PRU for spitting in the face of a teacher who was trying to restrain him after he had a confrontation with another student. He said that during those two years he spent his time with a group of similar drop-outs, and that they did little more than mess around drinking and causing a nuisance. It is an illustration of the extent to which boys like Alex want to belong to a positive education institution that Alex travelled for an hour-and-a-half to and from his home on the other side of London to be at the LBACP each day.

However, it should be emphasised that few of the students took boxing seriously as sportsmen. Alex and Hunter were the exception in pursuing amateur boxing careers. In terms of their sporting preferences, the students were normal: most of them liked football best. So we ran as many football sessions as we did boxing. Our students were *not* a self-selecting group of 'boxer drop-outs' who remained with us because of their love of boxing, Hunter and Alex excepted. Few students joined the project with a pre-existing interest in boxing; only participation in non-contact boxing was mandatory. We did not expect them to become members of the amateur club, and indeed none of the hundred-odd students I interacted with in the project did actually join the gym, except again for Hunter and Alex. What the students were provided with was a special form of *exposure* to the gym's social relations, in the structured environment of the LBACP. Over time, the students gained membership, of a junior kind, to the strong, overlapping solidaristic relations that characterised the boxing gym.

The students completed at least one boxing session a week. The majority of the time those sessions involved skipping, bag work and pad work. Bag work meant hitting a punch-bag for a three minute round, before moving on to a different punch-bag. Pad work meant that the pod leader donned a pair of pads and required the students to punch the pads in a series of different combinations. Pad work was definitely the most popular activity in the boxing sessions. It meant one-to-one attention from the pod leader and the satisfaction of trying to hit a real, moving target. During pad work, pod leaders would constantly encourage the students to improve their technique, correct the student's footwork, timing and head position. They would teach the students the difference between jabs, hooks and uppercuts; and eventually they would learn the non-verbal pad-signals for the different combinations of punches. After a series of combinations, the pod leaders would often without warning straighten out their arm in front of them, with the pad pointed at the student, and walk forward, forcing the student to jump out the way of the charging pod leader, mimicking the need to be footloose in a real boxing match.

Students work the pads

Music is blaring out of the stereo in the corner of the boxing gym. Two pods have been timetabled for a joint boxing session which Richard is running, so there are approximately 12 students around the ring. Three or four of those students are slouched on the benches on the edge of the gym watching the session, perhaps spaced-out from last night's excesses or glumly reflecting on why they can't be bothered.

The students begin with a warm up. Richard has them jogging around the ring, and they are required to touch the floor with their left hand at Richard's signal. Hunter enthusiastically tries to overtake other students whilst running around the narrow space around the ring, to the other students' irritation. After a few laps, Richard invites the students into the ring for a co-ordination game. The students pair off, put their hands behind their backs, and they are required to try to step on each other's toes. The aim of the game is to encourage quick footwork. Some of the students begin messing around, to Richard's distaste, but he sets them straight.

Richard then begins working the pads with students individually, spending three or four minutes with each one, whilst the other students work the bags. The students give their all whilst they're in the ring, smashing away with all their might. Richard's skin is shining with perspiration due to the heat of the gym and to the intensity of taking student after student on the pads.

'Right, everyone in the ring!' bellows Richard suddenly. Hunter eagerly jumps straight through the ropes in a diving motion, and rolls into the centre of the ring. The other students stop working the punch bags and

slowly get into the ring. Emre hangs back, and loudly declares that he 'can't be bothered' to do boxing in the ring.

'Everyone except Emre in the ring!' bellows Richard in response. He shows the students how to complete a hook, followed by an uppercut. Richard's movements are refined, flowing smoothly, as if they are powered by hydraulics. The students' enthusiastic, powerful, but ill-formed imitations follow. Testosterone flows amongst the students but is controlled. Everyone is pumped up by Richard's enthusiasm, and his prowess and experience at getting the students going is obvious.

Richard has ten students in the ring in a circle around him, and he moves around the circle receiving 'one-twos' from each student. He takes the opportunity to correct the students when he spots errors in their technique, and occasionally demands that a student complete the move again if they did not put as much effort as they could have into the punches. 'Now the jab!' shouts Richard. The shots hit his pads more rapidly now, with a 'snap' as the leather hits leather.

Paulo sits in the corner watching the session with one of the 'lady boxers' from the Haringey gym. He plays with his favourite gadget, a large watch that doubles as a mobile phone, only intervening when one of the students sitting on the side starts chasing another student around the gym. Out of respect for Paulo they quieten down. John Beckles, one of the other LBA trainers who spends most of his time lifting weights, wanders past the ring and corrects William's footwork.

As I watch from the benches, Darius walks out of the ring with his mobile clamped to his ear, clutching the boxing glove he has removed to his chest with his spare arm and smiling in his mischievous way. Before he gets far, Richard shouts after him 'Darius if you ain't back in ten seconds I'm gonna give you a red slip!' Darius grins in response, slowly getting back into the ring, tearing his phone away from his ear as if it were attached by Velcro.

Richard then remembers Emre, and having allowed him to take a few minutes break, also threatens him with a red slip if he does not join the rest of the students in the ring. 'Come-on Em!' cries Ricky, a tongue in cheek call that is then repeated by several other students. Emre grins roguishly and reluctantly drags himself into the ring to the sardonic cheers of the other students.

Just as the students finish cheering Emre's entrance into the ring, Darren unexpectedly arrives at the door, so they cheer for Darren's arrival as well. He pops his head into Chris's office to say hello before entering the ring to join the other students in the workout, bobbing his head and pushing his shoulders back. Sweat flows as the students intensify their efforts through to the end of the session, when they exhaustedly flop about on to the ropes and the benches beyond the ring.

Sparring

Although rare, sparring was probably the most important activity the students undertook in boxing, and explicit parental consent was required. It was generally only allowed at the end of a half-term as part of a sports day, and even then only when the students had acquired enough experience to be able to box properly. It was where the real discipline of boxing showed itself. It was necessary that the bond between pod leader and student was strong during sparring, because when the pod leader shouted 'stop!', it was important that the students did so. The 'stop' command was used for example to check that a student who just received a flurry of strong blows was OK, to call the end of a round, or just to stop the contest entirely because one of the students was being dominated by the other.

Boxing is as much about controlling one's emotions as it is controlling one's body. Wacquant again: 'In the squared circle, one must be capable of managing one's emotions and know, according to the circumstances, how to contain or repress them or, on the contrary, how to stir and swell them; how to muzzle certain feelings (of anger, restiveness, frustration) so as to resist the blows, provocations, and verbal abuse dished out by one's opponent, as well as the "rough tactics" he may resort to (hitting below the belt or with his elbows, head-butting, rubbing his gloves into your eyes or over a facial cut in order to open it further, etc.); and how to call forth and amplify others (of aggressiveness or "controlled fury," for instance) at will while not letting them get out of hand.'

Chris told me that sparring was important in the LBACP for the following reasons: 'Boxing, like all sports, can be used as a tool to make a more rounded and balanced person, and in boxing it's got

113

particular, peculiar aspects that give it advantages over other sports. There's a culture today that, if there's a problem with other people, you call your mates or you pull out a weapon. Well, in boxing, you have to stand in front of someone on your own and box them, there's rules and regulations, and people are watching. So I think for many of the students it's one of the most honourable things that they ever do, to actually stand up in front of everybody, to put their self-respect and reputation on the line, to stand in front of someone and get punched on their nose, *not* lose their temper, but actually think about how not to get punched on the nose again and try to land one yourself. So if it's a controlled environment, (we've never had someone hurt) then you can clearly use it as a tool, as a lever to try to move kids into the right direction.'

When there were serious disputes between the students, Chris sometimes threatened to use sparring as a means of resolving the issue. More than once, students were dissuaded from a conflict by Chris offering a boxing contest to resolve the dispute. In each case, the parents not only gave their permission for the sparring to take place, but were positively enthusiastic about it the idea. Far better to resolve the matter in a forum where there are set rules, and where both students are protected from serious harm, than to allow it to escalate into a street brawl where one or more of the students could be stabbed or worse. The students very rarely actually accepted Chris's offer, however, and after that the dispute was normally spent.

You can't save them all

Whilst joining the LBACP was the turning point in the lives of some of the students—such as Felix and Hunter—that was not always the case. Of our normal cohort, Chris once told me that he reckoned that our students could be placed into three categories of roughly equal size. First, there were those students whose lives were indeed completely turned around by joining the LBACP. In the second category were students upon whom we had some effect, even though they did not appear to change their behaviour that much. We did two important things for them, though. We were able to bring stability into their lives and prevent any further slide into serious criminal activity, even if they did not go completely straight. And secondly, we sowed the seeds of discipline, hope and self-belief that in a few years usually led to the young person being relatively normal. The mere fact of *stability* for those students, even when what they were doing was a poor performance by any normal standards, was an enormous improvement.

In the final category were students upon whom we had little effect. They appeared bent upon ruining their lives and though we could help at the edges, they had to learn the hard way. Jamie and Mitchell fell into this category. After being suspended for the incidents at Spurs, Chris told us in a staff meeting that he intended to visit them at home, in an attempt to work out exactly what was leading to their difficult and angry behaviour. Chris told us that 'the only way that I'm going to be able to get those two to sort themselves out is if they're in tears in front of me'.

Chris's account of the visits were revealing. When Chris visited Jamie, he was morose. Jamie had a supportive mother, and Chris said that there 'was even a man around the house, though he wasn't Jamie's dad'. Chris got a good feeling from the meeting, and decided that Jamie should return to the Academy a week before Mitchell, in order to see what Jamie was like on his own without Mitchell's negative influence. Although we had hope for Jamie, Chris's description of his home was not pleasant. It was an extremely cramped flat, with things strewn all over the place, Chris said, and no space at all for thought or quietness. But we hoped that Jamie could do well with us.

Mitchell was another story. Chris sounded very sad when he told us about the visit. Mitchell's mother, it appeared to Chris, had the mental age of a 13-year-old. There was no father around. When Chris sat down to discuss Mitchell's future with them, Mitchell's mother was busy having a tug of war with their dog and arguing with Mitchell's two sisters. She didn't seem able to appreciate the seriousness of the situation, said Chris. So Chris focused upon Mitchell. Unfortunately Mitchell didn't seem to care, and looked at the floor throughout the conversation. Mitchell gave the standard assurances that he would not be rude to the teachers, and would behave himself on site. But as Chris put it, his mind was on 'all the people he's got to rob, all the drugs he's got to take, and all the pornographic videos he's got to watch, rather than sorting himself out'. It was very sad, Chris said. He told Mitchell that his place had been booked at another project, which Chris had been told by the referring school was 'the dustbin of youth projects'. Chris told Mitchell that any slip up would lead to expulsion from the academy, but Mitchell just shrugged his shoulders in response.

Jamie returned to the Academy a week later. His morose outlook had disappeared and was replaced by his normal mischievous demeanour. The first I saw of him was when he entered the classroom and stole a calculator, before walking out again, thinking that I had not seen him. When he eventually returned, I asked him why his behaviour had deteriorated so.

'I dunno y'know, things have been bare mad lately. Some madness t'ings have been happening,' said Jamie. He didn't want to elaborate. Jamie behaved reasonably well for the rest of the week, but deteriorated when Mitchell returned. Mitchell quickly got himself into trouble by being rude to Carmel. After Carmel sent him from the class, Mitchell chillingly said, as Peter let him away, 'that woman's got me expelled from the LBA, the bitch!' Mitchell was expelled.

We had hoped we could still work with Jamie, but as it turned out, I never saw either of them again. Both of them had been charged with a serious assault and robbery that had been committed some time before they joined the LBA. They had been bailed until the court hearing, but they had breached their bail conditions and were imprisoned as a result. According to the accounts from Chris and the students, both Jamie and Mitchell had been present for the assault and robbery, but Mitchell was responsible for the severe beating that had been meted out to the victim. Tyrone was very happy to discuss the detail of the case in front of me. Speaking to Desmond, Tyrone said that 'Jamie'll take five for Mitchell. Jamie's tight with Mitchell. He ain't no snitch.' In other words, he was saying that Jamie would say nothing about how the attack took place in order to protect Mitchell.

As the sentencing for Jamie and Mitchell approached, their names came up in the classroom with increasing frequency. Then one afternoon Desmond, Tyrone, William and Darren disappeared for the sentencing itself. When they returned they were full of bravado about Jamie 'taking' the time for Mitchell. Tyrone mentioned that Mitchell had given Desmond a letter intended for Mitchell's younger brother. Tyrone said that the letter said 'crime doesn't pay', which made me rather sad. I asked Tyrone if I could see the letter and he vituperatively told me that I could not: 'you didn't even like Mitchell blud', he said, which I thought was fair enough.

The Manor Ballet Trip

One of the peculiar features of the school was the apparently sharp contrast between boxing and some of the cultural activities we took the students to. It seems appropriate, therefore, to end this chapter with an account of the LBACP's trip to the ballet.

When the opportunity to visit the ballet arose (via Civitas), I must say I was extremely apprehensive! Although by then I was experienced at organising trips for the students and cajoling them into attending, it was quite clear that everyone at the academy (staff and students) regarded ballet as a step too far. I decided to go ahead with the trip with only two students, and indeed two of the most mature students: Darren and George. A pod leader accompanied me.

The company we were to see was the Manor Ballet (now the London Russian Ballet School), which was based in Lambeth and led by Harriet Pickering. Manor Ballet was unusual in that it aimed to cater for deprived young people in Lambeth as well as more privileged participants. A trip to one of their shows seemed to be an ideal opportunity to show the boys something they would almost certainly never otherwise experience.

As expected, my proposal met with some scepticism from the students. However after some persuasion, Darren helpfully volunteered that 'you can't say you don't like something if you ain't tried it'. Since both the students were semi-serious footballers, I also told them that the ballet was a unique form of athleticism. However, the make-or-break issue in the negotiations were over how much money I would spend on their McDonalds meal on the way to the show.

'Whatever... we... want: yes?' George spelled out for the umpteenth time. 'As in, whatever, yeah?' I agreed, just asking them not to make themselves sick before the performance.

As we had only two students, I was able to relax and enjoy the performance. Darren and George sat quietly throughout, and seemed to appreciate it. There was a wide variety of ballerinas and ballerinos in terms of age, ethnicity and ability. The fact that there were novice dancers on stage, whose movements were clearly not as refined as their older counterparts, helped the boys appreciate just how hard it was to dance. It would be easy to assume that ballet was not very difficult if one had only seen ballet in Covent Garden, I thought. One pair of very young boys gave a performance that was deliberately comic, and went down very well with the audience.

The highlight of the performance was when one of the senior ballerinas began repeatedly pirouetting, to spontaneous applause. She kept spinning, and spinning, in an extraordinary display. Darren leaned over and whispered 'she must be dizzy you know!!'

The boys enjoyed the trip. George told me that he 'wouldn't mind doing that again', and Darren actually asked when the next performance would be. What appeared at first an extremely risky trip, was in fact a great success.

6

An Inspirational Individual

Rules without relationships ain't worth toffee, Tom... Remember that.

Chris Hall, December 2009

Pastoral and academic roles

Chris Hall, the principal of the LBACP, had overall responsibility for the running of the course and the welfare of the students. But since he was not a teacher, he delegated the academic elements of the course to me. Consequently, the day-to-day running of the school entailed a close partnership between Chris and me. The dynamic relationship between us was the driving force behind many of the innovations in the project.

Nonetheless, I should emphasise that the original vision of how the school would work was most definitely Chris's, and indeed that vision remained accurate as the school grew in size. One of the fundamental elements of that vision was the division between the 'pastoral specialists' and the teachers, where the pastoral specialists were the pod leaders and Chris. I call them pastoral specialists because their primary role was the care for the students, with the aim of improving their behaviour, though obviously the pod leaders and Chris had myriad other important roles (sports coach, teaching assistant and mentor to name only the most important). Most significant of all, one of those pastoral specialists, Chris Hall, was in overall charge of the project.

It is obviously unusual to have a non-teacher in charge of a school. But this novel structure accorded with the different educational aims that our school had, as compared with mainstream schools. We accorded priority to the socialisation of our students. This was because if the students were unable to sit still, listen, be polite, non-violent and so on, then whatever academic opportunities we offered to them were going to be wasted. Second, it was fundamental to Chris's vision that we could only get the students to behave themselves by making them want to do better academically. They would behave themselves, we reasoned, if we could persuade the students that it was sufficiently important for them to do so. The person in overall charge of this task had to be a very special, inspirational individual, who in the case of the LBACP was Chris Hall. It is therefore worth examining Chris and his methods in much greater detail. In this chapter I also discuss the visits Chris and I undertook to the parents of the students and a trip to the University of Oxford.

Some background

Prior to the setting up of the LBACP, Chris had been a boxing coach for nearly 30 years, whilst working in a variety of jobs, including as a warehouseman. He set up the LBA in 2000 after completing a degree in Sports Science and Leisure Management at Brunel University as a mature student. I conducted an interview with Chris in July 2010 and all the quotations in italics below are from that interview, unless otherwise stated. Chris told me the following:

My own time at school, I look back as being largely wasted—which is where I probably have something in common with a lot of the people we work with here. In 32 years [of coaching boxing], probably 95 per cent of people we have in boxing gyms are people that have wasted their education and have been disaffected in some way or another, and I feel I was largely disaffected. I didn't cause many problems, you know a few fights and stuff like that, but I just feel I went to school because everyone went to school. I didn't really understand why I went to school. I was never sat down and nothing was explained to me about that.

I lost my Dad when I was a baby. Perhaps if my father was around he would have been a bit more forceful in those areas; obviously mothers are more nurturing and caring, and as long as I was happy and healthy, Mum was alright. And she had a full-time job as well. I was able to get through GCEs, and even A-Levels, but nothing to the level I could and should have done had someone explained to me the purpose of all this. But no-one ever did so I just made of it what I saw.

Chris, then, could identify somewhat with the disillusionment with education expressed by the students at the LBACP. But Chris also had a positive personal story to tell about how he improved his life through education, because his degree was an important step on the road to setting up his own boxing club, the LBA.

A second way in which Chris could identify with the students was in having spent time in rough company during his time as a boxer and boxing coach. Chris once told me a story about his own boxing career, which was very successful: Chris won three national titles as an amateur. The story illustrated how terribly cruel some of the young boxers he boxed with could be. Chris was at a competition away from his home in London, and he and the other boxers on his team were staying in rooms with bunk-beds. One boxer was asleep in his bed when Chris and the rest of the boxers on tour returned from a night drinking. The sleeping boxer was on the top bunk, with one arm hanging off the side of the bed, with no side rails. One of the group pulled the sleeping boxer's arm, hard, which caused him to fall from the bunk on to the wooden floor whilst fast asleep, which left him with a broken jaw and fractured collar bone.

'They were horrible people, some of them,' Chris told me. He told me another story from when he was a boxing coach. The influence of the notorious criminals the Kray twins was still felt in the boxing community when Chris was a young boxing trainer, and Chris was unfortunate enough to have a confrontation with a man named Harry who was vaguely associated with them. Chris had provoked the confrontation by insisting upon adherence to the rules as to exactly when during a particular evening a boxer had to turn out to fight, because those timings conferred clear advantages in the ring. Harry had an interest in the boxer turning out early, but Chris refused to accede to Harry's demands.

Harry's tactic was an odd one, Chris told me. When he became angry, he would demand that one of his henchmen turn the light out. When the light was turned back on, someone would be laid flat out on the floor, having been knocked out by Harry in the darkness. It was obviously his way of avoiding blame or conviction for knocking people out. Lucky for Chris, when Harry had bellowed 'turn the fuckin' light out!' one of Harry's colleagues intervened, saying 'leave it out, Harry'.

As a result of confrontations like these, Chris had an authenticity that the students could identify with. For example, we once learnt about a fight outside of school that settled a dispute between two students. Chris said jokingly: 'I've had plenty of punch ups around the corner, and it's never done me any harm, I think.' Chris's personal experiences meant that he was not shocked or at sea when bad things happened.

Chris had a very strong moral compass, and a deep scepticism about the manner in which the modern state influences people's behaviour. He told me that some of his 'lady boxers', after having a child early in life, would have another one 10-15 years later in order, he suspected, to keep receiving benefits from the government. 'Everyone should get something', Chris told me, but he said that, in effect, paying people to be sick, unemployed or to have children is not just wrong, 'it's blinkin' ridiculous'.

Considering that Chris spent his time trying to persuade young people to respect authority (of teachers, for example), Chris was deeply cynical about actual figures of authority. For example, returning from the trip to Oxford (described below), we were stuck in traffic running in both directions up and down the road. 'You know what's happening here, Tom' he said. 'There'll be a police officer up at the top of the road directing traffic back down towards us.'

'You've got a bit of a love/hate relationship with the police, ain't you Chris?' I said.

'I don't trust anyone with authority, police, army anyone like that,' said Chris.

Although Chris had experienced the uglier side of boxing, for the most part he clearly saw the boxing fraternity as a moral counterpoint to some of the failings of government and society. Take, for example, the following discussion of the LBA after it was first set up:

> The LBA was set up in 2000 and we did the normal work associated with boxing facilities, such as becoming mentors and role-models, and father figures, for lots of young people that use the gym.

Boxing clubs have traditionally done this over many, many years and I think it is generally recognised in society that boxing has a very, very good effect on young people. It isn't just the activities themselves but it's the kind of people that actually get involved in boxing gyms. For instance if you want to take your child to a tennis lesson you're looking at 30 quid or ridiculous sums of money, but most kids can access boxing gyms for nothing, virtually, two pounds and stuff like that.

The reason is coaches give up their time willingly and voluntarily. There's an awful lot of difference between people who are giving voluntarily, as opposed to someone who is giving, but there is a price attached. It's a little bit like fostering these days, as foster parents traditionally were great-hearted people who gave, in every sense. Today you can get about £350 a week to be a foster parent—well that slightly changes the whole reasoning for doing it, i.e. if you take away the money, they wouldn't foster.

It's a bit like that in boxing gyms, they do it without the money, there's no financial interest for most boxing coaches, if not all of them virtually. So they've really got a good heart and they really do care for young people. I think they give one-to-one quality time and attention to young people in a world which is generally very busy. They probably don't get that level of attention elsewhere, and they probably don't meet people that believe in them in the same way that their coach does.

Chris's motivations for getting involved with the young people we worked with were not, however, in any way political. Chris was a born-again Christian, and wanted to use the LBA to do good for the community. When I asked Chris why he worked with the students, given how challenging their behaviour could be, he said the following:

I have to say the first reason I have to work with them is because it's a calling for me, it's something from God. I can't remember the exact day—I wish I could remember, but I can't—but I was walking through the gym and I actually had a revelation. It was: I've got to make this gym a blessing for the whole community, for every single person that comes here. I've got to make it a blessing. It needs to be a blessing.

So it just hit me, like a flash of light really: I must make this place a blessing. This all happened before the school, and I believe it [the school] was all part of that movement. We started literally from that point to take boxing into schools, and just broaden what we do to bring in more people.

123

I think that I've got a blessing, as far as relationships with young people go. I didn't realise it myself. It's my wife who actually brought it up. She said that everywhere I've been, all the clubs I've been to, we've flourished. That's not to say there's not bad moments, there's bad moments in everything, but generally speaking, I just feel called to do it.

I think it's a little bit easier for me to do it than most people because I get on well with them. I'm always aware that if I was born in a similar environment and circumstances to these students and to these people that walk into my boxing gym, I would probably be the same—probably worse—in terms of my emotional and behavioural difficulties.

Because, you know, parts of Tottenham and Hackney and even Enfield now, they're rough, and it's harsh. There's some that are bullied and are looking over the shoulders for the bullies, the bullies are looking over their shoulder for the other bullies that are after them, so there's a lot of tension whenever the kids just go from A to B...

I don't think it's actually them that are the problem to be honest with you. I think it's the environment that they're growing up in, and where you want to put the blame for that, everyone's got their own opinions. Certainly the government is first stop because the government is supposed to look after the environment that we grow up in, and some places are going wrong and no one particularly seems to care.

Chris did not wear his religion on his sleeve—on the contrary, he once told me that he is greatly sceptical of organised religion (in a similar tone to the way he said he was sceptical of the motives of the police). I knew that he went to church with his wife, who is Ghanaian, where Chris joked that he was the 'only white person in the place' each Sunday. But the image and persona that Chris projected within the gym was of an earthy, people-person. Chris kept his religion private. Despite working extremely closely with him for three years, the above is the only time Chris spoke to me in those terms. He did occasionally say that his confidence in the project's success stemmed from his belief that he was 'not of this world', but the other staff and I largely thought that he was pulling our legs.

Chris's outlook, then, was a compelling combination of realism and idealism. He was cynical and pessimistic in his analysis, but hopeful and determined in action. By way of illustration, contrast the two following conversations between Chris and me. First, after a particularly grating outburst from Russell whilst we returned from the trip to Oxford, I asked Chris in frustration whether he thought that Russell would ever be a normal person.

No, to be honest with you Tom. Most of these kids in the old days would have been fine, once they'd left school. The thing is, they just don't do social interaction. They can't handle it. Twenty years ago, once they'd left school they'd get a job in a warehouse or a factory, get their £300-400 a week, and be very happy. But these days it's either a professional, high-tech job that they ain't cut out for, or some face-to-face thing like retail. But they don't do people. They'll just never have a job, live off the state, have half-a-dozen crazed children with four different women, then die young. It's tragic. We just can't cope with them in our society in the way we could.

But that did not stop Chris from busting his gut trying to do the best for each and every one of the young people he worked with. The second conversation, regarding his work at the boxing academy:

The LBA has been here for 11 years, and over those 11 years we've worked with thousands and thousands of young people. From time to time some of the most extreme cases, who I really had fears for in terms of where they're going to end up, have come in and just made a visit off their own back and totally surprised me. People who I thought I hadn't made much of an effect on have gone on to do great things.

A particular lad from eight or nine years ago came in. I thought he was off the wall, and really heading to a bad place. He came in, and had done an access course at college and got into university. He was one of the extreme cases, you know, violent flare-ups virtually every day, and very hard to deal with. When I look at him, I think we're planting seeds that we don't see the harvest of. I'm sure that if enough good people keep putting positive things into these kids, the vast majority of them, by their late teens, will turn around.

It's a question of getting enough people to do positive stuff with them, and for them to spend enough time with positive people for that to take place. I think that the ones that I feel maybe don't get a good turn around are the ones that spend virtually all their time with negative people, because obviously if you're hanging around with drug dealers and burglars and people that commit violence all the time, then no one else gets a chance to have that input.

So engagement is a very, very powerful tool for us. Sometimes you may feel that you're not finding your way, but if you keep on, and other people are also willing to put that time in, then we can have a positive result. I speak to a lot of parents that are really concerned about their 14-year-old or their 15-year-old and I can reassure them, honestly, that most kids of that age group do get sorted out before they're 20. Not all, but the vast, vast majority.

Chris in action

One of the most important qualities required for successfully working with these students was honesty. Chris's position meant that he often had to be frank about his beliefs on some very serious topics, spanning the family, crime and indeed the most general questions of what life is all about. For Chris, being honest was a way of showing that he took the students seriously as individuals. Long after Felix had completed his time at the LBACP, I asked him to describe Chris. Felix told me that Chris was 'honest, supportive, kind, and... a laugh'. It is the best summary of Chris's qualities I have come across.

However, given the erratic and immature behaviour of the students, it was very tempting to fob them off with generalisations in order to avoid the risk of being ridiculed. It was tempting because it is much easier to avoid difficult questions than to tell students exactly what you think. Chris would never fob the students off in that way, and it could be a very tough role to play. This was particularly true when Chris was telling a student where his criminal activities were likely to lead. I recall Chris telling me about a long conversation he had with Emre, who at the time was in crisis after getting involved with the Turkish gangs on Tottenham High Road. His parents were very concerned for him, not to mention extremely scared, after several police raids on their home. I found out what Emre had been up to when he explained his lacklustre work effort by saying (of himself) 'daddy is tired': he had been in police cells overnight. Chris said to me after his conversation with Emre that 'it'll be hard to find anyone else who Emre will sit down with for an hour, especially telling him all the hard facts that I had to'.

To take another example, Chris often had to explain to new students the reality of what their schooling situation actually was. When Mohammed joined the school, he told the other students and me that he was hoping to return to his mainstream school if he behaved well at the LBACP. This promise was often made to the students but was generally speaking just not true, and the older students knew it. In Mohammed's case it was Lucas who set him straight initially: 'Blud they always say that shit but believe me, once they get you out, you ain't going back, fam. They is always saying that shit just to get yous out the door; but once you're gone, it's bye-bye.' I remember Mohammed looking cross and asking to see Chris. Chris was straight with him: 'In all my years working with students like you, Mohammed, I've got to say that I have never seen one actually go back. Once they've got you out, it's very, very difficult to get back in. I'm sorry.'

Honesty was just one strategy Chris deployed to build a positive relationship with the students. Chris formed his disciplinary policy around his own ability to build a relationship with the students. Chris once summed up his approach with the phrase 'rules without relationships ain't worth toffee'. When I asked Chris what he meant by this he said:

You have in our society lots of rules and regulations in everything, these days, and largely I think people have just had enough of it. There are so many rules, and so many regulations, and particularly in our institution, a lot of the kids have had it up to their ears. They don't have a lot of respect for rules and regulations because the rules and regulations applied to them are made by people they've never seen, they don't know, people they don't have a relationship with, and who they don't respect.

One of the crucial things for me in our organisation is that our rules are policed via the relationships we have with the students. If you threaten to suspend someone or remove them from a lesson in most mainstream schools, students would gulp, and stop what they're doing. But with the students that we work with, the extreme end of behaviour, it doesn't really mean anything at all, so to use formal rules as a lever to establish order doesn't really work.

You're much better off building a relationship with the student so the student actually wants to make you proud and happy, doesn't want to disappoint you or come into conflict with you, and therefore seeks to please you by listening to what you've got to say and then moving out of the room, and accepting that suspension...

127

It's not to say that rules and regulations shouldn't be enforced, of course they should. But it's a far easier way of doing it to build a relationship than to keep using the stick, because these kids have had the stick their whole lives in one way or another. It's just easier to build a relationship to get them to do it. In the same way, people beat puppies and dogs, loads of people do it, but I can't think of an animal more eager to please than a dog. They are so eager to please you it's incredible, but people still give them the stick and whack 'em. You don't really need to because innately they want to please, and innately all the students we have, they want to please, they'd like to be popular.

They don't know how to go about it, they probably haven't experienced it, but everyone likes to be popular, everyone likes to please people. So if you can build that relationship, and you can enforce the rules using informal power—which is the power that they've given to you, they've given you authority—I think that without exception all the students respond in a positive way to what I ask them to do. I don't think they did it because I was the principal of the school, I think they did that because they respected me and liked me enough to give me that authority.

And I think that's the way forward with this particular cohort. It's not always easy to get there, but if you persist and you're consistent I think everyone can get there and get to the point where they're happy to comply. And even though you will always still get the odd eruption of poor behaviour, and sometimes quite bad behaviour, they would still calm down and respond positively, if you have a relationship with them. If you don't, it just makes life very hard for you.

I think the reason it's hard for most people, and easier for me, is that I actually like all of the kids that we have, without exception, and some of them I like a lot. So it's easier for me to have a relationship. I think a lot of people actually don't like the kids, and therefore it's impossible to have a relationship. Although you try to pretend you like them, and have a relationship, the kids see through it instantly, they know that you're just trying to play them, and so it's not going to happen.

Chris therefore lent great weight to the *informal power* that his relationships with the students afforded him. What this meant in practice was that Chris expended a lot of energy trying to acquire the loyalty of the students through acts of kindness, small and large. I was most struck by this whilst I was watching Chris interact with Ricky one lunchtime. Ricky was certainly the most notorious student for moaning, which, given our cohort, was quite an accolade. Chris told me that Ricky asked him whether he could go home virtually every day, often on the grounds of illness, but sometimes for no reason at all. He just seemed to be rather miserable, except when he was ridiculing other people. That lunchtime, we were in the boxing gym, and Ricky had approached Chris in his tiny office in the corner of the gym. Ricky wanted to use the toilet (to 'bust a shit' as he put it), but he didn't want to use the toilets in the main gym. He asked Chris whether he could have the keys to the main sports centre building to use the toilets there. He did not like the toilets in the gym because the other students could see who went into those toilets. Chris told him that he could not have the keys, but that he would take him round to the sports centre to use his preferred toilet. This involved at least a five minute detour around to another building and back again, not to mention waiting for him to finish on the toilet.

As I sat there eating a sandwich, during the short 30 minute lunch-break, my immediate reaction was that I wouldn't have taken him. Chris, however, dropped what he was doing and walked him to the toilet without hesitation. Reflecting on this little incident, it was clear that the next time Ricky had some kind of disciplinary problem, Ricky would almost certainly bend to Chris's will, because Chris had gone out of his way to help Ricky where almost no one else would have.

This example also illustrates the importance of Chris being very easily accessible to the students. Chris, incidentally, never took a lunch break, to ensure that he was around during the time when most of the students were milling around and free to see him:

One of the biggest advantages that we had was that my office was right in the middle of the action, sort of on the frontline. My door was always [physically] open and the students were really grateful that someone was always available, and always listened to what they had to say. That in itself just solved a lot of problems—they felt that they could always go to the principal and express whatever it was, whether they thought they had been badly treated or whether someone was trying to take their £1.50. They didn't have to go up any long set of stairs, along the corridor, it was just there. You know they really used to make use of it, and I think that goes a long way to establishing a platform for rules with relationships because they could go to the rule-maker, which in life generally they can't do.

Almost as important as the small acts of kindness was a financial generosity that over time I learnt to mimic. When I started at the academy, I spent a lot of time being badgered for 50p, or to lend my mobile to the students so that they could ring 'their mum', as illustrated by Lucas's '10p' story in Chapter 4. Chris's approach, illustrated by giving money to Darren for staying behind for an after-school class, was generally to agree to the student's requests. What I started to realise was that 50p could mean quite a lot to a 15-year-old, especially those who were very unhappy and accustomed to hostility—but that 50p did not mean much to me at all, as an adult with a salary. A few pounds a week in loose change, and few of the minutes on my mobile, bought an enormous amount of goodwill from the students.

Chris probably spent ten to £20 a week on the students, but the return on that expenditure was certainly much higher than many of the other things that we spent money on. Moreover, what Chris emphasised to me after giving money to Darren, was that Darren and the others 'probably had a hundred quid stashed in their socks. So it wasn't really the money itself that made the difference. It was the fact that I gave the money to them that was important.'

In addition to acts of kindness and financial generosity in school, Chris was involved in the lives of the students outside of school. Chris described his role in the following way:

> It's never perfect, but I do the very best I can. There's not a lot that I wouldn't do for the students and for the kids that come to the boxing gym, within reason, you know. Sometimes it's difficult to find the time to go to court with them, and you know, I do what I can. I try not to be taken advantage of in terms of 'Chris, can you take me to Wood Green?', you know—'No I can't take you to Wood Green'—but if something's doable, or if something is a major issue, then I try and address it… I've been dragged into personal disputes of students, with gangs, and intervening to prevent problems with pupils from this school and estates, at some personal risk.

> [It] involves going to people's houses in the evenings. One of the things I normally say when I get there is: 'Look, let's talk properly, because I could be at home playing with my kids, but instead I'm sitting here talking to you and your parents. So I want you to be aware of that factor, and appreciate it.' So I do spend time with families trying to put things right, but I don't feel I can

work any other way, and you know, as I think I said earlier, what's taking place here for me, all of it, it's a power working through me. So I have to go with it. It's just giving up time in all sorts of situations, and going to housing estates at night in the dark.

Chris tried to avoid telling the rest of the staff about *all* of the scrapes that the students became embroiled in because the students expected Chris to hold much of it in confidence. However, the following are examples from my own experience of Chris sorting out the problems of the students, which give an idea of the time commitment involved. After school one day I happened to be present when Ricky burst into Chris's office in tears, saying: 'They punched me in the face on the bus and took my hat,' referring to Darius and Desmond. He was terribly upset. Chris got on the phone to Darius and said to him: 'Darius, if the hat don't come back then there's gonna be a big issue', which led to the return of the hat and an apology from Darius. Another time, someone using the gym found that his mobile phone had been stolen, almost certainly by one of the students. Unable to identify the culprit, Chris paid for a new mobile phone for the boxer to save any further trouble. And as described elsewhere in this chapter, Chris often went to court for the students or had to facilitate a truce between two warring students.

To do what Chris did required a certain ability to distance himself, in order to appreciate the humour and extraordinariness of the events that he was involved in. After working with him for a long time, I noticed that when Chris described a particularly outrageous outburst of anger or a particularly vindictive act done by some person, he would chuckle at the incident. I learnt to do exactly the same. Looking back, it was rather similar to the way in which I dealt with difficult episodes with my father. Getting those stories off our chests (and being able to laugh at them) served as a kind of therapy, a coping mechanism for dealing with the challenges that the students brought our way each day.

Psychological warfare

Chris's strategy was that once he had acquired the students' loyalty and respect, he could begin moulding—or socialising—them into mature adults. First, once Chris had a student under his wing, he would be sure to boss him around a little. 'Could you make me a cup of tea please Lennox?' Chris would say, getting the student to rush off to boil the kettle and attempt to make a cup of tea. It was important, Chris told me once, to establish dominance in this way by asking little things of the students, just for the sake of it. The students, by the same token, felt useful and valued by Chris. As Chris said, the students loved to receive approval from men for whom they had respect.

Chris also enjoyed, as I did, ribbing the boys a little to establish a relationship. It was important that the students could find you funny—even if my own efforts were seen as slightly unconventional. Often Chris's means of challenging the students were more purposeful. Each week, Chris would meet with a pod and run a lesson called 'discussion'. It was Chris's opportunity to set the tone for the week, deal with any grievances the students had, and discuss a topic intended to make the students think. The most memorable topic of those discussion sessions was whether love is a verb or not. Chris described the situation to me as follows:

> The reason we spoke about whether love is a verb or not was because I'm always talking to broken-hearted mums, sisters, dads and guardians. I wanted to get a point across. So I asked the kids: 'If you really loved your family and your guardians, would you really still go out and do whatever it is that you're doing that is bringing so much unhappiness?' And it was a discussion that was never ending, some would say yes, some would say no, and then most people, when it came up again a few weeks down the line, would swap—it was a very good topic. But love is a doing word, it's very easy to say 'I love you' to anyone, but really if you love somebody you want to show that you love them by doing things.

This question of whether love is a verb or not frequently spilled over into my lessons. The students talked very animatedly about whether they did, in fact, love their mothers—and whether loving their mothers entailed no longer 'doing their t'ing'. Getting the students to reflect on the consequences of their own behaviour was, of course, half the battle.

There were also other, more subtle tactics. For instance, Chris never swore when the students were present (and extremely rarely when they were not), so as to afford him legitimacy when he told the students to stop swearing. Similarly, he made sure never to lose his temper with the students when they did something wrong. This meant that when he did lose his temper (or pretended to), he could be sure of having a more profound effect as a result. I only saw Chris shout at a student once, in a dangerous situation where several students were attempting to gang up on another student — and sure enough, they scattered.

One of the most important set of questions that Chris had to have an answer to was about the purpose of education. 'What's the point? Why am I doing this?' was a perennial line of questioning, and it was important to have answers. When I asked Chris about this, he said:

> Well, the purpose of education, is to begin for the first time, personally, shaping your future, I believe. Up until you go to school, possibly even during primary school, largely it's just like 'do this, do that', and you don't really have any input. But once you go to secondary school, I think for the first time you can start shaping your own future rather than just drifting and going with the flow. I never really grasped that concept.

> You can choose what subjects you do, you can be looking around at what you actually want to get into in terms of a career, you can choose a profession, and you can study towards it. Unfortunately, as it wasn't explained to me, I didn't do any of that, and always chose the easy subjects, the subjects where I knew the classes would have the most girls in them.

In an attempt to help the students to avoid a similar fate, Chris frequently told the students what the purpose of it all was. He was selling the ideas of *self-determination* and *self-improvement* to the students: he told them to take control of and better their own lives using education. This impulse ran throughout everything we did in the academy. These ideals do, of course, fit well with the individualistic, self-willed characteristics required of boxers.

We sold these ideals to the students with a large dose of realism. The students needed qualifications to get ahead in the job market, regardless of whether they found what they were doing in class stimulating, useful or otherwise. We were explicit about the importance of credentials: 'Yes, if you want to work in a garage, you will probably find you need a GCSE in maths. It's just a piece of paper,' I would say, 'but it's a piece of paper that employers use as a signal for the fact that you can add up, even if the qualification says you can do much more than that.' Our message was: 'Society views education instrumentally, and you need to know that.'

The primary way we encouraged the students to re-engage with education was by linking it with the world of work. But quietly, we would also suggest to the students that learning is worth it just for its own sake. We wanted the students to enjoy learning. We also wanted them to appreciate culture that they might not regard as relevant to them, such as classical music. Chris played the radio station Classic FM in the gym every morning when the students came in, and I frequently played my favourite piano concertos from my laptop whilst the students were working. After a while, the students even put in requests. Robert was a big fan of Luciano Pavarotti's rendition of *Nessun dorma* and would wiggle his head in time to the music.

In my lessons I tried to use algebra as a means of showing that learning for its own sake was enjoyable. Algebra is perhaps the most notoriously frustrating and confusing topic in elementary mathematics for students like those at the academy. Moreover, the students could quite plausibly tell me: 'I'm never gonna use this ever again in my life, am I, Tom?'

The first, and most important step in responding to that student's challenge was to teach them the rules of algebra from scratch, step-by-step, to make sure that they really understood it. If they listened, all of the students were capable of doing so. As I mentioned in Chapter 4, even Felix and Ricky could do algebra. In those small classes, where I could give the students lots of attention, algebra was actually one of the easier topics to teach. Then, once they understood some algebra, it gave me space to suggest to the students that: 'Even though algebra is not very relevant to everyday life, it is satisfying once you get it, isn't it?' More than once I had to teach a boy the meaning of the word 'elegant' when I was explaining why algebra was enjoyable.

Moments like those gave me an opening to try to show my own enjoyment of learning to the students in other ways. Generally it would involve my telling the students a random fact that (hopefully) they found interesting. Some facts were very simple — like telling the students why every four years we have a leap year. The facts that really seemed to hit home were those that connected the students' rather brash world with something they would regard as much more stuffy, like history or politics. For example, Robert once claimed in a lesson that the word 'fuck' was a French word. This set me off explaining to Robert that he was talking about etymology, the study of the origins of words. By way of introduction, I told them about the phrase 'excuse my French', which is often used to excuse swearing, and implies that the French language is somehow vulgar or dirty. Then I told them about a traditional (albeit false) explanation for the origins of the rude version of the V-sign hand signal. The story is that during the Battle of Agincourt, in which England was fighting the French, the French threatened to chop off the index and middle fingers of any English longbow men they captured, in order to disable their ability to use their longbow. So the English longbow-men flashed their two fingers at the French, as an insulting way of saying 'I've still got my fingers...'

The point of all this was to show the students my love of learning. Their usual reaction was to tell me that I ought to be on the TV show 'Mastermind'. But hopefully, in a similar way to the stories that Mr Dunn told me in Tamworth about his 'perfect moment', some of the spirit of what I was trying to get across stuck with the students. The other main method we used to try to broaden the horizons of the students was taking them on cultural trips to the ballet, the theatre and university.

The Oxford Trip

Towards the end of each academic year I took a group of Year 10s to the University of Oxford. We used the summer term at the end of Year 10 to concentrate on building relationships with the students who were about to enter the all-important Year 11. We were to visit Corpus Christi College, where I studied for my undergraduate degree, before going on to a training

135

session with the Oxford University Amateur Boxing Club in the debating chamber of the Oxford Union.

The students were interested in the fact that I had gone to a 'posh' university and when we began promoting the trip to the students, I was asked a lot of questions along the lines of: 'Did you really go to Oxford then?' They found it quite confusing, because they generally assumed that having gone to Oxford, I ought to be rich. Yet I was working with students who had been removed from mainstream school. No sane person, they thought, would teach in a rough area after the opportunities they assumed Oxford offered. Laura took a closer interest than most in my career choices, and once said to me: 'Why the fuck would you want to work in a shit-hole like this if you went to Oxford? You is mugging you'self sir, swear down.'

Another incident in which Oxford came up was also with Laura. I had been trying to win her over—buying her a jacket potato with cheese and beans one lunch-time—but I was not having much success. During one memorable lesson she had refused to sit at a desk. She insisted upon sitting on a chair in the corner of the room that did not have a desk. Sometimes I would put up with this kind of thing to give the students a little space, but I felt at the time that Laura was just trying to undermine me. So I insisted that she sit at a desk. She refused again, blankly. I persisted, which led her to explode: 'Do you think I'm some kind of fucking dog that came out of some dog's fanny? What the fuck, man!'

I sent her out for that outburst. Her response to being sent out was violently to push over the nearest table, walk towards my desk, and venomously kick my bin with all her might, which smashed into tiny shards of black plastic flying across the room. Ervis ushered her out of the room, perhaps fearing another 'William' incident, but then she poked her head around his side and shouted pointedly at me: 'We're not in fucking Oxford now Tom!' Despite the violent context, it remains one of the funniest things any of the students have ever said to me.

A few weeks later we were on our way to Oxford. Laura, Ricky, Russell, Suma, Hunter, Craig and Robert attended the trip. Russell, Hunter, Robert and Ricky were all in their own ways 'star students'. I expected the difficult students to be Laura and Suma.

Suma was not a rude or malicious student, indeed he was charming, although rather silly. But he really disliked academic lessons, and particularly maths. He avoided doing work, and frequently left the class in *frustration at being badgered to study. I had recently decided to cut him some slack, however, after a telephone call to the boxing gym from his grandfather, who was looking after him at the time. The call was primarily intended to inform us that Suma was not going to be in that day because he was unwell. However, his grandfather also mentioned in passing that Suma was also very upset because 'he had seen something terrible whilst he was on the bus the other day. His father, who as you know does not live with Suma or his mother any more, assaulted Suma's mother whilst they were on the bus. Suma is very upset, I'm sure you understand'. This went some way, I felt, to explaining Suma's agitated state in school at the time.*

When we arrived in Oxford, after a long trip in the minibus, many of the students were restless. So we took them for a walk around Christ Church meadow, a beautiful pasture in the centre of Oxford, which serves as flood-land for the River Thames, or the Isis, as the river is known at Oxford. I had always found the meadow to be a very special, tranquil place where I could collect my thoughts. I looked at the meadow from my own college, Corpus Christi, almost every day when I was studying there.

The students generally seemed to like the meadow. 'This is even bigger than Alexandra Park!' said Craig, betraying his parochial knowledge of open spaces. We took them to G&D's, the popular ice-cream bar in the city, to use up some time before taking them into the college. 'It feels like I'm in another country' said Robert, which was exactly the lesson we wanted the students to take away: that not everywhere is like Tottenham and Hackney.

Upon entering Corpus, Hunter and the other students insisted that they had entered 'Harry Potter land'. Hunter asked me: 'Where's Gryffindor?' We met with two friendly undergraduates who had been asked by the college to give us a tour. They happened to be two rather pretty females, and entrepreneurially, Robert and Russell attempted to separate the girls, one each, in order to chat them up.

We went for lunch in Corpus's sixteenth-century hall, where the students were offered roast beef, a Cornish pasty or vegetarian lasagne. The students were soon telling me that Oxford students 'must be the best fed in England'. Robert and Ricky had a serious conversation about whether it was sensible to eat the stuffing that had accompanied their beef—something they had never come across before. They agreed to eat it simultaneously as a dare, but Robert pulled out at the last moment. Ricky mumbled to Robert, with his mouth full of stuffing, that it was 'alright you know', which eventually led Robert to try a little of the stuffing.

Our next port of call was with Corpus's tutor for biochemistry, Dr Mark Wormald, for a discussion about life at university. I knew Mark quite well, as we had worked together on admissions to Corpus when I was an undergraduate.[1] We met around a large table in the Reynolds Room, the most ornate and formal meeting room in Corpus.

Mark introduced himself and told them a little about his job, before inviting questions from the students. Initially they were very quiet, declining to volunteer any questions or comments, so Chris told the students they had to ask a question each.

They began stutteringly, asking how long Mark had been at Corpus, whether he was a millionaire, and whether he was famous (only amongst a small band of biochemists, Mark told them). Hunter then asked: 'What's biochemistry?'

'Good question', Mark responded, before explaining that biochemistry is concerned with what is going on at the atomic level in living things. This led Craig to ask: 'Does smoking give you cancer?'

The students listened intently to Mark's explanation of the links between smoking cigarettes and cancer. Robert, smiling as he spoke, could not resist asking whether 'smoking weed' had similar effects. Mark addressed the question directly, saying that although he knew much less about the evidence on cannabis, the general story was that although the risk of cancer was much lower, there was emerging evidence of other health issues, particularly mental health issues, associated with cannabis use.

Suma asked: 'How hard is it to get into Oxford then? To get into a place like, what is it, Corpus?'

'Very hard,' Mark responded, giving some statistics which illustrated the low odds of getting a place, even for applicants with good A-level grades. 'Only a few of the very best manage to get a place at Oxford. It's very similar at other universities like the LSE, Imperial and Cambridge, of course.'

'Oh right,' Suma replied thoughtfully. 'My granddad went to Cambridge.'

'Is it?' Laura asked in surprise. 'Whrarr,' she added. The students never ceased to shock me with odd bits of information like this. Suma's meek offering led to a discussion of what it was like to be a student at Oxford.

Robert asked about tuition fees, so Mark patiently explained how they worked. Robert's main concern was whether it was possible to purchase a place at Oxford for his future son 'when I'm a Premiership footballer'.

'No,' Mark emphasised whilst chuckling, 'places are allocated on a strictly academic basis.'

'Aww, peak,' said Robert.

'But it's not only academic work that students at Oxford spend their time doing, although it does take up most of their time. Many of our students are off around the country competing in national sports competitions, including at football.' Russell suddenly looked up, and interrupted.

'What, they let you leave?'

'Yes,' Mark said indulgently, 'as long as you complete your academic work you are more or less free to do what you want.'

'So, what,' Russell began, 'you can get drunk n'that?'

'Yes Russell' I interrupted. 'I spent a fair amount of time doing that. You get a room of your own you know,' I added, returning to a familiar theme, 'and it's the quickest way to leave home and get your independence.'

'So you can take girls to your room?' Ricky interjected. Mark nodded.

'Any girls?'

'Erm, yes,' Mark confirmed, telling them a story about St Hilda's College, at the time the only single-sex college in the university (for women). The legend was that at a fire-drill early one morning at St Hilda's, more boys than girls emerged from the student accommodation looking bleary eyed and mildly embarrassed.

The students found the story very amusing and we then concluded the session to walk over to the Oxford Union for our boxing session with the Oxford University Amateur Boxing Club (OUABC). On the way to the Union, the students were astonished to see that most of the bicycles in Oxford were not chained to anything—the locks were used to immobilise the wheels and the bikes were leant against the walls of the colleges. 'This is crazy' Robert said, 'just three gangs from Hackney', he said, listing the names of the gangs on his fingers, 'and they'd all be gone in a day, I'm telling you!'

When we arrived at the Union we met with Richard Pickering, OUABC's student president, who had organised the session for us, and arranged for OUABC head coach Des Brackett and five other Oxford

139

students on the boxing team to join us for the session. After all the sitting around the students were keen to let off some steam. We pushed the leather benches and dispatch box to the sides of the chamber and the students gathered for a warm up on the wooden floor where thousands of the great and good had spoken. Des conducted the warm-up, having the students and boxers jump up and down, twist their upper bodies, do press-ups and some shadow boxing.

We had enough trainers for each of the students to get one of the OUABC staff each to do pad work. The students passionately whacked away at the pads as they did back in Tottenham. They particularly enjoyed practicing 'Haymaker' punches, which are very wide, looping punches intended to throw as much bodyweight as possible behind a punch in the hope of a knock-out blow. There was a lot of laughter and fun during session, although half-way through Laura declared that she was 'sick of this' and grumpily sat down, complaining that she was too hungry to be doing boxing training. The boys, however, pushed harder and harder, and by the end were dripping in sweat.

It was a successful session, although Russell insisted on making a big show of leaving the room 'to do a fart' during the warm-down. Des told me that the students were 'much better than I expected'. At the end of the session I took photographs, including shots where Robert and Ricky posed with the busts of Michael Heseltine and Roy Jenkins, which stood against the wall of the chamber. Laura cheered up when Chris told the students that he was going to buy them all a KFC for doing so well.

I overheard the students in conversation whilst we left the chamber and walked across the yard of the Union. 'You gonna come here there then?' Ricky asked Robert.

'Yeah, but you gotta work towards it, you can't just come, like' said Robert, before turning towards me and declaring: 'I ought to start listening to Tom's lessons!' I laughed and told him that would be great.

Suma then approached me and quietly thanked me for organising the day. 'I'll come to your lessons now and not mess around, because today was good. Thanks!' Even Laura became effusive about what a great day she had once she received her KFC.

Teaching after Oxford

The trip to Oxford went very well indeed. In the weeks afterwards, whenever Robert saw me he insisted upon loudly greeting me with a positive 'Hey, Tom!' He had visibly warmed to me. Although Laura was still loud and obnoxious, she made a big effort. Suma was almost a different person—polite, sensible, totally different to the whining, difficult student before the trip. The only student who complained was Russell, who was unimpressed by the racial mix in Oxford, complaining that 'the only black girl I saw had a moustache and dry elbows'.

I had tried to invite the students into a world in Oxford that I knew and loved, which contrasted so starkly with their own. I wanted them to know that there were places away from their own areas of North London which were safe and secure. Certainly, the experience of visiting Oxford stuck in their minds. The students would often refer to the trip, request to go again soon, and made jokes about the experience. For example, I often played football at lunchtime with the students. Whenever I scored a goal, or went around a player, the students would refer to my 'university skills'. In another example, a few months after the trip to Oxford, I was encouraging Craig to improve his time on the times-table grids, possibly to improve upon the time of the top person in the rankings, who was Darren. I said to Craig: 'We're going to knock Darren off his pedestal, right Craig?'

'That's some Oxford humour, innit Tom?' Craig said, quick as a flash, which was his way of saying that he did not know what a pedestal was.

Unfortunately, we were only able to take a small number of students on each trip, and whilst we were having a positive effect on those students, other students were sometimes deteriorating. Lennox was one of those students, and his behaviour was so bad that like, Mitchell and Marcel, he eventually had to be expelled from the course. Lennox's story is worth telling, however, for two reasons. First it illustrates how far Chris was prepared to go for the students, particularly the ones almost everyone else found it hard to care for at all. The second reason is that Lennox's self-destructive

141

behaviour illustrates the tragedy in the lives that some of our students led.

Lennox had been previously been expelled from the LBACP for being threatening to Pete Quentin, my predecessor as mathematics teacher. This was quite early in the life of the project, when the school was much smaller in size, and before I arrived. Lennox kept appearing at the gym, begging Chris to allow him back on to the course, so Chris decided to give him another chance.

Lennox was always on the edge. He was the exact opposite of 'low-hanging fruit'; students who were easy to work with and to reform. If we had to run the school based on the principle of 'payment by results', Lennox would have been one of the first out the door. But for Chris, he was exactly the kind of student whom he wanted to help.

Lennox's mother, allegedly, was dying of cancer, and had been for some time. Perhaps as a result of the pain of his mother's illness, or for other reasons, Lennox was constantly trying to get the better of the other students and of the teachers. The problem, as mentioned in Chapter Five, was that he did not have the brutal streak in him to back up his confrontational words. The other students ostracised and victimised him because of his behaviour. For example, I remember Darius once mentioning in class that he had 'bang-dropped' Lennox the previous evening in Manor House, an area just south of Tottenham (i.e. that Darius had punched Lennox, who then fell to the floor). When I asked Darius why he had done this, Darius simply said 'cos he's dickhead, innit?'

In my lessons, Lennox yo-yoed from outright hostility to being very pleasant. One lesson that went well ended, for example, in him writing down his *MySpace* web address on a piece of paper and inviting me to visit the site. At other times, he was very confrontational. In an attempt to illustrate to Lennox how much work he had to do, I once pointed his attention towards the tick sheets. He did not like this at all, looking at me angrily before saying: 'Are you dumb? What are you showing that to me for?' When he was like this, he was very hard to get on with. Another time, I asked him to stop shouting at me, and he retorted that he was not shouting, but then asked rhetorically: 'Do you want me to show you what happens when I start shouting?'

Chris, however, kept faith with Lennox throughout, and even said that he liked him. Sometimes I did not know how he managed it. As he was at the academy before I joined, Lennox would often trot out his 'I was here before you' line, as if that allowed him to misbehave. One incident in particular stuck in my mind. During a lesson, Lennox had refused to give up his mobile phone, claiming that he was using it as a calculator, despite the fact that he was not meant to be using a calculator. According to the rules of the classroom he had to leave the class for refusing to hand in the phone. When Peter arrived, Lennox refused to leave, so Chris had to collect him instead. I think that Lennox was expecting that Chris would conciliate him and let him stay in the lesson. When Chris arrived, Lennox explained to Chris what had happened, that he had his phone out but he was using it as a calculator, and said that I was being unreasonable and unfair. Chris listened patiently to Lennox's account, but then told him that since a teacher had asked him to leave, he had to leave.

'Come on Lennox, let's go' said Chris, matter-of-factly. Lennox looked at me angrily.

'He can't win. He always wins.' He looked menacingly at me. 'You know you've got to get the bus home don't you?' said Lennox, trying to be intimidating. Richard laughed at him, trying to win him round.

'What are you talking about bruv? Where'd that come from?... Come on bruv, let's go!' Lennox walked out with Richard and Chris.

Lennox's threat about the bus was not serious, but I was dismayed that he saw his being sent out the class as a 'win' for me. Later, Chris explained to me that teachers are amongst the few people who can't fight back—the other students just beat him up. For example, at one time Lennox and Robert appeared to be best friends. But for some unknown reason, Lennox went about the academy saying that he was going to stab Robert, because he had been 'chatting shit'. This went on for almost a week, until Robert decided that he had had enough. I was walking from my classroom through the car park to the boxing gym, and I saw a group of the students surrounding Lennox and Robert, who were fighting, but in a very strange way. Robert kicked Lennox in the stomach, which caused Lennox to fall to the floor. Then Robert kicked Lennox whilst he was on the floor, before the staff were able to intervene to stop the fight.

The fight was strange because Lennox did not fight back at all. He seemed almost to invite the violence against him. Consequently, unlike most incidents like these, the action unfolded very slowly. When I first saw them, I didn't think they were fighting at all. It fell to Chris to support Lennox after the 'fight', when Lennox's tears flowed uncontrollably.

I also learnt about incidents outside the academy. During this period, Tyrone and Marcel robbed Lennox of his phone. In response, Lennox had organised for one of his cousins to put a gun to the head of one of Tyrone's cousins, with the message that if the phone was not returned, there would be serious consequences. As a result, Chris had to organise for Tyrone's and Marcel's mothers to club together to buy Lennox another phone in order to settle the matter.

Even after this incident, though, Lennox continued to hang around with Marcel and Tyrone. This was, I suppose, always going to end in a further humiliation for Lennox. What happened was that Lennox had a large amount of cash in the back of the very small Nike bag that he carried. For some reason the bag was open, and Desmond, Tyrone, Marcel and Darius each took turns to steal a banknote from the rear of Lennox's bag. Marcel finally caused all the coins in the back of the bag to spill onto the floor, leading to a scramble for the cash. In the heat of the moment Lennox threatened the life of Marcel. But once he had done this, being the coward that he was, he dared not to travel to school, and so I did not see him for some weeks, until the issue blew over.

The offence that finally ended Lennox's time at the LBACP involved drugs. Drugs, along with weapons, were one of the 'red lines' that Chris made clear to the students would lead at least to suspension and probably to expulsion. In the middle of his English lesson, Lennox had passed a small ball of cannabis wrapped in cling-film across to another student, saying 'try this'. There was no alternative, given all his previous offences. With great reluctance, and in the knowledge that he was probably ruining what was left of Lennox's life, Chris had to expel Lennox from the academy. What was extraordinary, though, were the lengths to which Chris had gone to give the boy another chance.

Visiting the students' parents

The first parent I met at the LBACP was Darius's father. I met him in the car park outside the boxing gym, after I saw him give Darius a very stern and dignified dressing down. Darius's father's name was James. James was a black man with a Jamaican accent and he struck me as very intense. Darius was obviously in trouble for some reason. James kept saying to his son: 'Are you a man, Darius? Are you a man?' Darius meekly responded in the affirmative. So James continued: 'If you are a man, why would you behave like this? This is not the behaviour of a man!' After the bombardment, which went on for quite some time, Darius looked humbled.

Darius, like several of the other students, had lived with both his mother and his father at different points during his life. Some of the fathers said that they felt they could not look after their sons because they feared that they would hurt them if the boys stayed with them, so bad was their behaviour. But James wanted to give it another go for the sake of his son. Over time, we developed a cordial relationship. I frequently bumped into him on Tottenham High Road and he came into the school to monitor Darius's progress very frequently.

Later in the year, Darius's behaviour began to deteriorate seriously. Once I had been in the job for a while, I was able to spot when something was wrong with a student. Rather than just having the occasional bad day, their behaviour became gradually worse over a period of weeks. 'Going off the rails' was generally what we called it. Normally it would be Chris who contacted the parents to find out what was going on, but I had to contact James on an unconnected matter to do with permission slips, and happened to mention to James that Darius was not doing very well.

James sighed heavily, and said that he was not surprised, before apologising for not getting in touch sooner. What had happened, he told me, was that Darius's mother had kicked Darius out of her house at the same time as James was evicted from the house that he was living in. So Darius and James were effectively homeless. They were staying at various friends' houses whilst James looked for a new place for them to live. They did not have any keys to the flat in which they were staying, and could only enter late at night. This meant that Darius was roaming the streets of Tottenham, getting into trouble, because he had nowhere else to go. It was hard enough supervising Darius when they had a home of their own, James said. He told me he felt that he had already overstayed his welcome at the place where he was staying. 'You really find out which of your friends have got the right intentions, when you're in a place like where we're at', James said. 'It's alright when you've both got money to go an buy an espresso, but when one of yer don't, then you find out what's up.'

The reason Darius was climbing the walls, then, was because he was homeless. James was trying to find council housing but the only places that had been offered to them, almost a month after they had become homeless, were in Wood Green. The problem was that Darius was a Tottenham boy. Although Wood Green and Tottenham are both in the London Borough of Haringey, for young boys like Darius—and many of the better behaved children in Haringey too—they might as well have been opposite sides of a 'peace-line' in Belfast. Moving across the ill-defined boundary between the two areas was simply unthinkable. James complained bitterly that the council was not taking into account the needs of his son. He also felt that, as a single father, he was not getting the same level of help that a single mother would receive. They were finding it difficult to eat properly, James added quietly. But he could not bring himself to come into the academy to explain what was going on because he felt ashamed. I could barely believe what I was hearing. I called Chris to tell him what James had told me and Chris said that he would do what he could to help, starting by making sure that Darius ate properly every day.

When I next saw James, a few weeks later, he told me that he and Darius were living in temporary accommodation. He showed me a picture on his mobile phone of where he was staying, which was a dreary garage that had about a dozen washing machines dumped in front of it. He told me a humiliating story about being allocated his accommodation. Apparently he was told by text message, late in the evening, where he was to be staying. But when he arrived at the accommodation, the manager said that he did not know anything about Darius and James staying there that night. This led to a fiery argument, during which the accommodation manager had threatened to call the police. James had been forced to hold his tongue and grovel with the man to check the records again. Eventually a fax came through confirming their permission to stay that night, but the experience had made James bitterly angry. He felt powerless, he said. Until only a few years ago, he ranted, he had been a drug dealer, selling heroin. Now he wanted to make sure that his son did not go down the same path but he was finding it nearly impossible to do the right thing. The housing arrangements in London are 'fuckry', he said angrily, and he surprised me by saying that he was considering standing as a councillor in the forthcoming local elections for the Conservative Party.

It was to deal with situations like this better that I suggested to Chris that he and I ought to visit all the parents of the students in their homes. We generally did this in August, just before the students were due to begin a new school year. We visited both the new students and those who were already with us. The visits served several purposes. Primarily, it allowed us to get to know the parents of the students. We made it clear that we wanted to have strong lines of communication and gave them our mobile numbers, whilst taking down theirs. In the case of new students, it was useful to get off on the right foot with their parents present before their son or daughter joined the academy, otherwise there was a danger that the first time they heard from Chris would be when he had to inform them of something naughty the student had done.

Knowing the students' parents was very useful. For example, one morning Chris received a phone call from a blocked number who claimed to be Desmond's father, informing him that Desmond was not very well that day and so would not be coming in to school. However, Chris was suspicious of this sick-report because it did not sound at all like Desmond's father's voice. So Chris immediately rang Desmond's father on his mobile, and asked whether he had just called in to report Desmond sick. Of course, he had done no such thing—it was one of the other students pretending to be Desmond's father.

The visits also allowed us to deliver certain important messages to students and their parents. To the Year 11s, we emphasised the importance of their examinations at the end of the year. We would discuss what kind of college course the student would like to take, what kind of work experience would benefit them, and what kind of job they wanted. For those older students, we were trying to make them realise how important for them Year 11 was, in the hope that they would take some time to consider their future seriously. There was no better way than meeting with them in their own home with their parents.

Chris and I visited all the parents in a marathon two-day stint. We travelled in Chris's car, in which I was in charge of sorting out the satellite navigation device, while Chris drove. Walking around the estates where the students lived, Chris and I received some very funny looks. Chris pointed out with some humour that, as both of us were dressed smartly, we looked like police investigators. As usual, Chris's mobile phones went off at very regular intervals. Chris's ringtone was so loud and distinctive in the academy that the students often sang the ringtone to themselves as they walked around. Often Chris would finish a conversation on one of his phones, only for the other phone to ring with a different parent trying to contact him.

The vast majority of the meetings were very positive and constructive. Most of the visits were fleeting, a maximum of ten or 15 minutes each. However a few of the visits gave me an insight into the life of the student in question and caused me to feel enormous sympathy for them. The most vivid example of this was visiting Ricky's house. Ricky's parents lived together in the upstairs flat of a house in Tottenham. Most of the flats that I visited were well maintained and clean, but Ricky's was unfortunately neither of those things. Ricky's brothers and sisters were playing in the side-street by the house when Chris and I squeezed up the staircase to their flat, past a pile of broken furniture. Ricky's mother was a large black lady, who was wearing a white dressing gown when we arrived. We sat down in the front room, perched on the edge of a sofa whose springs were extremely loose. Ricky sat on a seat on the other side of the room looking sullen. His mother offered us tea, which I refused, but Chris asked for a glass of water. We began our pitch about the year ahead, and the importance of Ricky doing well, when Ricky's father charged into the front room wearing only a pair of white underpants. He demanded to know who we were, in a sort of friendly way, but I could not help noticing that he smelt strongly of cannabis. Ricky's mother scrunched up her face in embarrassment, and Ricky looked at the floor.

We explained that we were from Ricky's school, a boxing academy. 'Yes, a boxing gym!' he exclaimed. 'That's good, you know, because Ricky is *too fat*. You gotta get him into the gym and get some weight off that boy cos he is *too fat*.' Ricky looked mortified, his mother even more so. Chris jocularly promised that there would be plenty of opportunity for Ricky to do exercise, but Ricky's father painfully pushed the point again. His eyes were dilated—he was clearly high as a kite, despite the fact that it was only 11a.m. in the morning and we had arranged the visit in advance. Chris and I soon left, incredulous at the father's behaviour and having a much better idea of why Ricky was the way that he was.

A second difficult encounter was at Laura's house. The positive effects from the Oxford trip had lasted for a few months, but like Darius, Laura's behaviour had been slowly deteriorating in the months leading up to the home visit. She had become more 'street'. She talked a lot about going out partying and getting into fights. Chris had been working with Laura and her mother very closely, visiting their house frequently to try to sort Laura out. By the time of the visit, Chris and I knew what had gone wrong, or perhaps, what had happened as a result of things going wrong: Laura was pregnant. She was only 14. Laura's mother had told Chris in confidence about the pregnancy, and it was at this visit that Laura's mother planned to formally tell us of the pregnancy in front of Laura. At the time of the visit, Laura had known she was pregnant for two weeks.

Laura lived on a council estate in Hackney, in low-rise blocks. When we arrived Chris said that he recognised the estate from a previous unhappy visit: 'Do you know, Tom,' he said, 'that this is the site of the only time I have ever been shot at?'

'What?' I asked.

'Yeah, probably about 20 years ago I was visiting one of my boxers who lived about here. I knew he was into some dodgy stuff, and he kept going on about leaving the country, but when you've got a decent boxer you try to hold on to him, you know? Anyway I came looking for him in the estate, and as soon as I'd knocked on the door a couple of men came from the other end of the estate and started firing a gun at me! I tell you, Tom, I've never run for my life like that before, but I did that day, oh yes...'

We met with Laura and her mother in the front room, which like most of the other students' homes was pleasantly decorated and had a large TV in the centre of the room. Her mother kindly provided us with tea and biscuits, and we discussed the weather. Laura sat at the end of the room with her arms folded across her chest, not saying anything. When we were all settled, her mother explained, slowly, that Laura was pregnant. Chris soothingly told them that we would do everything that we could to support them. He also asked whether the father of the child was going to live up to his obligations, in a sensitive but semi-serious way, which made Laura break a smile. She didn't know what was going to happen with the father, Laura told us.

The eye-opening moment in the visit was Laura's mother's reflections on the situation. 'You see,' she said, 'I've been out of work for 26 years now, and I thought it was about time that I got a job, so I'm going to college in September, or, was. But now with all this, I don't think I'm going to be able to go.' Laura had an older sister, which probably explained the gap between Laura's age (14 years) and the amount of time Laura's mother claimed to have been out of work (26 years). It did seem an extraordinarily long time to have been out of work, or at any rate, an extraordinary thing to say.

Most of the students lived on council estates, like Laura, and most of them also lived only with their mother. I came to know about half of the families of the students, and of those parents whom

I knew, three-quarters were single-mothers. Quite often, though, there was a grandmother or grown-up sister involved in the care of the child as well. But it would be fair to say that a large majority of the students did not have males living with them, and when they did, they were rarely their fathers.

Chris's theory was that often the student and his mother were engaged in a struggle for power, and that usually the student won. Around 14 years of age, boys often shoot up in height, strength and confidence, and demand more independence—to stay out later, to not do their homework, and so on. Often it would come down to question of physical strength. The boy would say 'what are you going to do to stop me?' and, given his advantages in size, strength and aggression, single mothers found this very difficult to cope with. The corollary of this argument was that if there was a man around the house, he might possess the authority to face-down the newly eager boy.

That is not to say that the single-mothers I knew did not struggle very hard to keep their sons in check. One mother told me that once, she happened upon her son openly smoking skunk in a deckchair in the back garden. 'Alright mum?' he said, defiantly, whilst taking another drag from the joint. Her response was to pick up a length of wood from the floor, and run at him, whacking him over the head with the length of wood, drawing blood. The boy then ran off in terror, and perhaps also in shame. Mohammed's mother, when we visited her, complained of violent outbursts of anger and rage from her son, which led her to call the police on a regular basis. It became so bad for Mohammed that he spent periods of time in care, because his mother no longer felt she could cope with him. Tyrone's mother threatened to take Tyrone to a psychiatrist, saying that she thought his bad behaviour stemmed from a mental illness.

But it was very difficult for them. Marcel's mother, whom we met before he was expelled, was a nurse. But Marcel, being who he was, pushed her very hard. I was present once when Chris was speaking to her on the telephone. Chris said afterwards he could hear Marcel swearing at and insulting his mother in the most obscene way in the background of the conversation. In another example, I once overheard Darius and Darren talking about staying with their

151

mothers. If they brought a computer games console home, or any other piece of electrical equipment, their mothers would not let them keep it in the house unless they could produce evidence of purchase: 'receipt and box', Darren said, imitating his mother, 'or you can take the bumba-rass t'ing outta here', which caused Darius and Darren to descend into giggles. Moreover, relations between the mothers and fathers of the students—such as in Suma's case—were sometimes so bad that it was much better for the student that their parents did not live together. This was one reason why it was so important for the boys who joined our school to have strong, positive male influences in the shape of Chris and the pod leaders. Chris often became a father figure for the students he worked with.

Why did it come down to violence and physical strength? It seems to me that dealing with stroppy teenagers is hard enough for settled families who live in wealthy, peaceful areas. The tools of persuasion and bribery can take you much further when there are relatively few problems for a family to deal with. But where the kind of difficulties experienced by Lennox (whose mother was dying of cancer) and Darius (whose father was effectively homeless) enter the equation, relations have a much sharper edge. Many of the families faced financial pressures and had lives that were complicated in unbelievable ways. A few of the parents of the students would probably have lost some of their moral legitimacy in the eyes of their sons by their own actions—Ricky's father, for instance. Moreover, when there is just one parent, conflict is much more personal. When two parents raise a child, the two adults can support each other's views and maintain a common front in support of what is best for the child. In the same way that the presence of pod leaders in my classroom de-personalised my conflicts with the students, for a parent to be able to say 'we have decided' is much easier than saying 'I have decided'.

What Chris emphasised to me, though, was the strong influence of the areas in which the students grow up. Given the prevalence of violence just outside of their homes, especially amongst young people, it is perhaps not surprising that violence, or the threat of violence, reared its head at home as well. The influences of 'the street' will be discussed more fully in the following chapter. What particularly struck me, touring some of the estates in Hackney and Tottenham, was the scale of the concentration of people into what were very small plots of land. The green spaces, where available, were generally very small. But many of the students I met wanted to get out of their flat as much as possible.

Visiting flats like Tyrone's, you could understand why the students would want to get out on to the street. Tyrone lived alone with his mother in the ground floor flat, in a patch of estates in Stoke Newington. I've never been in such an extraordinarily small flat as Tyrone's. It was like putting together two student-sized rooms with a bathroom, and filling it with a lifetime's worth of possessions. About half the living room was just a large pile of stuff, heaped on to what was probably a sofa—just because there was so little space. The house I grew up in, which I regarded as very small, was a mansion in comparison. Tyrone's flat was very claustrophobic. After the visit, I surmised that one of the causes of Tyrone's caustic talkativeness was simply that in that flat he couldn't escape interacting with others all the time. It was impossible for him to have any personal space inside that flat.

When all the children from those flats spilled out into courtyards and small patches of grass this produced a lot of young people in one place with not a great deal to do. Indeed Chris and I bumped into a number of our students driving around the estates. One of those students was Russell. When we spotted him, Chris slowed the car and I drew down the window. When the car stopped opposite Russell, Chris said out the window: 'Alright Russell?' He stiffened as if preparing himself for a confrontation, but then relaxed when he saw it was Chris and I, and invited us in. Within the flat we met an old Jamaican man who was Russell's grandfather. The flat was very brown, largely through age, but also because of a passion for leather on the part of whoever had furnished it.

Russell's major problem was his punctuality. When we told his grandfather this, he heartily complained that early every morning he 'runs 'is bath, make 'is breakfast, and call up stairs, but he just don't get up!' He was a real character. He told us that Russell's mother and sister lived in the house too, and that they all looked after Russell. Russell's other quirk, which I did not mention to his family, was his fascination with the technicalities of thievery. Half of the questions I received from him in mathematics were about security devices. He was very disappointed when I told him about the 'smart-water' and dye devices that security companies use for transporting cash from banks and shops.

Although he was exceptionally keen to do well in maths, and badgered me for after-school sessions (despite finding it hard to turn up to the scheduled sessions), Russell really was not very clever. For example, he was a fan of one of the newer slang words in the student's lexicon: 'political'. This was used to describe something as unfortunate. It was very similar in meaning to another slang word they used: 'tense'. He once said in the class: 'if everyone lost their watches, and no one knew the time, that'd be political, wouldn't it?' Or another time: 'If I have to go outside, and it starts raining, it's gonna be political'.

Richard tended to reply such insights by saying: 'Yeah, deep thinker, Russell is. Ain't you Russell?'

'Are you dumb blud?' Russell would reply, 'don't chat shit.' Chris thought that Russell was the kind of child that, if he grew up in a supportive family in a nice area, may still have been not very clever, but would also have been pleasant, polite and diligent. As it was, something had led Russell astray.

Whilst some of my experiences with the parents of the students gave a negative impression of their parenting skills, I knew from my own experience that such a snapshot view could be very misleading. Catching a parent on the wrong day could throw good parenting into a very bad light. Conversely, an experience with Russell, documented in the next chapter, suggested to me that visits which gave a relatively good impression could also mislead. The majority of the visits were very positive. Hunter, Craig, Felix and Tyrone all lived only with their mothers, who all worked and who gave every impression that they did the best for their child in the circumstances. The students whose parents were together also all made a positive impression. Robert, Emre and Lucas' parents all lived on council estates and appeared to be on the ball. Emre's father was a strict Turkish man and Robert's parents were very much on his case. Visiting the parents of the students was not like watching *Precious*, the film quoted at the start of the book—it was not a tour of parents who seemed abusive or crazy. The negative stories were the exception, but of course, parents who appear normal are not that interesting (or easy) to write about.

The difference that the visits made to the behaviour of the students, and our relationships with their parents, was enormous. I recall thinking at the start of the second year of the school, when we had met most of the parents of that year-group in August, that they were behaving like 'angels'. They returned to school with a sense of purpose and vigour. The effect wore off somewhat, over time, but it made an enormous difference to be able to start the school year on the right note. It was particularly useful to me as a way of cajoling the students into behaving properly, because I could credibly threaten to speak with their parents—I had their mobile number stored on my phone after all. I remember once Felix jokingly said to me: 'don't forget Tom, I know where you live'—because I had told the students the area of North London where I lived. But I was able to respond by saying: 'no Felix, *I'm* the one who knows where *you* live.'

The last stop on our schedule of visits was Darius and James. Darius and James were living above a shop on White Hart Lane, opposite a council estate. When we visited them, I was relieved to find that although the apartment was sparse and whitewashed, both James and Darius seemed far more settled than earlier in the year. James continued to lecture Darius on the importance of planning for his future, with only small interjections from Chris and I to affirm the message. We were hopeful that Darius would have a productive year; being as intelligent as he was, we wanted him get to high grades in his exams. Given the chaos and unhappiness that had plagued the lives of Darius and James in the months preceding that visit, Chris and I were both very pleased that they had managed to find a little peace.

Riding on the bus back to my own flat, I thought about the catch-phrase of one of my teachers at Tamworth: 'you know who I blame'. Perhaps he was right about some of the students. But not all, most definitely not. In any case, the purpose of those visits was not to blame anyone, it was to see what we could do to help the students, regardless of their circumstances. Take the following example, where the influence of the student's family background can, I think, clearly be seen. One afternoon I was discussing jobs with my class. A short way into the discussion, Ricky perked up and said: 'job? Nah, I'm just going on benefits! Who here's on benefits?' he asked the other students, before sharing a high-five with Suma. In one conversation, they had fulfilled all the negative stereotypes that drive calls for stringent welfare reform. But I could see from their downcast expressions that despite this joke, they knew that getting a job would bring meaning and purpose into their lives. Their problem, they knew, was that they currently stood at the back of the queue for all jobs worth having, and it was for this reason that they were wavering about whether to bother standing in line any longer.

7

The Classroom and the Street

'Education cannot compensate for society.'

Basil Bernstein. (1970) New Society, 15, 387, 344-347

Travelling to the LBACP each morning on the 259 bus, I passed a number of familiar landmarks. As I approached Tottenham, the first was the Woodberry Down Estate. Enclosed within a loop of the New River, Woodberry Down was split down the centre by the dual-carriageway Seven Sisters Road. Its row upon row of 1940s blocks running parallel with the road, with boarded up windows and young men walking muscle-dogs outside, was the image of a challenging estate. It is due to be demolished and completely re-built over the coming decade. Further up Seven Sisters Road was the South Tottenham area of Tiverton, where Tyrone, Desmond, William and Darren grew up. Tiverton produced our most challenging students, and at the stop outside Tiverton Primary School, one or two school students would often join me on the top deck, playing R&B on the loudspeakers of their mobile phones.

At the top of Seven Sisters Road there was a Wickes Buildings Supplies, where each morning around a hundred men gathered in the hope of finding work. The vast majority of the men were Eastern European, and over time several Polish shops established themselves to serve their needs. It was a labour exchange, a market in its crudest form. The men sought cash-in-hand casual labour, and stood outside Wickes in the hope that a builder would drive up and say 'I need two of you for a job'. Just around the corner, past Seven Sisters Underground Station, was a large Tesco's, which was the focal point of the area. There were several regular loiterers outside the front of Tesco's, including a young Asian man with a rug displaying the pirate DVDs he was selling, a beggar who had lost his legs, and occasionally, a group of men gambling over a shuffled-cups game.

As I rode up Tottenham High Road, amongst the mothers taking their children to school, people going to work, and sixth-forms students heading to one of Tottenham's two colleges, I would occasionally see a man in the *Star Trek*-style black robe. For several days he marched with a blond wig on the end of a pole in one hand, and a school bell in the other hand, which he rang solemnly. Chris and I assumed he was a patient at the St Anne's hospital in South Tottenham, which catered for people with mental health problems. Approaching the gym, the bus passed a shop that was once raided by armed police for allegedly selling guns. The shop's shelves were largely bare, and what products they did sell were given arbitrary prices at the checkout. A hundred metres from my stop, I would pass the patch of pavement on a side-road where, by lunchtime, the local drug dealers would be plying their trade.

Although just landmarks on my bus ride to work for me, these were real, daily obstacles for the students. They could not help but interact with them, and be influenced by them. And although we tried our utmost to create a safe, insulated environment from those influences outside on the street, it was not always possible to do so.

For the most part, the students regarded the boxing gym as a sanctuary. For example, Darren once spent an entire day asleep on a gym mat in the weights gym, after what we assumed was a night of mischief. But unfortunately, sometimes the students brought problems upon themselves that we found it difficult to deal with. William was one of the most prominent victims of this tendency. One lunchtime, he remained with Carmel and me in the classroom to continue some work, I suspect in search of shelter. Darren and Desmond were eating their lunch outside the classroom, which was unusual. In an earlier lesson, Darren had accused William of 'linking up' with Mitchell's girlfriend. Mitchell was still in prison. William had denied linking up with her, but Darren continued with his accusations whilst they lay in wait for William to get his lunch. 'All I did was talk to her!' William protested, but Darren didn't believe him, insisting that they did 'link up' (which I presumed meant kissing). Richard happened to be on the scene, and tried to sort the problem out himself. Darren produced a text message which he claimed to be from Mitchell's girlfriend, asking Darren 'not to tell anyone' about William and Mitchell's girlfriend linking up. Richard asked to see William's mobile in order to check that Darren's text message was in fact from Mitchell's girlfriend, and the numbers matched, to Richard's surprise, confirming Darren's accusation.

Then, suddenly, Darren, Desmond, Mohammed and Tyrone swarmed into the room and surrounded William, who looked terrified. William glanced at Darren to his right, just as Desmond, who was to his left, swung a punch that connected sweetly with William's cheek.

'No! Get out!' I yelled to the attackers, as William curled himself into a ball on his chair to protect himself. Several more blows rained down upon William before Richard, Carmel and I surrounded William and forced the boys out of the classroom.

The incident was traumatising for me because it had occurred in the classroom—a place that before the incident I had hoped the students regarded as cut off from the street. Evidently, it was not. Although Mitchell was in prison, he still had his friends to do his work for him. Soon afterwards I remembered that Mitchell's girlfriend was pregnant—indeed given the timing of the incident, she must have had quite a bump. So what was William doing 'linking up' with her? It seemed an exceptionally foolish to thing to do. Another question was why Mitchell's girlfriend had confided in Darren. Surely she knew that it would get out if she told Darren what she had been up to? Did she tell Darren in the knowledge that William would get a beating, as a way of ending the relationship? The mind boggled. Desmond and others were suspended for several weeks following this incident.

In a staff meeting later in the day, we conducted a post-mortem of what had gone wrong. It was clear that Richard had made a mistake in trying to sort out the incident himself. The protocols of the academy stated that he (or indeed, I) should have told Chris about the situation, who would then have had the opportunity to deal with the situation. But this was probably one situation that was beyond even Chris's powers of persuasion—consequences were sure to follow from William's actions, whether in school or not. In fact, it was probably for the best that the incident happened in school, in the middle of my classroom. If it had occurred anywhere else, the beating inflicted upon William would have almost certainly have been much worse.

Special arrangements had been made for William the next day so that he did not have to sit with any of the students who assaulted him. Tyrone complained loudly that William was receiving special treatment, 'just because he got banged, yeah'. But in the event, William did not change his timetable, and joined the class with Darren. There was surprisingly little tension. They got on with their work. Although Darren had been talking the day before about going to William's house to 'do something', the score had been settled in the classroom.

Gangs

Each lunchtime the students gathered outside the front gate of the sports centre, many of them smoking cigarettes. Many of the people passing by might have thought that they were a 'gang'. Congregated youths, particularly congregated black youths, have such a powerful social stigma attached to them that just being in groups is enough frighten and intimidate, regardless of the true character of the group. This stigma is painful for the young black boys who have nothing to do with gangs. For example, I once asked Felix about some of the groups of students in the school, whilst asking him about the impact of gangs.

'Look yeah,' Felix interrupted impatiently, 'they would be called a gang in the white society, but in the black society, they'd be, like, a group of friends, I personally think.' Felix, as we shall see, knew the difference between a gang and a group of friends. Nevertheless, the students in the school sought each other's protection because they had to get to school and back every day, and avoid getting mugged, stabbed or chased by the other young people on Tottenham High Road—some of whom most definitely were in gangs. The distinction is important to bear in mind through the following discussion.

The stories that I heard about the students of mine who were (it seemed) involved in gangs were chilling and surreal. Mohammed, for example, was once kidnapped by a rival gang. They tortured him and made a video of him on a mobile phone whilst torturing him. They forced him to distance himself from his own gang and to say disrespectful things about them. When they released him, they put the video on *YouTube* for all to see, but with Mohammed's gang particularly in mind. Unfortunately for Mohammed, *his own gang* then kidnapped him, tortured him and forced him to swear allegiance to his original gang whilst being filmed for a video which was then put on *YouTube*. Even prior to this incident, Mohammed had a real problem just getting to school on time, for the simple reason that he was up all night with his gang. Afterwards, he attended so infrequently that I barely saw him.

Marcel was another student who appeared to be involved in gangs. Before he was expelled, I was having an argument with him about whether he needed his mobile phone in the lesson. 'What if someone in my family got shot?' Marcel argued. 'I'd need to know, blud.'

'Well you'd just have to wait a little longer to find out, Marcel' I said.

'No,' disagreed Marcel, 'I need to know *now* so that I can go get my gun and do something about it.' With most of the students, I knew they were bluffing. They were pretend-gangsters. But not with Marcel—he probably did have a gun somewhere. What was really scary, though, was not that a few of those young people had guns. It was the fact that almost all of the students *could* get hold of a gun, very quickly, if they needed to. They knew the drug dealers on their estate, they knew who the most dodgy characters on the High Road were, and they knew which of their friends were connected in the drug trade. For example, after we had both left the academy, one of the pod leaders told me story about Emre, who came into school one day with a black eye. The pod leader asked him what was up.

'Some beef with the boys round these parts,' said Emre. 'But it's alright though,' said Emre, lifting up his shirt, 'I got it covered.' Emre had a pistol tucked into the belt of his trousers.

'Fucking hell,' said the pod leader, 'you wanna get rid of that thing Emre, you can't be bringing that shit into school. Where the hell'd you get that thing from anyway?'

'The garage blud,' said Emre, referring to a shop near the academy where many of Emre's friends hung out.

'Well fucking get rid of it, you stupid cunt,' said the pod leader.

'Yeah,' said Emre, smiling, 'you're probably right'. Emre left the school and did not return that day.

Gang rivalries occasionally meant that a student was limited in his choice of school. For example, we once had a student called Ali join the school, but he only lasted for a single lesson. Caroline told me that Emre had asked her about him, and when Caroline told Emre that the boy's name was Ali, Emre chuckled in his special, 'bad-things-gonna-happen' manner. Ali soon asked to see Chris and informed him that he could not stay at the school. Ali was presumably someone who Emre was entangled with on the streets of Tottenham.

Why did students like Marcel, Mohammed and Emre become involved in gangs? There were a number of reasons. Sometimes it was about personal safety—the students needed friends to travel with to avoid being mugged, but this was true whether a student was in a gang or not. What I think led some of the students to want to go out and 'beef' with other young people in gangs was a raw *unhappiness* in them.

Mehmet, for example, returned from his spell in Feltham to tell us that he actually enjoyed his time in prison. Whether he was trying to wind us up, or simply did not value his freedom, I am not sure, but what he said certainly annoyed Chris. It could also have been part of his macho, weight-lifting identity to say something like that. Certainly, Mehmet had always been very keen to be seen as masculine and was always talking about sex. For example, Mehmet once returned from the toilet, finished a conversation on his mobile phone, before telling us that he had a lot of skunk in his trouser pocket.

'Why would you say something like that?' asked Richard, exasperated. Mehmet said that he was only joking, before taking a plastic wrapper out of his pocket which contained a number of condoms. Richard asked why he had brought so many with him. Mehmet explained that girls were 'always telling me that they love me. And you gotta say "I love you" back, right?' Richard truculently replied: 'No, you don't.' When I once asked Mehmet what career he was interested in, he told me in all seriousness he was looking into becoming a porn star.

The thing was, Mehmet was gay. But growing up in his strict Muslim family, and hanging around with young men who were very homophobic, had clearly led Mehmet to bury his true identity under an edifice of chauvinism and toughness. The first sign that something was really wrong with Mehmet was when he came into one of his mock exams stoned and probably drunk, although this was not immediately obvious to us. Mehmet was entitled to a 'reader', who would read the questions to him during his examination, who in this case was one of the newer pod leaders. This new (male) pod leader told me that Mehmet made 'some pretty homoerotic approaches to me'. Mehmet said to the pod leader: 'I really like you y'know'. At the time I thought he was probably just winding us up.

Unfortunately we found out for certain after being informed that Mehmet had tried to commit suicide by stepping out in front of a train. He had been sectioned under the mental health act for his own protection. Mehmet clearly couldn't deal with the internal conflict between who he was and who he thought he ought to be. No wonder he tried to prove his masculinity, or what he thought ought to be masculine, by doing terrible things in gangs.

Suma was a slightly different case. He was not a gang member, so far as I could tell, but he lived an existence pretty close to the edge of gangs and the street. He once disappeared for a weekend with a friend of his to Brighton without telling his mother or grandfather, and told me about how he was arrested by the police on suspicion of vandalism (which he said he was innocent of, this time) and was driven home in a police car. Another time, he was explaining to me about the teardrop tattoos we saw on the faces of some rough-looking men we came across on a school trip. 'Usually, when you're in a gang, and someone close to you like a friend dies, then you get one on the left.' Teardrops on the right hand side of the face meant that the person with the tattoo had killed someone.

Suma was also the victim of the worst case of a lack of parental care that I came across. Since his excursion to Brighton, he had not stayed with his mother for over a month. He was sent to live with foster parents, but he fell out with them and so stayed with his grandfather instead. On the morning in question his grandfather had rung the mother to tell her that he could no longer cope with Suma's behaviour, saying that he was totally out of control. Suma's mother rung Chris, saying: 'Could you ring social services to tell them that Suma doesn't have a place to stay tonight please?'

Chris said: 'No, that's not really my responsibility, you ought to sort that out.'

'But I've been trying to get through to them all day, and I'm busy you know!'

As Chris pointed out to her at the time, 'we're all busy'. But Suma was her son. She made it sound like Suma's entry into her world was an inconvenience. How neglected must Suma have felt? I was teaching him later that day, and I recall watching him, in the full knowledge that he had no place to stay that evening, and feeling angry. He was behaving very well in school at the time, just following the trip to Oxford that seemed to change his attitude towards me. This latest catastrophe, I thought, would no doubt mess everything up for him once again. If Suma turned to a gang for support, and to vent his feelings, would it be a surprise?

Having said that, I did not know what Suma had done to lead his mother to treat him in that way. I did not know what other influences upon Suma's behaviour there were. I did not know the full story about Suma's father. But I didn't doubt that whatever occurred must at times have made Suma feel truly awful.

Filled with such negativity, I think those boys were looking for men whom they could respect, who would accept them as they were. Boys who are that unhappy are attracted to one another because they want similar things and they share common feelings. Gang members would accept each other for who they were, when teachers, social workers and most other people would not. Indeed, it seems to me that there are only two types of people who are able to accept a boy with all that negative energy. There are other people who share in that pool of negativity; and there are people with exceptionally open hearts, who would care for the students regardless of that negativity. I am obviously thinking of gang members on the one hand and people like Chris on the other. The problem is that there are many more gang members available to boys like Suma than there are people like Chris.

Most teenagers would reject the opportunity to join such groups, for the same reason that most young children are a little scared when a teacher tells them to do something. In both cases the boys react in the 'socially correct' way because they have been socialised by their parents to act in that way. Teachers and other authority figures rely upon that relationship between children and their parents when they assert their authority over children. But with our students one of two things had happened. Either the student was not properly socialised by his or her parents, or that socialisation was disturbed by some other force—such as the brutality of the street, or some problem within the student.

Take Felix, who arrived in the UK at 12 years of age unable to read or write. His embarrassment at his low ability led to him to misbehave in school, and eventually to hang around with a gang. This pattern was very common indeed. A few of the 'gangster' students really only had one problem: their reading. Felix described his behaviour within his gang in the following way:

'It's because of the people I'd been walking around with, socialising with. Let's say you're new in a gang, you're just a wannabe, yeah. So you gotta move up. It's like, say everyone smokes and you're the odd one in the pack that don't... You do things. I remember this yute who used to do that... obviously you gotta...'

'Do things to prove yourself?' I asked.

'Yeah, basically. And when you go home you think, "why did I do that, like? This guy didn't even really do nothing to me, I don't understand."' What Felix said illustrates the importance of peer pressure, and his own yearning for acceptance. For some of the students, though, there did not appear to be any issue that drove them to gangs. Emre did not appear to have anything fundamentally wrong with him, but as his teacher, why would I necessarily know? Emre seemed like the kind of alpha-male who, if he went to a posh public school, would have been a successful sportsman and then a cut-throat businessman. But growing up in

Tottenham, his impulse to be the top dog drove him in a different direction.

The worst moment during my time on the project that involved gangs occurred during my third year. Two alumni of the LBACP made an appearance on *Crimewatch*, a BBC television show that asks for the public's help in finding criminals at large. *Crimewatch* were trying to find someone who was responsible for an unprovoked stabbing of a man at a Tottenham bus stop that I knew well. It was a chillingly brutal and frenzied group attack on an innocent bystander that was captured on CCTV, after which the group ran on to a bus. The two former students had already been convicted and were serving time in prison at the time of the *Crimewatch* appeal, although that was little consolation. The students did not commit the stabbing itself.

As you might imagine, the images caused quite the sensation in the school ICT room when they were released. They watched the video on the *Crimewatch* website repeatedly. 'Normally you get stabbed for a reason blud,' commented Robert, who was watching the video for the fifth time, 'but this is just some stupidity, man. How can they go stabbing mans for no reason, blud?' Laura was characteristically withering: 'Black boys would do anything.' Darren, appearing typically well-informed, told me that the reason they couldn't find the person responsible for the stabbing was that 'he's already in the clink for somefink else blud, that's why they can't find 'im'.

This anecdote served to remind me that no matter how sympathetic I felt for an individual student's circumstances, acts such as those featured in the *Crimewatch* appeal could never be justified.

Postcodes

The language that dominated the gang violence was structured by postcodes. That is, the postal codes that Royal Mail use to organise areas of London into relatively small districts for the purposes of delivering the mail. Postcodes are generally centred upon towns. So for example, N22 is centred upon Wood Green, N15 on South

Tottenham, N17 on North Tottenham, and E9 on Hackney. The borders between postcodes areas are more arbitrary. Gangs generally used their postcode as a badge of honour, even if there were a number of different gangs within that postcode. The students I knew were all highly aware of the boundaries between postcodes and which postcode corresponded to which area. For example, I remember once showing a large map of London to Lucas, who read around the map using the postcodes, rather than the actual names of the places. Similarly, we once played a game of hangman on the board, at the end of a lesson. Over two games of hangman, the words that the students chose were of course 'Hackney' and 'Tottenham'.

The use of postcodes by young people is in part a form of slang, designed to exclude adults. Adult awareness of postcode boundaries is relatively low. They are occasionally used to refer to areas where there are specific institutions that share the name of the area, such as Wimbledon (SW19), or the political institutions in Westminster (SW1). Pubs and restaurants are occasionally named after the postcode they are located within, and a 1990s pop group took their name, East 17, from the postcode of Walthamstow, their home town. But the way that the young people we were dealing with used postcodes was of a completely different order.

The term that the students used for being beaten up or robbed when travelling alone was being 'caught slipping'. For example, Robert, who was from Hackney, was once standing on the edge of an estate with a friend, when he was approached by two older boys on mopeds. They asked Robert where his friend was from, and the friend responded 'fields', meaning London Fields, an area of Hackney a mere ten-minute walk from where Robert and his friend were standing. The boys on the mopeds produced a gun and shot Robert's friend in the leg before driving off. This was probably a gang initiation—someone had to be shot for the boy to join the gang. The cause of the violence was gangs; but *who* the putative gang member shot was based upon postcode loyalties. What was depressing was how insular and territorially constrained this fear of travelling to unknown areas made the students: to travel alone outside your own area was potentially a 'slip up'.

Within the territories defined by those postcodes, gangs tended to target anyone who looked like they could be a threat—that is, who could be involved in gangs. And for 'fun' they would also often target anyone who looked vulnerable or particularly strong (especially tall boys). However, overall, it was probably the boys involved in the gangs who were the biggest victims of the postcode-related violence.

One of the ways the gangs identified each other was through the internet. The story about Mohammed and *YouTube* above is a case in point. Gangs frequently made *YouTube* videos of themselves rapping about defending their territory and their honour, which often began with an image of their postcode (e.g. N15). Quite often the gangs would film themselves in 'enemy' territory as a provocation to other gangs. They also used social networking sites, albeit in a different way to most users. During the time I worked at the academy I saw the students move from holding *MySpace* accounts to holding *Facebook* accounts—except that none of the students used their real name on their profile, often using their street name or an entirely made-up name instead. Darren told me that he tried to avoid appearing in the *YouTube* videos or *Facebook* photos related to gangs: it was a sure way to get targeted by other gangs. And as the students knew, the police could see the content on social networking sites just as easily as rival gangs could.

One of the ways that we responded to the postcode violence problem was to adjust the opening hours of the school. The students were expected from 9.30am, with lessons beginning at 10am. Arriving at that time meant that our students were travelling after all the other mainstream school students were already at school. The school day finished at 2.45pm, which allowed the students to get home before mainstream school students were on the buses.

Drugs

One afternoon I was in the newsagent opposite the academy buying some chocolate, when two young black boys sauntered into the shop after me. The boys were speaking to a large Asian man, who said to the boys: 'I been selling skunk for four years blud, it ain't about

168

weed no more, I ain't sold that shit for time. So you wannit, or what?' The boys bought a can of Red Bull before leaving with the man.

This anecdote in many ways summed up the drugs problem I saw amongst the students who were sent to the academy. Skunk was by far the most prevalent drug the students used, and it was almost freely available to them. A few of the students became involved in more serious drugs—Desmond was in trouble with the police at one point for, as Darius put it, 'dashing a bit of white' (dealing cocaine). But skunk was by far the biggest problem. Chris had the following to say about skunk:

What really annoyed me [was when] the Labour government reduced the category of cannabis a few years ago. Literally up to that point we hadn't had a major problem, but the very next year we immediately had big problems. So I think there's a correlation between that law, which I know has now been reversed, [and the skunk problem].

It was the seed that the following year caused an enormous amount of problems—not everybody, but we had quite a cohort of skunk smokers. In the early days, before they came here, they're clearly into football, and they've got quite a lot of energy to do this and that. But once they start smoking skunk they don't want to do anything, they start acting stupid, they lose their rational behaviour, they sort of just sit there in lessons and can't participate.

Overall they also become a bit more belligerent. One of the most worrying things was also that they then came into contact with all sorts of criminals. We've had lots of examples of students that smoke skunk falling into debt, and then having to do all sorts of things to pay back the criminals. If someone gives them £20 of skunk of Monday, £20 of skunk on Tuesday, they don't care. Then £20 of skunk on Friday. But then the following week they owe them £60, and they're kids, so £60 is a lot of money. Then, once the threat of violence is given, they then will maybe rob someone else, or take something from their home or their aunt's home. Then it escalates. So what started off as what they regarded as a fairly innocent activity becomes a major deal.

What was really striking was the correlation between aggressive, irritable behaviour by a particular student and their usage of skunk. George, for example, had a torrid time in the lead up to one Christmas. But when he returned, he was much more sociable, considerate and calm. It was no surprise to me when he said that he had made a New Year's resolution to quit smoking skunk and that he had lasted 12 days.

Mohammed was another heavy user of skunk. Chris once visited him at home during a winter that saw heavy snow. He made the visit to tell Mohammed and his parents that his skunk problem was extremely serious. Sitting in his car after he had completed the visit, Chris told me he saw Mohammed walking off down the lane in the heavy snow, hood up, shuffling determinedly along the road in the darkness. Why else would he go out in that weather, late in the evening, Chris asked me rhetorically, than to get his fix? Skunk was a qualitatively different drug to the weed that I had seen my friends at Graveney smoke, and the destruction it wrought amongst the students was extensive.

A miscarriage of justice?

I received a call from Chris, who was away on a course. He told me that Russell was coming in from his home in Tottenham to see me. He had been summoned for a court appearance that day, but had not yet managed to get there. Russell had asked Chris to ring the court to let them know that he was delayed, but initially Russell did not know which court he was supposed to be attending ('unbelievable', said Chris).

Soon after Chris had rung me, Russell burst in the room. 'I'm upset, man,' he said. 'I'm upset! I gotta be at court at 10 and it's like, what time is it Tom?'

'It's 11.30 a.m. Russell,' I said. Russell was sweating. 'Chris told me that the court knows that you're coming now though, right? 1 p.m. is when you're supposed to be there.'

'Yeah, but I can't get to court. My sister, man, that dumb bitch, she says she needs £10 petrol money to take me, and I need £2 bus fare to get to her flat in Edmonton.'

Russell required a family member, or a responsible adult, to accompany him to court because he was under 16 years of age. His grandfather was out somewhere (he did not know where), and he had not told his mother that he was due at court.

'I'm fucked man, I'm just gonna wait here until they come and arrest me. Fuck it... I'm upset, man, this is tense.' I tried to persuade him to speak to his mother, but he said that she was out at work and couldn't take the time off to take him to court anyway. He carried on dejectedly for several minutes. I rang Chris, and he told me that Russell had to attend court, and that I should take him if a family member would not.

So I took Russell to court. When we arrived, just after 12 p.m., Russell said that he recognised the court from a previous appearance. When we entered the waiting area, Russell suddenly became very tense and quiet. Before I had the chance to speak to Russell an usher told us to go into court.

Russell and I filed into a small courtroom, and Russell was forgiven for being late. The three magistrates were sitting at a bench made of oak above us. We sat on the leather benches below. Russell was not required to stand in the dock, and knew to remain standing whilst the magistrates' clerk (the legal adviser to the magistrates) read out the charges. He was charged with possession of a small amount of cannabis, which had been found upon him by a police officer a few weeks previously.

In front of me was a crown prosecution service lawyer, and to my left was a representative from the Haringey youth offending team. I found out later that it was Youth Court day at the Magistrates' Court. Youth Court days are subject to restrictions upon who can attend and what can be reported from the day's proceedings. Every Thursday the Haringey youths accused of crimes went down to Highgate to appear before the court.

The magistrates considered Russell's history and whether he might need to consult the duty solicitor. Since Russell was currently subject to a referral order (i.e. had to attend youth offending team sessions once a week) they decided he did have to see the solicitor. I was asked what my relationship with Russell was, so I explained about the LBACP.

The magistrate then unexpectedly began a lecture on the economics of boxing. She pointed out that she knew that of the 900 registered boxers at one of the local boxing associations, only 25 could make their living solely out of boxing. Since only a few of the boxers were educated, she said, there were moves to ensure that there were computers installed at the rear of the gym to help with their education.

I responded by saying that yes, many of the professional boxers who worked at the LBACP earn money with us whilst doing their boxing training at the same time. The magistrate pointed out to Russell that smoking weed and a career in boxing were not compatible. She then praised me for coming to court with Russell, saying that the magistrates used to get school reports (but not any longer).

We then went to see the duty solicitor. We filed into a small consultation room surrounded by plastic windows, with a female solicitor called Shirley. She asked Russell about what happened. Russell did not respond well to her questions—he seemed to regard her as the enemy. He told her that both his parents knew he had to come to court (which I knew was a lie), but that both of them were at work so couldn't accompany him. Then he told her that his mother had recently been diagnosed with cancer. He didn't know the details or the diagnosis, but Russell said that he had been smoking the cannabis for 'personal use to relieve the stress' associated with his mother's diagnosis.

Shirley asked Russell to describe what happened. Russell told her that the 'feds' had noticed a group of young people loitering near a garage, and had approached them. Russell claimed that a friend of his cousin had given him some Rizla (tobacco), cigarette paper and so on, which also included some cannabis. He claimed that he didn't know that the cannabis was in the pack. This obviously didn't square with his claim that he used the cannabis for personal use because of his mother's cancer.

Shirley asked how many brothers and sisters he had. He put up his left hand and began counting, saying the names as he went. 'Jamal, Jordan, Jeffery... five brothers, yeah'.

'And how many sisters?', the solicitor asked. The left hand went up again. 'Candice, Rianna, Susan... four sisters, I think. Erm, yeah, that's it I think, four'. Shirley asked how many lived with Russell.

'Only the younger', Russell said, as the rest of them were grown up.

We returned to court only to be bailed for lunch, and were required to return at 2 p.m. At this point the reason for Russell's suddenly quietness as we entered the court building became clear. The Wood Green boys were at the court. Russell was terrified of them. He said that they knew his name but didn't know his face, so as long as he kept quiet, he would be safe.

One of the other Tottenham boys in the court was not so lucky. A fracas broke out in one corner of the court. The security guards, two rather elderly-looking but large black men, intervened and placed the Tottenham boy in a separate room. Several minutes later, the police arrived.

I took Russell out with me for lunch and offered him his choice of meal — sandwich, fried chicken, whatever he wanted. He wasn't hungry, he said. I ordered my own lunch, just as the Wood Green boys walked into the cafe. Russell looked mortified. All six of them walked in and ordered sandwiches. My food arrived, and Russell sat perfectly still in front of me, watching me eat, terrified, and trying not to attract any attention.

Luckily, the youth offending team, who were seven strong, were sitting on the seats opposite us, and I pointed this out to Russell. The Wood Green boys would not do anything with the youth offending team within the cafe, surely? I told Russell to relax.

When we arrived back at court, Russell let out a big sigh of relief, only to tense up again when he realised that he still had to negotiate his actual court appearance. When we went into the court, Shirley asked for an absolute discharge—an unusual course of action, she said, but perhaps appropriate given the circumstances of the case. An absolute discharge meant that Russell would plead guilty, but would not receive any punishment. She explained Russell's story that he smoked cannabis to ease the stress stemming from his mother's illness, and emphasised how well he was doing in school. The magistrates asked for a report from the youth offending team. They said that Russell was doing well and had only missed one appointment. He had yet to undertake reparations for his car burglary conviction, but generally he was doing well. Normally, the additional conviction would had led to more serious sanctions — such as a curfew, or a longer referral order—but the solicitor argued that in Russell's case this appeared to be inappropriate.

The magistrates then returned to the subject of the LBACP and told me what good work we must have been doing. 'Would I like to add anything?' they asked.

I had realised that I might have to say something just as the youth offending team finished speaking. I had something of a dilemma, because I thought that Russell would benefit from a punishment. His disorganisation that morning had shown me how seriously he took the court's proceedings, and half of what he talked about in class was related to crime. I also knew exactly what the effects of the drugs that Russell had been caught with were. An absolute discharge would not do Russell any good at all. But since I was in court, and there to support Russell, I could hardly say that I thought that they ought to punish him to the full extent of the law. That would make me a 'snitch' to all the other boys in the LBA and irrevocably turn Russell against me. And moreover, I would look an idiot after giving up half my day to be with him in court.

So I said that Russell was doing well in school in general, and was very enthusiastic about his mathematics GCSE, so much so that I found it very difficult to accommodate his desire for more mathematics sessions, and that I hoped that he would do well in the future. All of that was true, of course. The magistrates put their heads together and decided upon an absolute discharge, on account of his good behaviour. Russell had got off!

I put it to the solicitor afterwards that I had saved Russell's bacon. She said that I had: things would probably have been very different if I hadn't turned up. Russell also recognised this. 'My saviour!' he kept saying.

Walking out of the court, I asked him whether his mum had cancer. He said she did not, grinning guiltily. So on top of everything else, Russell had allowed the solicitor to tell a lie in open court. What a cheeky boy, I thought. He had managed to get off because his and his family's disorganisation meant that I had to take him to court, which led the magistrates to clear him!

Russell felt better, and was very hungry. 'My belly hurts bad, man,' he said, 'it feels like it's going to explode!' I bought him some fried chicken and asked what the 'beef' between the Wood Green boys and the Tottenham boys was all about. Russell said that it had started with the 'olders' over something, but now continued amongst the 'youngers' over 'some dumb stuff man, for no reason like'. He also told me that he had been 'beefing' with Darren lately, and that he thought they were going to have a fight sometime soon. I put it to him that it was ever since he had stolen away with that 13-year-old girl that he had problems with Darren. 'Yeah,' he said, grinning.

I told him that I was thinking about going swimming that afternoon. Russell said he hadn't gone swimming in years. He asked me if I was going to the baths in Tottenham, looking hopeful that I'd take him with me. I wasn't, unfortunately, but I suggested to him that he could go on his own. The Tottenham baths are not far from where you live, I said. But I knew *somehow that he wouldn't go. He couldn't. He couldn't risk being 'caught slipping', even a few hundred metres from where he lived.*

As I suspected, Russell's absolute discharge did not encourage him to behave himself. Rather, he saw the school as a means of getting out of trouble. A week after my experience at the Magistrates' Court, Russell missed an appointment with the youth offending team. He asked Chris to get him out of this 'dumb situation' by ringing them up and telling them that Russell was at school. Chris refused to give him an alibi, so he asked me to do it, on account of the fact that he had been working hard in maths. I told him that I couldn't lie to the youth offending team—he'd just have to learn to turn up to his appointments.

I found my experience in court to be very frustrating. After all, it is one thing for adults to use destructive drugs like skunk. It is a quite different proposition for a person under 16, or even 18, because they are not mature enough to know what they are doing to themselves. How Russell could walk away from court after being caught with drugs, without any further intervention, was a mystery to me. To my mind, it should have been treated as a very serious issue. I had seen drugs (particularly skunk) ruin the lives of several of the students in the academy. Surely, I thought, Russell should have had professionals crawling all over him? Not in this case.

It illustrated what I came to regard as a more general problem with the youth justice system. The young people seemed systematically to be treated more leniently than adults who entered the system. The system seemed to presume that the young person, up on their first brush with the law, would be so scared and intimidated that they would cease any offending behaviour, and that civil society was capable of guiding the young person away from crime. That might well be the case for boys growing up in secure households and in areas free from malign influences. But most of the boys who have contact with the youth justice system are in precisely the opposite situation.

If the discussions of the students were anything to go by, it was only once they were put on electronic tags and subject to an evening curfew that they were really deterred from further criminal behaviour. I often heard students say 'nah I can't get involved in that cos I'm on tag'. They valued time with their friends, and so effectively taking it away by a tag and curfew order was a real punishment.

Perhaps as a teacher I just felt overwhelmed by the number of incidents that seemed to occur without effective sanction or resolution. This was especially true when the students became seriously injured as a result of their criminal activities. For example, despite extracting himself from the postcode/gang violence some years before, after he left the academy Felix was seriously stabbed near his home by boys from Wood Green. Some months after the stabbing, I took him to see a specialist literacy tutor and he explained what happened. The conversation came up as we passed an old lady being wheeled into an ambulance.

'Y'know, those ambulances are bare high-tech, I saw that the last time I was in one o dem' said Felix.

'When was that?' I asked, ignorantly.

'When I got stabbed, innit?'

'Oh' I said, in embarrassment. 'What happened?... Where did they stab you?'

'They stabbed me all in the arm, in the back, and you see this mark on ma face' he said, showing me a scar about a centimetre long, 'they stabbed me there as well.'

'God, that must have been awful,' I said.

'You know, it's funny,' replied Felix, 'getting stabbed don't hurt that much. It's all the shit they do to you in hospital that really hurts, all them needles 'n shit. You know they have this thing they stick in you to see how deep the wound is? S'long man, s'long. Not that I'd wanna get stabbed again though.'

'Why did it happen... do you know why?' I asked.

'Yeah man, it was cos of some old stuff, old beef from time ago when I was, y'know, rolling with the wrong kinda people. I used to be with the grey gang innit, and stuff happened, innit.'

'Oh, I see' I said. 'If it was some old beef, why didn't they just let it slide—why were they still after you?'

'Cos some people ain't got nothing to do but get beef innit? It was all from time ago. What happened, yeah, was that my friend's little brother went down Wood Green and nearly got robbed by the green gang [centred roughly upon Wood Green]. Ting was yeah, me and my friend were cool with the Wood Green boys. So my friend an' me went down there to sort it out, like, an' say waguwan, thought it was cool? So we went down to Wood Green, like, and it was alright, 'cept that they started at 'im cos he's got an accent, like. They was taking the piss, like, so he says, y'know, "waguwan, what you laughing at me for?" So, in the end, we got into a fight, and I joined in like, cos he's my friend, innit? And the beef was from there, like.

'Once, right, I went to Wood Green to Blue [a clothing shop] to get some jeans. There's ain't nothing in Tottenham for jeans, so I got to go there, innit? They was waiting outside for me, cuz. And they was bait about it too, they spuded me and said waguwan. But then they was following me innit, and so I said to them, "yo, I thought all that beef was cool though, bruv?" But it weren't, so I got rushed that day. And it just went from there, things happened, y'know.'

'That's horrible, Felix' I said. We talked about girls and clubbing for a while, and he told me that he loves to 'go West End'. He liked the glamour of the area and the smart clothes that everyone wears when they go out there. 'I don't tend to get none though in West End,' he said, meaning that he does not pick up many girls, 'cos I dress different, like, with hoodies and all dat'. He said that there was a lot less 'beef' in West End than in clubs in North London. He used to go to dances a lot, he said, but didn't bother any more because 'there's always beef. Some people, they're just staring at you, looking for beef all the time, like. It's annoying, man. It gets very annoying.'

We passed Haringey Magistrates' Court on the bus, and I explained my recent experience with Russell to Felix. 'Russell musta been wetting his pants' said Felix. He told me about all the 'beef' that is generated every Thursday with the youth court. 'People wait for you to get your sentence, after they've got theirs, then they have beef. This area is hype.'

Much later after my visit to court with Russell, I returned to Haringey Magistrates' Court and spoke to one of the people who worked there. They told me that the conflicts between the Wood Green boys and the Tottenham boys had become so serious that from September 2009 a permanent police presence was deployed at the youth court as a result of a very serious incident. Early in September, someone entered the court waiting room, exactly where I sat with Russell, brandishing a sword. He attacked one of the boys waiting in the court, chopping off several fingers. Given incidents like this, you can understand why students like Russell and Felix felt scared.

Mobile phones

Part of the story in the growth of postcode/gang violence is the rise of the mobile phone. As young people carry around increasingly valuable devices on their person (mobiles, ipods, and so on), the incentive to rob other young people on the street has grown. This is one of the reasons why street robberies are so common today. Mobile phones were the primary currency that the students used in bartering, and many of those phones were acquired in muggings. For example, Darius once requested to go to the toilet. Normally I declined to let the students go 'to the toilet', because what they really wanted to do was have a conversation on their mobile phone. But Darius placed three mobile phones on the table and said that he would leave them in the class whilst he went to the toilet, so desperate was he to prove that he needed the toilet rather than to use his phone. But when he got up to leave for the toilet, a fourth mobile fell out of his pocket. Darius giggled and ran out the class with the phone.

One of the consequences of this rise in robberies was that the students hid their mobiles in a very unconventional place: in their underpants. They called this 'ballsing' their mobile, because it was the only place on a person that a gang generally would not search during a mugging. Another consequence was the racial dimension to the muggings. Due to the disproportionate numbers of young black boys in areas like Tottenham being involved in muggings and gangs, police and authority figures were easily tempted into thinking, when a young black boy was mugged, 'oh well he's part of it all anyway'. If a white boy were mugged, it might well be treated more seriously. The boys were aware of this. Darren once said, for example, 'I only rob boys that look like me'. Why? 'Because no one cares. I've been seen robbing other black boys before, and people'll just sat in the car, like, watching, then drove off.'

Parents purchased mobile phones for their children because of the peace of mind it provided. The direct parent-child link was enormously cherished by the parents of our students. The problem was that mobile phones connected young people to everyone else as well. When a parent gave a mobile phone to a child, they no longer controlled access to that child. With a landline telephone, parents act as gatekeepers, and so are able to exercise some control over who their children interact with. Not so with mobile phones—and indeed the internet—which provided an independence to the students that often they were not ready for. For example, I remember sitting with George, helping him with some coursework once, when he received a phone call from his mother. 'Yes mum' he said, 'I'll be home soon,' being as sweet as George could be. Just a few seconds later he received a phone call from someone else, and his whole demeanour changed into his mischievous, street persona. He arranged to meet with the person on the other end of the phone, and agreed that the other person would bring 'the stuff'—almost certainly some skunk.

The way that mobiles allowed the students to transcend geography and contact each other regardless of where the student or caller were, was extremely disruptive. For example, after a particularly poor set of test results, I brought Lucas, Darius and George together to explain to them how to revise. During the session I asked them 'what is the biggest barrier to revision for you?' They all agreed that the distractions from their mobile phone were the biggest obstacle to their revision. Darius told me that his sleep was often disturbed by people ringing him up late at night.

Chris put it this way: 'I think the whole package [mobiles and computer networks] is very disruptive to their lives. We could have experienced a good morning in the academy and then suddenly someone gets a text from so and so, from a friend who's getting agro at another school. The next minute, three or four kids want to run out and get down there in the middle of the school day.'

179

Mentoring

One of the techniques we used was to give the students mentors. A friend of mine from university, Jimmy Moreland, volunteered to mentor a student. Chris and I chose Lucas, because he had a good prospect of doing well in his examinations if, and only if, he could avoid the temptations of the street. Lucas was interested in business and Jimmy worked for one the major consultancy firms in the City of London. We hoped that Jimmy could provide inspiration and guidance to Lucas.

For the students, there was a special quality to having a mentor from an external organisation come in to speak to them. Jimmy had a different kind of authority and pull upon Lucas, that I and even Chris were unable to emulate. Somehow, as a teacher, I was not seen by the students as being in the 'real world'. The same advice about trying hard in school, and so on, had a quite different impact coming from Jimmy than from his school teachers.

Jimmy and Lucas met fortnightly before school began, at 9am, as this was the only feasible time Jimmy could meet with Lucas. Lucas was used to arriving at school at 10am, and had a time-keeping problem anyway, so it required a special effort on Lucas' part to make it in for each session. Lucas' record was a good one—of the approximately 16 sessions that were arranged, Lucas only missed one, and was very rarely late.

Jimmy decided to approach the mentoring as he would in any normal professional situation, using the approach used by his firm whereby goals were set and the sessions were used to reflect upon how the 'mentee' was progressing towards those goals.

Jimmy used the first session with Lucas to set those goals. He told me afterwards that it was quite difficult getting Lucas to come up with any suggestions, despite being very keen on the arrangements overall. Of course, Jimmy had in mind some targets for Lucas, based upon what I had told him about Lucas's performance in school. It was important, though, that Lucas came up with the targets, so that Lucas could get used to setting himself goals and trying to meet those goals.

Eventually, Lucas stammered that he wanted 'the teachers to say I'm a good student', which Jimmy modified to the teachers saying that he was 'a good student when he left the school'. The second target Lucas came up with was to get a good score in the behaviour rankings each week. Indeed, in the weeks after that first meeting Lucas had a long streak of outstanding scores in the behaviour rankings. Finally, Jimmy suggested to Lucas that something about time-keeping might be a good idea, which Lucas agreed to.

Reflecting upon the sessions after Lucas left the school, Jimmy told me that overall he very much enjoyed them. He certainly never felt physically threatened by Lucas. However, due to the nature of the exercise, Jimmy always felt slightly that he was diving into the unknown, and therefore that he had to be a little tentative with Lucas. For example, Lucas had a habit of keeping his earphones in his ears at all times. Although Jimmy wanted to do things professionally, he told me that he never quite built up the courage to ask Lucas to take those earphones out.

Overall, the mentoring had a very positive impact. Jimmy spent much of his sessions explaining to Lucas about what it means to have a professional job. He told Lucas that having a job meant that you had to do what the boss says and be at work every day at 9 a.m. Lucas took a deep breath, exhaled, and said '9 a.m .every day boy, damn...' It was, I think, an important step on the road to Lucas accepting some of the realities of employment.

It was difficult, though, to remove the 'street' element from Lucas's behaviour. For example, one morning Jimmy came in for a session with Lucas, which seemed to go well, finishing about 9.30 a.m. After the session, I saw Lucas receive a phone call, before he borrowed Robert's bicycle to go off somewhere (which was not that unusual an occurrence).

I was teaching him first period, at 10 a.m. Lucas strolled into class late, at about 10.15 a.m., eating a meal from Burger King. I was somewhat irritated by this because he had only just finished the session with Jimmy.

'Lucas, can you finish that outside please?' I said. 'How can you be late, anyway? You only just finished a session with Jimmy. What were you doing?'

'Giving a little middle finger' Lucas boasted, smirking. Lucas's pod leader shook his head.

'Well done' I said sarcastically, 'I hope you've washed your hands.'

Lucas had apparently had a sexual encounter with a girl on the High Road, who had bought him a burger in return. Lucas said she had initially offered him a KFC, but he had held out for a Burger King, and he assured me that he had washed his hands in the restaurant. When I told this story to Caroline, she told me that the reason students like Lucas and Darius were often late in the mornings was that they were visiting girls at their parents' houses, for sexual purposes, because the morning was the only time that the houses were free, as the girls' parents were at work.

Jimmy, of course, found this hilarious. He said he was thinking that since Christmas was approaching, he would offer to buy Lucas an alarm clock as a present. When Jimmy offered the alarm clock to Lucas, he responded somewhat absent-mindedly 'oh yeah, I could do with that'.

Jimmy was always struck by the extent to which Lucas was ignorant of the news. In particular, what was striking for Jimmy was Lucas's ignorance of the financial crisis that shook the world economy during the 2008/9 academic year. Jimmy, of course, was working right in the thick of the events that were unfolding in the financial markets.

Jimmy told me that the time that he realised that he was making a difference was when, one cold November morning when it was raining, Lucas was standing outside the gym with his hands in his pockets, waiting for Jimmy and me to arrive. That session, Lucas confided in Jimmy that he was worried about an upcoming court appearance where he was accused of a robbery that he may or may not have committed. The victim kept changing his story, so Lucas was hopeful that he would get off. But Jimmy could never be entirely sure of those positive effects. For example, Jimmy attended a student awards ceremony, because we had invited him to the LBACP's Christmas lunch held straight after the assembly. When Lucas saw Jimmy, he bounded up to him and asked: 'Why aren't you at work?' Jimmy could only laugh at this. It was a nice moment, however, when Jimmy was asked to give Lucas some of his certificates within the ceremony.

As the end of Lucas's time at the LBACP approached and his exams loomed, Jimmy organised a special mentoring session at his firm's offices in central London. I was to take Lucas down to see Jimmy after school. During the day, however, Lucas was not behaving well. When he entered the class, he was muttering rap music under his breath as usual—talking about 'bitch niggers' and muttering darkly about Hackney boys. I tried to snap Lucas out of this by reminding him that we were going to visit Jimmy that afternoon, which brightened his spirits.

'You'll be safe with me travelling down to the City, Lucas. There ain't no heads in the City,' I said, mocking his worries about being 'caught slipping' on the way down to visit Jimmy. In retrospect, that was not a wise thing to do.

Lucas responded by saying: 'Yeah well I'll have my "best friend" with me innit, so there won't be no trouble, sir.'

'Well you won't be bringing your "best friend" down to Jimmy's office, Lucas' I said sharply. By his "best friend" Lucas meant his knife. Lucas did not respond.

Later in the day, I met with Lucas to take him down to see Jimmy. He was still in a funny mood. At Seven Sisters Underground Station Lucas looked at me and said: 'You know I've got my best friend, yeah?'

I looked at him and sternly told him that if he did have his 'best friend' he better go outside the station and get rid of it, or I would not take him to see Jimmy.

'Alright, alright...' Lucas said, before walking off outside the station apparently to get rid of the knife. When he returned, he smiled and said he had god rid of it. 'Probably, anyway,' he continued.

I had to be stern with him again, and lost my cool a little. Lucas interrupted me and told me that he was only joking—he had got rid of it outside. We continued our journey. I did not feel I could cancel the visit to Jimmy's office on the grounds that Lucas might have a knife, and I certainly could not search him.

Jimmy worked in a shiny, purpose-built office that was modern and impressive. Lucas and I were given visitor passes by the reception desk and met with Jimmy on the ninth floor of the building. Jimmy had arranged to meet in a room that was intended only for meetings with his clients. I sat in a waiting room reading one of the copies of the Financial Times *that were scattered around.*

Jimmy told me that this final session went very well. They discussed the impending GCSE examinations and how to revise for them. They had recently been improving Lucas's CV and they went through a final version of the document. Jimmy made recommendations to Lucas about work experience and how he could start on the path to getting on to the business career that he was keen on. When they had finished, Jimmy took Lucas over to the window to look out on the impressive views of the London skyline that were available from the ninth floor. 'It's just like an estate, innit?' Lucas commented.

On the tube journey home, I asked Lucas whether he actually had his knife with him during the whole of the visit. He nodded. Suffice to say that Jimmy was not quite as amused by this story as by the last one I told him.

When I asked Lucas, a year after he had left the academy, whether he really had the knife, he became very embarrassed. He said that he was only winding me up and that he didn't know how he could behave so badly when he was younger. Who knows where the truth lies?

The most important benefit from the mentoring sessions with Jimmy was that Lucas was able to interact with someone who could tell him how the world worked, and in particular, how to get a job. It was a little like my experience at Wimbledon. Lucas was gaining from interactions across class and cultural barriers that he would never normally have surmounted, and without a doubt that was priceless.

Settled in the ring

Darren had been saying to me for some weeks, regarding Russell: 'I'm gonna hit this nigger'. Darren was the alpha-male in the school, his pre-eminence undoubted except by Russell, the stubborn boy who refused to yield to Darren's attempts to dominate him. The problem was that Darren came with a group of other students who were supporting him: Desmond, Darius and, at the time, William. Russell was much more of a loner. Despite Chris's attempts to placate Darren, his patience with Russell was rapidly wearing thin.

One afternoon, I spotted Darren menacingly approaching Russell outside the five-a-side football pitch. Desmond, Darius and Mohammed were standing behind Darren, urging him on. Darren's fist was clenched behind his back, in the same way it had been when Darren threatened me in Devon. I rang Chris and told him what was going on, whilst walking over to them. When I reached them I told Darren that he couldn't attack Russell. He would be suspended, I said, and that was the last thing he needed with his exams looming.

'Yeah but this prick owes me money!' said Darren, making reference to a watch that had been broken, for which Darren blamed Russell.

'No, weren't my fault!' shouted Russell back.

'Don't chat shit man' said Darren, angrily. Darren was about to move towards Russell when Chris arrived.

I knew that this was not the first time that Chris had been forced to separate Darren and Russell. 'Two big boys like that,' he once told me, 'neither of them backing down, there's always going to be a scrap at some point'. But for the moment, he was trying his upmost to placate Darren, who remained angry. Russell did not help matters by muttering: 'I'm gonna bang him up bruv, I'm gonna bang him up.'

After strenuous efforts on Chris's and my part to keep the boys separated and to calm both the boys down, Chris turned to Russell and said: 'Russell, do you want a one-on-one in the boxing gym with Darren?'

'Yes bruv! Let's do this!' said Russell forthrightly.

Chris turned to Darren: 'Do you want a one-on-one, Darren?'

'Yes man, let's do this' said Darren, business-like. Chris walked Darren and his henchmen to the boxing gym, whilst I escorted Russell. Chris asked the pod leaders to keep an eye on the other students whilst he dealt with Darren and Russell. Both were found boxing gloves, head guards, and mouth guards. Chris had previously told the boys that if they continued their belligerency that he would have them spar each other. He had spoken to both the boy's parents, and they were very clear that if boys continued the spat then Chris should see to it that the matter was settled. The sparring consent forms signed at the start of the year lay in the office.

Chris stood in the middle of the ring and reminded the students that this was a boxing match, and that they had to follow the rules. If one of them decided they no longer wanted to participate, that was the end of it, the other student had won, and the issue had to be over. Darren nodded, whilst his eyeballs continued to bore into Russell. Russell agreed, bashing his fists together, which, with the boxing gloves on, made a snapping sound.

The students edged to their corners and Chris called them in for the first of three rounds. Chris brought his hands together and said: 'Box'. Darren stepped forward and swung wildly for Russell, who blocked the blows with his guard, holding his left glove high up by his left cheek. Darren pursued Russell around the ring with fervent anger, attacking with all of his strength. Russell continued to defend and Darren was only able to land body-blows. Russell edged around the ring taking the blows.

The bell for the end of the first round rang and Darren's henchmen cheered for what they saw as a victory. He grunted in acknowledgement as he took on a little water. One of the pod leaders advised Russell to open up more on the inside, but he wasn't really listening. He was too focused upon looking at Darren and steeling himself for the round ahead. Sweat pored off Darren's forehead and he grunted through his mouth guard before spitting into the spit bucket in the corner of the ring.

The bell for the second round rang a minute later. Darren surged out of his corner again but this time was visibly more tired. His legs moved sluggishly, and he no longer held his arms up to defend his face. Darren swung with his left but Russell ducked out the way, before opening up on Darren's inside with two powerful upper-cuts. Clearly surprised, Darren backed away and began to protect himself with his boxing gloves. Russell was a different fighter in this round and used his tightly packed strength to push Darren around the ring. Darren's initial flourish had faded and Russell took advantage.

Russell's brawn was rapidly triumphing over Darren's height and aggression. Matters came to a head when Russell charged at Darren but was rebuffed by Darren's guard. Russell lost his balance, and began to fall backwards, and Darren lowered his guard slightly. But as Russell fell backwards, he swung a wide looping punch with his right hand that caught Darren on the chin, snapping his head sideways. Chris intervened: 'Stop!'

Russell backed away. Darren was defeated, and leant unsteadily on the ropes, and he held up a boxing glove to signal his submission. Chris would not have him continue in any case. Without the normal bravado or celebration, Russell exited the ring, placed his gloves, head guard and mouth guard on to the benches and walked with a pod leader to the bus stop.

Darren looked at me: 'I lost, didn't I Tom?' I told him that he didn't have the better of it. Chris made him agree that the problem between him and Russell was over and dealt with, which he reluctantly acknowledged.

This incident made a strong impression upon the way I thought about boxing and the street. Soft-liberal critics would doubtless say we were 'brutalising' Darren and Russell by allowing them to settle their differences in the ring. But this is a rather blinkered view of the situation. Russell and Darren had already been brutalised by their treatment by gangs and the other adults in their lives. There was a rawness in them that caused them to want to fight in the first place. From a pragmatic perspective, if the issue had not been settled in the ring, then Darren and his side-kicks would have beaten up Russell on the street. The beating could have been a serious one. Then there would doubtless be reprisals from Russell's friends upon Darren, and then Russell would stop coming to school for fear of being caught by Darren. The cycle might have continued until one of the students was stabbed or worse.

What Darren and Russell had agreed to was an honourable method of resolving their differences. Most young people today resolve their differences by recourse to weapons or gangs. Through these brutalising means, boys who feel powerless are able to exert power and humiliate their victims. This was, it seemed, exactly what Darren had in mind before Chris and I intervened. There was no honour there. For Russell and Darren to have put their pride on the line, in a one-on-one, was a practice that harked back to a more civilised time.

It was also something I had seen at camp in the United States of America during the summer mentioned in chapter three. Two boys, very similar to Russell and Darren, had irresolvable differences that some of the lower-level staff decided had to be sorted out in a one-on-one fight. It was not quite so civilised as Russell and Darren's boxing match, as the fight took place without boxing gloves or head guards, behind one of the sleeping billets. The only rule was that they broke when told to. Fighting is, I hope I have illustrated in this book, something different to boxing. But nonetheless, as with Darren and Russell, the issue was resolved after the bout and the boys felt they had satisfaction.

It would of course be a more pleasant world if the boys had felt able to resolve their differences in a less violent way. But young men being as they are, I don't think there will ever be a situation where contact sports like boxing are no longer needed as outlets for aggression and other feelings. But it was the boys' experiences during their young lives, in the world that as adults we had shaped for them, that had led Russell and Darren to feel a need to fight so keenly. As adults, it is our responsibility to change our world so that boys feel more secure and happy, and so require recourse to fighting as infrequently as possible. But it also seems to me that it is right to provide appropriate and honourable ways for boys to settle their differences without recourse to the cowardly methods of weapons or gangs. Boxing did just that for Russell and Darren.

8

Boxing Clever

Don't let it be forgot,
That once there was a spot,
For one brief, shining moment,
That was known as Camelot.

Lyric by Alan Jay Lerner from Camelot
by Alan Jay Lerner and Frederick Loewe (1960)

The exams

The GCSE examinations were the culmination of a programme of socialisation as much as education. Each half-term we would take a day out of the normal timetable and make the students sit mock exams. This was necessary because without training and experience in the discipline required for exams, the students were all likely to be sent out for being disruptive. The first time we ran the mock exams was always a blood-bath: all bar one or two students would be unable to sit still through the test. But by the time of the real exams, the students knew what to expect.

The lead up to exams is stressful for any student, but our students tended to react particularly badly to the pressure. Often, after putting some genuine effort into their studies during the revision period, the students developed wholly unrealistic expectations of the grades they could achieve in the exams. The problem was that a few solid weeks of work rarely compensated for the prior years of academic neglect. William and other students' frustrations often manifested themselves as an argument about whether they were to sit the 'higher' paper (where grades of A* to D were available), or the 'foundation' paper (which had a maximum C grade). The problem with the higher paper was that if they failed to get enough marks for a D grade, they would fail outright. So the higher paper was not a sensible gamble. Few of the students accepted this fact without at least one temper tantrum.

Unfortunately, two of my brightest students, Darius and Lucas, went off the rails in the weeks leading up to the exams. Lucas disappeared somewhere for several weeks. Upon his return he explained to me that he could only remember that he had gone to a city beginning with 'P' and that it was several hours away by car. I found out from Darius's father, James, that Darius had fallen out with him again. James said that he had not seen Darius for five days, that he was not answering his phone, and James didn't know where he was. Chris managed to contact Darius via some of the other students to make sure he was OK. Darius was living with his mother on-and-off, but mostly staying with friends. No wonder he was wild.

Some of the students did better. Darren, serious as always, solemnly attended revisions sessions with Desmond grudgingly in tow. George's parents regularly arrived at the school requesting previous examination papers for George to practise. But despite our best efforts, they were the exceptions rather than the rule.

My own preparations for the examinations were more prosaic. I had learnt that if the pens that we distributed to students during the exams possessed their lids, then those lids would become projectiles. Similarly, the rubbers had to be allocated sparingly, and only on demand, lest they be cut into tiny pieces by rulers and chucked about. Reducing opportunities for misdemeanour did not, of course, eliminate it entirely. Even when we had persuaded a student to hand in one, or even two of his mobile phones, they usually had a third that we did not know about.

Nor could we entirely prevent the chaotic world outside the doors of the academy from intruding on the exams. For example, Darren once arrived on a scooter for one of his English exams. It turned out that he had borrowed the scooter from a friend. I found this out when the friend turned up at the school requesting the keys to the scooter, on the grounds that he had to get to a job interview. I was required to convey the keys from Darren in the exam hall to the stranger outside. There was, however, some light relief. Ricky sat through most of his mathematics exam with his trousers around his ankles, exposing the shorts he was wearing underneath. He looked like he was sitting on the toilet.

Attendance for the exams was good. Our feeder schools told us that it was an achievement simply to get them in the room for an exam. The students who did not attend had either already disengaged from the course or had suffered some crisis on the day of the exams. Collette, for example, failed to attend one of her English exams because of an incident on the bus on her way into school. She had been travelling on a child ticket, but without the card that proved her entitlement to do so. She shouted at the ticket inspectors, who called the police. The police searched her and found a small amount of cannabis in her possession. She was arrested and missed her exam.

The weather had an important influence on the students' performance. If it rained, the drops of water hitting the roof produced a soothing sound that helped them concentrate. They found silence very difficult to cope with because it was something they rarely experienced. And provided they made it into school in the first place, if it was raining, the idea of leaving the exam seemed quite unattractive. When the sun was shining, by contrast, the students ached to leave, especially in the afternoons. The roof's beams and plastic sheets would creak loudly as they expanded in the sun's heat, mirroring the students' rapidly disintegrating patience.

Once the torture was over, the students did not hang around. Lucas bid his goodbyes by fly-kicking his biro in the direction of its container, smiling at us, then walking out the door muttering 'have a good summer innit'.

The GCSE results achieved by the students at the LBACP are displayed on the graph below. It shows the grade achieved in each of the 132 GCSE examinations sat by the 41 students who sat exams during the three years I taught at the LBACP. In the second and third years the students also sat a BTEC First Diploma in Sport, and the students achieved one distinction, four merits and eight passes. Although those results would be unimpressive for a mainstream school, one head teacher who referred students to us described the results as 'awesome'.

Figure 8.1: Aggregated results of 132 GCSEs
taken by 41 students at the LBACP between 2007-2009, by grade

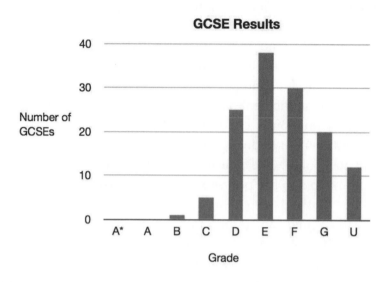

Where are they now?

I have not made a systematic survey of the destinations of the students, and so the following is impressionistic only. It is a mixture of my own experiences and news channelled to me through Chris and other former staff members.

I will start with Lucas. You will recall that his father was a drug dealer. Perhaps it is not surprising, then, that when his GCSE results were released, he had under-performed. He got a collection of D grades rather than the Cs that he was easily capable of. I was rather worried that Lucas would blame me for his bad grades, as he was in the habit of blaming me for his bad behaviour. To my surprise, he did not. He was in fact pleased to have got Ds rather than Es. He was in school partly to print copies of his CV, which he had prepared with his mentor Jimmy Moreland, and partly to search online for an apprenticeship. Whilst his CVs were printing, Lucas mused: 'I'm going to miss this place you know. However much I hated it at the time, I'm going to miss it.'

Kind of you to say that, I told him.

'Yeah, well it's true. Hopefully the year below will get even higher grades—some As and stuff.' We moved on to searching for jobs for Lucas. There were very few available and many of those Lucas could have done were ruled out because of the area in which the job was based: 'bare problem, man, with these boys there man, bare problem'. Several years later, Lucas still does not have a job. He is planning to study sports abroad, if he can, though I fear his convictions may scupper that too.

Many of the students at least started at college after leaving the academy, though I know some of them were soon kicked out for fighting. The students who were most successful in their GCSEs, Darren and George, are studying at good colleges. Some of them have gone on to work for Chris at Footsteps. Another student works in a bowling alley near the Olympic park in Stratford. A year after leaving the academy Craig told me that he had a part-time job at Londis, which is a small-scale supermarket ('I'm not ready for full-time yet', he said when we met). I bumped into one student who was clearly addicted to skunk whilst at the LBACP but now is clean and working. Other students are working for family members. But I fear that many, if not most, of the students have merely joined the millions of unemployed who have borne the brunt of the consequences of the financial crisis that began in 2008.

As far as their criminal activities are concerned, in 2009 the police told us that our students had much lower rates of offending than equivalent students who had been excluded (though I cannot verify that claim myself). However, I know that at least one of the LBACP's former students was imprisoned in the wake of the 2011 summer riots and I have heard rumours of several other students passing through the criminal justice system as adults.

I have also had some contact with the parents of my former students. Darius's father once came into the boxing gym to speak with Chris, and whilst he was waiting I caught up with him. He said that he had 'started living, rather than just existing'. He was still very angry and disillusioned about the way he was treated when he became homeless earlier that year. 'You can't change shit in this world apart from yourself, Tom,' he told me. 'Can't change women, can't change kids, but ya can change yourself. A leopard don't change his spots, if y'know what I mean, but he can stop hunting if he don't want to no more.'

The student with whom I have had most contact since leaving the LBACP is, by far, Felix. Felix's big problem was that he simply could not read, despite the additional lessons and extra attention we had given him at the LBACP. Felix had shown a sincere desire to learn and improve himself, so after he left the Civitas staff, and particularly my line manager, Robert Whelan, kept in touch with him and offered him academic support. Robert gave Felix lessons at the Civitas office at the end of Robert's working day for a time, but ultimately Westminster was too far for Felix to travel regularly for lessons, and it was clear to Robert that there was some underlying difficulty with Felix's reading that prevented him progressing.

Therefore, the Civitas dyslexia fund paid for a trip to a specialist dyslexia assessor, who confirmed that Felix was severely dyslexic. Obviously, it was a disaster for Felix that this had not been picked up when he arrived in the UK in his early teenage years, or, for that matter, in Jamaica. We travelled to Surrey for his assessment. On the way it transpired that Felix had never used a lift in an underground station before. He had lied to his girlfriend, who was studying at university, about where he was going because 'I don't want her to look at me differently, you know?'

When we met the assessor, she asked me why we were getting him assessed, given that he was 18. I told her that we hoped to get Felix some specialist tutoring. Felix agreed: 'I want to learn the basics, not no fancy words, just the basics. I never been taught the basics. Cos the thing is, if you can't read, you can't get no job. I want to go college and not make the mistakes I made back in school.' On the way back from the assessment, Felix explained some of the practicalities of being unable to read. He cannot read text messages properly, for example. So he can't tell whether his girlfriend is cheating on him or not—he couldn't tell if another man had text messaged his girlfriend saying 'I miss you', because he just couldn't reliably read the text. And even if he did suspect something, he wouldn't question a text that she received, for fear of his poor reading ability being exposed.

The dyslexia fund paid for specialist tutoring for Felix, and I spent some time with him one-to-one so that he could practise his reading. The assessor had told us that Felix had great difficulty with learning sounds and mixing sounds within words. He would only be able to learn words by rote, as pictures, in the way one learns Chinese. 'Sounding a word out' was not something Felix would ever be able to do. The key, then, for Felix, was that he spent a large amount of time practising reading, so I offered to help him with that task.

During that time he told me some difficult things about his life. 'I came up hard, y'know' he said. 'I don't show it, but it was hard, man. When I first come 'ere, with my uncle, we were sleepin seven in a bed.' I asked him how that was possible. 'We all slept on the width way, y'know?' he said. Felix's mother came to the UK before he did and sent money back home whilst Felix lived with his grandmother in Jamaica.

He told me: 'I just can't put my finger on when I didn't learn to read. I can't remember whether I went to primary school. I know I went to school in Year 6, 'cos I came over here in Year 7. I just can't put my finger on it.' He told me a story about his primary school in Jamaica. Latecomers would be lined up outside the headmaster's office in order of lateness. The punishment, caning, would be worse the further down the line of latecomers, Felix told me, so the students would barter apples and homework tasks in exchange for moving places in the line.

During the period I was working with him on his reading, Felix rang me to tell me that he had an 'anger problem'.

'An anger problem?' I said.

'Yeah.'

I probed him further. 'What's making you angry, Felix?'

'Well, anything. I get angry at stupid little things. And my girlfriend says that I'm pushing her away.' I told him that I would feel angry at being excluded from the rest of the world in the way that he was; if I didn't have a job and found it hard to see a positive future for myself. I told him to get down to the boxing gym and take his anger out on some punch-bags, and that he had to enrol on a college course to continue to improve his reading. I also remember asking him whether his girlfriend could help him with his reading. He was obviously uncomfortable with the idea. 'She'd just judge me' he said. His mother worked seven days a week as a hairdresser, so she couldn't help really, he said. She was 'not the best' reader anyway, he said.

I held our reading sessions at my flat in North London, where I learnt that he drank tea with at least three sugars. Once Felix had arrived at a session (he was not very punctual), his appetite for reading was indefatigable. We would practise spellings, and after the sixth or seventh attempt Felix was able to spell 'course', 'sneak' and 'stupid'. 'Stupid' was the spelling that evaded him the most, but this only redoubled his determination to learn it. Our sessions together usually lasted at least an hour and a half, and usually two hours. In one session, after over two hours of reading, he stopped and said: 'Tom, I've got a headache. Reading is exhausting... I never knew it could be so tiring. I ain't never read for this long before—I didn't know it could give you a headache! Now I know what my girlfriend is going on about when she complains that uni is tiring!'

In the film *Precious*—which portrays teaching methods which are as close to the way we worked at the LBACP as I have seen on-screen—the teacher asks her students to write letters. So I had Felix write letters to me and to Robert Whelan at Civitas. Robert and I once took Felix out for a curry, because he told me that he dreamed one day of owning his own restaurant where he was the chef, but Felix had a limited repertoire of dishes that he knew. He had never tried curry before, he said. In Felix's letter to Robert, he said that he was looking forward to the curry, but was not sure that he was ready to go on a literacy course at college. We agreed that 'worried' was the most appropriate word to describe his feeling about college—the word 'shook' was 'a bit ghetto', he said.

Felix enrolled on his college course after lots of encouragement, and for the first time in his life he was the star of the class. He enjoyed the course and was hoping to start a catering course in addition to his literacy studies. Felix joked that his college course had 'bare immigrants, man'. I had returned to studying, and both Felix and I were fortunate that friends of mine in the Islington Labour Party, Jan and Laurie Whelan, were able to continue to help Felix with his reading.

Felix told me that he had started writing out his text messages out by hand before he sent them, and that he had finally nailed down the spellings of the majority of the most frequently used words. His text messages stopped being in text-speak and began to read more like the way older people often text—in full sentences and with correct spellings. The only problem he was facing, he told me during a reading session, was that some of his old friends from his area were trying to get him involved in gang violence again.

'These guys, yeah, they're trying to get me into some bad stuff again, man. It's crazy 'cos, he's like 21 or suttin, you know, and he's behaving like he's 16 or 17 or something, going out on beefs and shit... He's got two kids! They was telling me, yeah, that I started the war that ended with me getting shanked. But the truth is, it's been going on for years. I've left the gang man, but he wants me back. They're going on road to get this guy, and they want me come' Felix said, as his Blackberry went off for the third time in the reading session. '"Stand up for your endz blud!" he says. But I don't even live in Tottenham, I live in Hornsey, so what's he talking about?'

'Can't read mate'

Felix was not the last teenage boy from Tottenham whom I taught to read. A year-and-a-half after I left the LBACP, I returned to work with Chris at Footsteps Football Academy. Civitas paid me to tutor the boys at Footsteps who were weakest at reading, as I had done voluntarily with Felix during the summer after I finished working at the LBACP.

It is difficult to emphasise how shocking it is to meet teenagers who cannot read. They are not many in number, but they are great in need. Perhaps unsurprisingly, there are concentrations of them amongst students who have been permanently excluded from mainstream school. I soon got over the shock of working with teenagers who couldn't read, but those feelings were soon replaced by sadness and anger. Sad for the boys who struggle through school with a dark, confidence-destroying secret: that they are unable to read or write. Angry at our education system because it allowed those boys to reach their teenage years without giving them the time and effort that was required to help them to read. The work I did only took place thanks to private donations, else those boys would probably never have been able to read.

That is not to say that it is easy to teach teenage boys to read. Far from it. But the problem with those boys is generally not so much an incapacity to read, but the boys' own fear of confronting a problem that, whether they realise it or not, has completely undermined their education thus far and ruined much else in their lives. When I sat, one-to-one, with those boys and tried to persuade them to work on their reading with me, they often had a kind of 'mental block' against doing so. I found it akin to asking a small child to talk about the death of a parent or sibling, so sore was the topic and so unwilling were the boys to address it. Deep down, they wanted to read, but so many other fears and experiences of failure got in the way of that desire expressing itself. I found that it took around six months of work with those boys—at a rate of two days a week—to help them gain some confidence in their reading, and in working with me, at which point their reading ages were rarely much above that of a seven year old, but they were no longer illiterate.

Whilst working with those boys, I was often reminded of a young man I met when I was a teenager. During my sixth-form years, each Saturday I worked as a sales assistant at Wickes Building Supplies in Croydon. I was once asked by a young builder to help him find a particular type of paint. After taking him to the relevant section of the store, I showed him a tin of what I thought he was looking for. He said 'can't read mate, what does it say?'. He was obviously just as embarrassed as the boys I taught in Tottenham, but had learnt to live with his disability. I wanted to help the boys in Tottenham to avoid having to live like that. I know that Civitas will continue to fund a reading tutor in my place at Footsteps, as I move on to other things. I just wish other boys with reading problems had the same opportunities, or better, that the problems were better dealt with by primary schools, removing the need for extraordinary measures.

Rules and relationships—what next?

One must be very careful about what should be regarded as 'success' for a school like the LBACP, given the challenges these students faced. For example, Darius was another student who, despite the high hopes we had for him, slipped just below that arbitrary metric of academic success that is the C grade at GCSE. But nevertheless, D grades were a tremendous achievement for a student like Darius, given all the difficulties he had faced in his life. Chris had the following to say about those difficulties:

Darius was a lot of work. He was probably one of the most resource-using kids we had. I got to know his mum and dad very well. So yeah, it took a lot- but earlier you asked me who I am most proud of. People like Darius and Lucas. We managed to get them through their GCSEs, through school, and they got good results. You have to be able to do whatever it takes, and some kids are really, really hard work.

At the end of the day, my philosophy is that when I was young, we still had pornography, drugs, gangs, crime, knives and girls. They were all there. But the way I explain it to people is like this: it's like a corridor, and all those doors were there, but they were locked, so we couldn't get in. When someone did get in one of those doors it was incredibly big news- if someone had a picture of pornography at school it was like wow, that boy in 5E has got that! It was incredibly big news. If someone saw a knife, it was incredible. But today, those kids have the same corridors, the same doors, but there's no lock on them. They can, if they choose, just get involved in pornography, crime, girls, knives, gangs, if they choose to.

Whereas it was a lot easier to get from one end of the corridor to the other end of the corridor when I was younger, now it's much more difficult. But I still think if we can get them from one end to the other, and they haven't gone too far off-track, then they'll just naturally come back. So it's getting them before they're too far gone that it's the challenge. And then I do believe that they will almost without exception get sorted out.

To continue Chris's analogy, what we gave the students at the LBACP was a vision of what could lie at the end of that corridor. 'Rules with relationships' was not just a temporary measure. It gave the students a vision, an example of how the students themselves could choose to live, and so gave them something to strive towards.

In the final weeks before I left the school, I took the remaining Year 10s to see *Billy Elliot* at the Victoria Palace Theatre. It was a wonderful production that all the students enjoyed. Following on from the ballet trip, the boys suddenly became very enthusiastic about dancing. Robert even declared, after seeing the show, that he wanted to try some ballet. 'I'm serious about this ballet thing you know!' he told me, 'I used to go to dance classes before I got kicked out of school.' Robert managed to persuade some of the other boys to come as well. Ricky said he would come: 'niggers can say what they want. I'll slap them in the face'. The only problem was that a ballet trip meant travelling to Clapham, South London, which worried Robert a great deal.

In the mathematics lesson during which the boys professed their desire to do ballet lessons, Robert made an odd request for music. I had been experimenting with playing classical music in the classroom, with mixed success. Robert has requested the title soundtrack to 1982 film *The Snowman*, entitled 'We're walking the air'. Robert explained that he used to watch the film every Christmas at school, and that he loved the music. 'There's no speaking in it you know,' Robert reminded me. When I played the track, the discussion returned to the issue of travelling to Clapham to do some ballet. Robert suddenly looked thoughtful.

'You can't control your dreams, can you Tom?' Robert asked.

'No Robert, I'm afraid you can't. Your subconscious controls what you dream.'

'Aww, that's tense,' said Robert. 'If I could, I'd be on that, boy. This morning I woke up after dreaming about being caught slipping by some of them Pee-Wee boys [a gang]. They grabbed me by the neck, then banged me in my face; bang, bang, bang... it's tense, boy!'

They even *dream* about the violence on the streets, I realised.

The LBACP could not rid the streets of London of violence. But we could, and did, foster dreams in the boys to replace the nightmares Robert spoke of. It was this spirit of cultivating positive, realistic dreams; this spirit of self-improvement, and belief in self-determination, that was most important about what we had tried to do in the school.

Yes, I believe that we ought to pay teachers as professionals, and thereby systematically attract the same calibre of people who today become doctors, lawyers or bankers. And yes, we should definitely pay teachers who teach the most difficult students significantly more than those who teach students who present fewer behaviour problems.

But the point of spending all that money on teachers' wages, the point of education itself, should not be to give the students a slightly higher grade in their examinations—although that would make for a fairer education system. The point of it all should be to show the students a way to live, an ideal of what it means to be a grown-up, so that when the students are ready, they can live out that ideal for themselves.

With me in the class, after Robert's saddening revelation, were copies of the students' essays from their English examinations. Reading those essays, I thought, here's to the triumph of dreams over nightmares.

Darren

Dear Chris,

This is Darren Thomas in Yr 11 who just so happens to be one of the few students you have at the London Boxing Academy.

I decided that I would inform you on the plans and dreams I have for my years to go. I would hopefully leave your academy with at least four Cs so I can then progress on to the next platform which is college. In college I will be studying BTEC National Diploma in IT/Business but may soon choose other academic subjects so I can take or re-take GCSEs next year. My chosen career has been to own or be a part of, a big organisation supplying everyday appliances whether it be as small as an ant or as tall as the Big Friendly Giant. I have thought about this for a number of years as it will be an excellent store as you may get whatever you want, whenever you want.

But on the other hand, if I fail my GCSEs I will then go into learning a trade as I have had many references from the older generation. They say that's where the money is nowadays. I will also look into moving out of the corrupted area of Tottenham, London. I was thinking about moving more to Essex or Sussex to see new faces and spend more time with my family than with friends.

I will keep you posted about what happens after leaving secondary school. I will also look into turning my education to my main priority.

Yours Sincerely,

Darren Thomas

Desmond

If you are coming to the London Boxing Academy in September you might be worried and have a few questions like: do you have to be tough and know how to box? No you don't have to be tough. You don't even need to learn how to do boxing if you don't want to. Apart from boxing you can do other stuff like football and basketball and table tennis. And the subjects they do here are English, Maths, Art, ICT, and a Sports BTEC. The LBA has a good environment. It has a weights gym and a common room. The students are friendly. There are teachers that can put you through with your coursework and the lessons are interesting. So if you want to come to the London Boxing Academy, we will welcome you with open arms.

Collette

If I could live anywhere I would live in a quiet area in England. I would like to live in a mansion so I could invite my friends and family over for sleepovers. Even though I would want people to live around me I'd want to have the house in a secluded area, with lots of grass and a swimming pool. I would want there to be local shops and colleges because I hate walking to far places.

The reason I would want to live in a mansion is because that's my dream house and it's very spacey. The reason why I would want the area to be secluded is because there's always a lot of friction between me and neighbours. I like the quiet because I'm very shy and timid so it just goes with my personality. The pool is mostly for fun and exercise because I eat quite a lot. I would want lots of grass for things like quad-biking or horse-riding and things like that. I would like a local college so that I wouldn't have to rush.

George

Dear Newcomer,

I am writing to you to talk about my school and why I would advise you to come here. First of all, I would recommend you to come because the school starts at 10 o'clock and that means you can get the extra one hour's sleep. Also the school is full of friendly and kind students who will be your friends.

During the period you are at the school you will go on many fun activities e.g. go-karting or Devon for a week but you will also do fun activities like football, tennis, and badminton tournaments. You also do activities like visiting Oxford University and getting big talks by the police.

What's really good about the school is that there are only around 30/40 students altogether. You will have about five other people including yourself in your class and this is good because you get more learning than you would if you was in a main stream school or college.

The teachers at this school are nice as well and if you do a little thing wrong they won't moan at you like they would in a normal school. The teachers are also always there if you need someone to talk to about things.

I really enjoy the school because you don't get in as much trouble because the teachers know how to calm you down and also because there is a mix of sports and lessons in one day—not just all lessons. I also like the school because the teachers and students respect each other and look out for each other.

In this letter I have told you all the reasons why I think you should join the school and I am looking forward to seeing you if you join.

Yours sincerely,

George

William

I would like to live on a tropical island because I like lots of water and sand. I love wild life. It makes me feel at home. I like to have lots of space. Because I spend most of my time by myself I like peace. The reasons for my choices are there's not a lot of people so there's lots of fresh air. And no litter on the floor so it will be clean.

It has always been a dream to live on an island. So I won't have to be near gang violence. And no conflict. I think this is everyone's dream. No TV, no phones, no nothing. Just silence—one with nature.

Suma

It was breathtaking—setting foot in the pilot's seat knowing that lift-off was not far away. First of all the engine was turned on and before long the propellers started spinning to allow us to gently climb above the clouds.

The experience felt magical—I looked down at the clouds and they looked like giant balls of steam then I looked up to see the crystal clear blue sky.

After flying for ten minutes or so, the pilot said to me if I 'want to have some fun'. I replied 'yes' and the pilot then showed me how to do the loop the loop and told me to have a go. I gripped firmly on the control stick and pulled back hard until I had finished the loop.

Before long my time was almost up so I had to turn back towards the runway, slow down and prepare for landing. I handed the pilot the controls and he pushed the nose of the plane down and touched down on the runway.

Robert

In this time and age it worries me that youths as young as the age of 13 are getting into gang violence and even murder. It's very disturbing and upsetting when you hear another youth has been killed as the results of gang violence and then when you hear a minor at the age of 13 years old has committed murder wouldn't you think the situation is getting out of hand? I am a black youth who lives in a borough consumed by gangs. I'm sick and tired of these deaths especially of the ones I knew. The government are always the first to criticise black youths but do they really care? They say they're trying to put an end to this senseless violence but does it really look like they're trying? In my opinion the government aren't doing anything to stop all this. They just go on about building more youth centres so youths can get off the streets but little do they know what actually happens in youth centres.

The fear of going places you apparently don't belong is ridiculous. Ten years ago I could've gone anywhere I wanted but nowadays if I was to try to pull that off I would probably end up in hospital or dead.

The truth is people join gangs for protection and in actual fact make new friends but sometimes it may be because you have no choice because of where you live. Youths of today kill other people to gain respect and make their name known throughout their borough and they find it fun to be arrested. This is probably because people would then fear them when they get released and they feel they have power and have gained respect.

I don't know how to stop the situation from getting worse but all I know is this must end soon before it's too late.

Darius

I would love to live on my own island where the weather is hot and in winter it snows. Where there is food such as cows, chickens, lamb, goat, fruits from all over the world. Somewhere you don't have to care where you come from or colour or even region, only where great people live, such as inventors, musicians and sportsmen. Where you can be yourself and be able to do whatever you want. Where you live from your own food so no money is

204

involved, no laws but if you kill someone you will be executed on the spot. Where women are faithful and men and kids have respect for their elders and vice versa.

Lucas

If I could choose where to live I would choose the outskirts of London — not too far out but close to the city so if I wanted to go in the city it's not too far to travel.

I would choose to live on the outskirts because it would be much more quieter there than in the city. In the city it's too loud. I would want to be somewhere peaceful and quiet. Also the people there are friendly and welcoming. I could have new neighbours and meet new people so it would be better socially.

Living out there would be better because there would be no trouble there and I would be away from the danger that's in the city. In the city there is too much violence so it would be better to escape it and start fresh.

Postscript

The character in this book known as 'Felix' was killed on 11 July 2012.

His real name was Kemar Duhaney. He was stabbed in the chest, and died after five hours of open-heart surgery at the Royal Free Hospital. The man charged with his murder appears to be the former partner of a girl Kemar was seeing at the time. He allegedly stabbed Kemar after confronting him at her house. Kemar was 21 years of age.

Kemar's death came long after I had finished the main body of writing for this book. The prominence of Kemar in the narrative reflects the fact that he was the student whom I knew best. I went out of my way to help him because he was so rewarding to work with: he was charming, warm and positive. His death was a terrible shock for everyone who knew him. It was a tragedy. This book is dedicated to his memory.

Rest in peace, Kemar.

Notes

1: Boxing and Exclusion

1   PRUs are schools set up by local authorities to fulfil their statutory duty to provide education to all children resident within the boundaries of the authority, and specifically to provide for children who have been excluded or who are unable to find a place at a mainstream school.

2   www.civitasschools.org.uk

3   http://riotspanel.independent.gov.uk/wp-content/uploads/2012/03/Riots-Panel-Final-Report1.pdf

4   BMA (1993) *The Boxing Debate*, London: BMA (2007) Boxing, an update from the Board of Science, London.

5   The Amateur Boxing Association of England, *Whole Sport Plan: Achievements and Outcomes 2005-2009 and Beyond*.

6   Taylor M. and Gibson O., 'Off the ropes, and back into the ring — boxing makes unlikely comeback in schools and clubs', *Guardian*, Sunday 15 November 2009.

7   Ogg, T. with Kaill, E., (2010) 'A New Secret Garden? Alternative Provision, Exclusion and Children's Rights', Civitas, online publication 2010. See also the excellent *No Excuses: A review of educational exclusion* by Eastman, A., Centre for Social Justice, 2011.

8   *Schools, Pupils, and Their Characteristics*, Department for Education, January 2010.

9   Ofsted is the Office for Standards in Education in the United Kingdom, which charged with maintaining standards in schools and children's centres, partly by formal visits known as inspections. See http://www.ofsted.gov.uk/

10 Taylor, C., *Improving Alternative Provision*, Department for Education, 2012.

11 *Permanent and Fixed Period Exclusions from Schools and Exclusion Appeals in England, 2009/10*, Statistical First Release, Department for Schools, Children and Families, 2011.

12 There were also three students who attended the project on a short-term placement (i.e. 1-2 months), who never intended to stay longer than this

period, and so I have categorised them as having completed the course, in the sense that they completed the course intended for them.

13 A General Certificate of Secondary Education (GCSE) is the standard academic qualification sat by nearly all school pupils in the United Kingdom, normally at 16 years of age.

2: We'll Always Have Devon

1 The EMA has now been radically reformed and largely abolished by the Coalition government that entered power in 2010.

2 A match-maker is responsible for arranging fights that are appropriate for each boxer's level of experience.

3 Terri later became the English teacher after Carmel left the project at the end of my second year at the LBACP. She was the match-maker for the Haringey Police and Community Boxing Gym, which is discussed in chapter 5.

4 Chic-King was the local fried chicken shop in Tottenham. In fact, Chic-King does the best fried chicken in London.

3: A Bit of Background

1 Machin, S. and Vignoles, V. (eds), *What's the Good of Education? The Economics of Education in the UK*, Princeton University Press, 2005.

4: Teaching the Unteachable?

1 i.e. to teach without Qualified Teacher Status.

2 Shepherd, J., 'Academies to become a majority among state secondary schools', *Guardian*, 5 April 2012; http://www.guardian.co.uk/education/2012/apr/05/academies-majority-state-secondary-schools

3 Harrison, A., 'Academies told they can hire unqualified teachers', BBC News Website, 27 July 2012; http://www.bbc.co.uk/news/education-19017544

4 e.g. see Roberts, M., *Skunk 'bigger psychosis risk' than other cannabis types*, BBC News website, 1 December 2009; http://www.news.bbc.co.uk/1/hi/health/8386344.stm

5   In the fourth season of *The Wire*, a fictional educational experiment for 'corner kids' (i.e. children involved in drug dealing) attempted something not dissimilar to the LBACP. The teachers find that it is relatively easy to get their students to talk animatedly and articulately about 'what they know', i.e. drug dealing. The challenge is to take the students a step further and get them to be animated and articulate about topics that are not based on their immediate experience.

6   For this reason, the LBACP appointed a literacy tutor, paid for at first by Civitas, in order to give one-to-one tuition in reading to the students. I was later employed by Civitas to help Chris's new project, Footsteps, by tutoring the children most behind at reading .

7   The Waterstones in Gower Street is the best bookshop in London for teaching and educational purposes.

8   The multiplication grids contained the numbers 0-12 in a random order along the left-most column and the times tables that were being tested along the top-most row, and the blank squares in line with those numbers were for the students to write the answers.

9   The other breakthrough in the novel was during a physical education lesson when Braithwaite was teaching boxing to the students. The main rebel in the class challenged Braithwaite to a boxing match, which Braithwaite won.

5: The Boxing Gym

1   A match-maker is charged with making sure fights are between boxers of the correct weight and of relatively equal experience.

2   A sixth form caters for students who are 16-18 years of age. 'Lower school' in relation to a sixth form refers to students who are 11-16 years of age. A school with a sixth form is normally composed of a lower school and sixth form as a single institution.

3   For example, British gold-medal prospect Frankie Gavin failed to make his weight for the Beijing Olympic Games in 2008.

6: An Inspirational Individual

1   Dr Wormald was the tutor for admissions in 2005/6, the year I was the Admissions and Access Officer for Corpus's undergraduates, which

involved helping both with the logistics of the undergraduate interview process in December and with access visits by students whom we wanted to encourage to consider applying to university.